WARRIOR MIND

STRATEGY AND PHILOSOPHY
FROM THE MARTIAL ARTS

Dick Morgan

AuthorHouse™
1663 Liberty Drive, Suite 200
Bloomington, IN 47403
www.authorhouse.com
Phone: 1-800-839-8640

This book is a work of non-fiction. Unless otherwise noted, the author and the publisher make no explicit guarantees as to the accuracy of the information contained in this book and in some cases, names of people and places have been altered to protect their privacy.

© 2009 Dick Morgan. All rights reserved.

No part of this book may be reproduced, stored in a retrieval system, or transmitted by any means without the written permission of the author.

First published by AuthorHouse 7/8/2009

ISBN: 978-1-4389-3048-0 (sc)

Library of Congress Control Number: 2009900560

Printed in the United States of America
Bloomington, Indiana

This book is printed on acid-free paper.

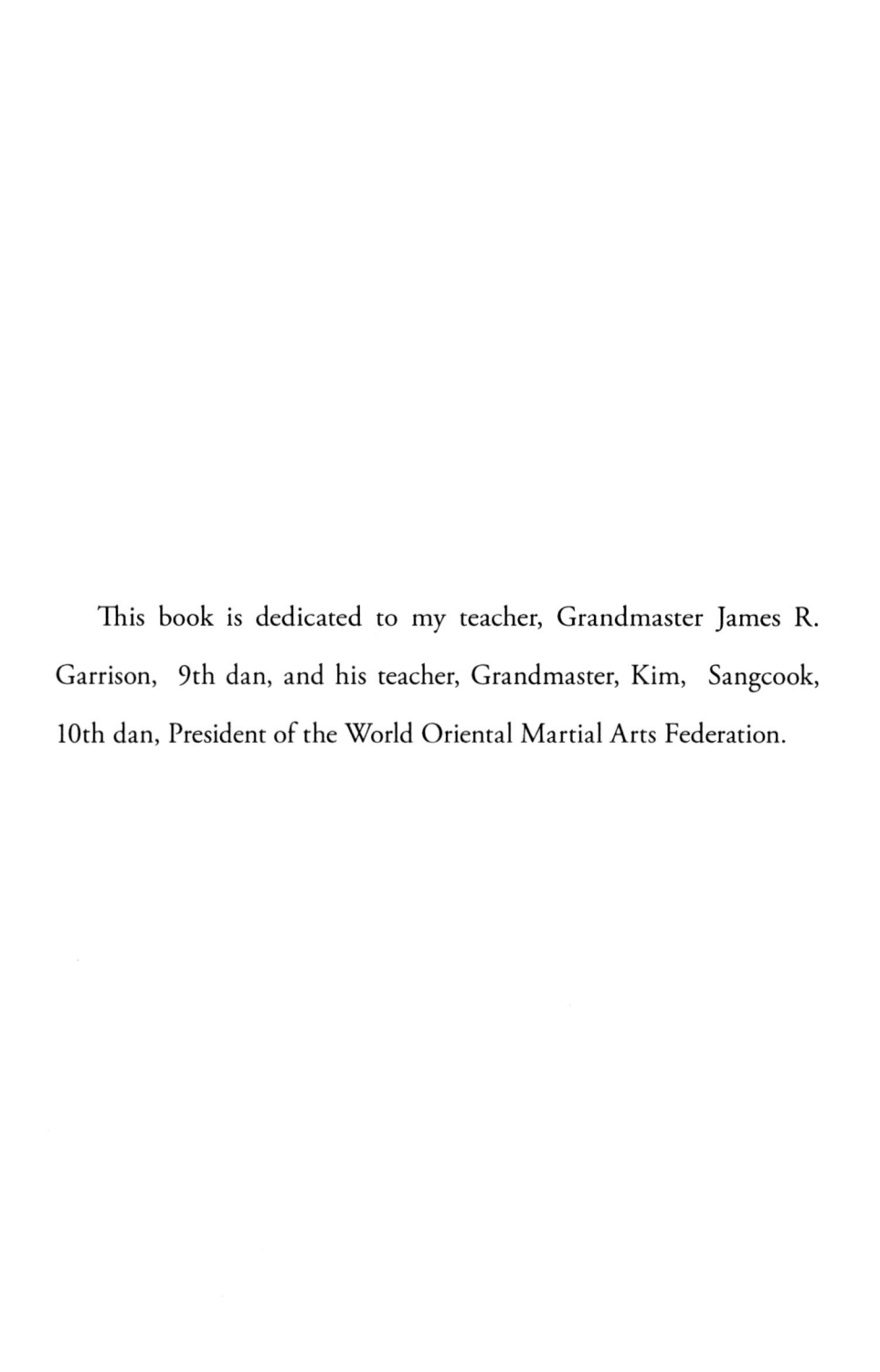

This book is dedicated to my teacher, Grandmaster James R. Garrison, 9th dan, and his teacher, Grandmaster, Kim, Sangcook, 10th dan, President of the World Oriental Martial Arts Federation.

TABLE OF CONTENTS

Forward ix

Introduction xiii

Chapter 1 1
    True strength comes from within.

Chapter 2 17
    The Mind and the Body are One

Chapter 3 44
    Breath control expands awareness

Chapter 4 73
    Move from the Center

Chapter 5 108
    All energy is directed toward attaining one's objective.

Chapter 6 154
    Do Not Resist Force; Blend with it.

Chapter 7 193
    Seek the Angle of Best Advantage
    Zen Koan: Father and Son
    Angular Advantage

Chapter 8 250
    Step into the Void Precise timing creates and exploits gaps in an opponent's defenses.

Chapter 9 286

Flow with Change

Chapter 10 336
Honor Your Spirit

Bibliography 389

Forward

There is no doubt that Richard Morgan is a warrior as well as a master of the martial arts. He is a retired firefighter and an E.M.T. (Emergency Medical Technician) who spent his life on the front lines helping citizens. He is a Vietnam Veteran serving in the U.S. Navy during the height of the war, and he is an award-winning author and poet.

Richard Morgan started practicing with us when I was a senior instructor at the Sang Cook Kim School of Martial Arts. He was a legitimate Chinese Kenpo black belt: lean and mean and as focused and dedicated as any student I had known. Without any prompting, he put on a white belt and began to practice with a beginner's mind. That was in 1974, and he has continued to be a dedicated student as well as an exceptional teacher. He now has his own school in N.E. Portland, OR., but travels to the main headquarters' school to train at least once a week.

Over the years he has traveled with me throughout the United States, offering his expertise to students as well as instructors. Our teacher, Mr. Kim S.C., often said that the measure of a true teacher is one that gives the same or more energy to new students as to senior ones.

Master Morgan is such an instructor. He willingly shares his extensive knowledge with the beginners as well as senior students. Master Morgan has compiled his knowledge in this volume.

This book is a result of his life work and his vast experience. I was with Master Morgan for most of his incredible journey. His insights and observations are priceless, and his ability to condense them in this book speaks to his writing expertise as well as his observational skills. This is a must read for new students as well as a valuable resource for master instructors.

James R. Garrison, MSW, LCSW

9th Degree Black Belt

V.P. World Oriental Martial Federation

Owner/Director Pacific Rim Martial Arts Academy

Grandmaster Sangcook Kim

Grandmaster James R. Garrison (right) and Master Dick Morgan

Introduction

The first time I entered full-contact sparring competition was perhaps the worst moment in my martial arts career. I was a new brown belt, in my early twenties, muscular, ambitious, and headstrong. I had told my instructor, a Kenpo black belt, that I wanted to enter the Northwest Regionals, that I wanted to compete.

"You are not ready," he said.

I told him I thought I was. I was athletic, limber, and strong. I ran three miles, lifted weights, and spent half an hour doing kicks of every kind every day. I could break multiple pine boards with a punch; I did my forms religiously. I attended class three times a week. How could he say that I was not ready?

"You are not ready," he simply repeated without explanation.

My instructor did not compete, at least he had not competed in the time I had studied under him. I thought to myself, this man doesn't know about tournaments, or maybe he didn't want me to outshine him in the *dojo* (training hall). I decided to compete anyway, despite his attempts to discourage me.

The day of the tournament, I arrived at the school gymnasium where it was being held promptly at its beginning, 10 AM. I listened to the explanation of the rules and began my warm up routines. But even though there were six event rings running simultaneously, time seemed to drag by slowly. There were forms competitions for every style, every age, and every belt level for both boys and girls, men and women. By the time the forms competitions were over, it was early afternoon, and I was becoming impatient. Then the non-contact sparring began. Again there were separate events for each sex, each age group, and each belt level. By the time non-contact sparring was over, it was late afternoon, and I was tired and hungry.

When full-contact sparring began, again I had to wait through all of the children and all of the lower ranks. I sat on the bleachers and watched the younger contestants and the lower ranks sparring. Some of the colored belt contestants were pretty good fighters. Occasionally, someone connected with a powerful kick, and his opponent would hit the floor, dazed or unconscious. I prayed that wouldn't happen to me!

By the time the men's heavy-weight brown belt full-contact sparring began, I was sore from sitting too long. I had warmed up multiple times, and now my muscles were stiff. As I climbed down off the bleachers and got into the line-up, I began to look over my fellow competitors.

A few appeared older and overweight; I hoped I got one of those as my opponent. A few others were lean and muscular, youthful and fierce-looking. I didn't want one of them facing me!

As it turned out, the number of competitors was uneven, and I got a "bye," meaning I would not compete until the second round. With mixed emotions about this turn of luck, I sat with the other competitors and watched all of the first-round sparring matches. Some of the competitors were very good; I saw some phenomenally fast and strong kicks. One fellow was knocked out of the ring by a side kick to his chest and could not stand up afterwards. Several people on the sidelines shouted encouragement to the kicker, calling him "Champ." When I asked a fellow contestant about the young man, I was told, "That the guy who won last year. Try not to fight him."

But as luck would have it, the young man with the strong side kick and I were paired up in the second round. I stepped up to the mark on my side of the ring, crouched into my fighting stance, and looked toward my opponent. He was very relaxed, pumping his shoulders and looking directly into my eyes. When the referee told us to get ready, my opponent stepped to his mark and took a loose stance, emitting a strong, loud *kihap* (spirit yell), never taking his eyes off of my eyes. His *kihap* unnerved me; I had felt its reverberation all through my body. This young man opposite me was an experienced fighter, and I was going to have to really defend myself or he would hurt me. I had begun to review all the blocks in my head when the referee shouted *"Sijak!"* (Begin!) My opponent strode forward and executed a fake front kick, followed immediately by a quick roundhouse which had such force that even though I blocked it, he knocked my own forearm into my face. I threw a roundhouse kick in return, but my kick was so slow and stiff that he was out of range before the kick was fully extended; he didn't even bother to block it.

I was in serious danger here. I was desperately hoping he wouldn't hurt me, and began to imagine all the ways in which he could. And while I was picturing him in my mind doing something, he stepped forward and executed a high crescent kick that swept up over my right arm and hit me square in the right ear. I did not fall down, but my vision swam as the right side of my face began to throb. The kick had such force that my vision was affected, and now there were two opponents looking back at me. The young man, my opponent, took out his mouthpiece and said calmly to me, "Keep your guard up." This was just great; my opponent was so sure of himself, he was giving me self defense tips.

When the referee came over to see if I was alright, I told him I couldn't see, that I didn't want to fight any longer. The referee held up my opponent's hand, and I stepped out of the ring in disgrace. When I sat down with the others, my instructor appeared out of nowhere and bent down toward me. "Are you alright?" he asked.

"He beat me," I said.

"He didn't beat you," my teacher said. "You beat yourself. I told you that you weren't ready. Now you will have to remember this moment until you figure out why." He looked at my face, moving my head gently. "You'll be alright," he said, and stood up. When I turned around to ask him what he meant, he was gone.

I will never forget that moment, and keep it with me as a reminder of the starting point of my martial awareness, the moment I began to realize that martial ability was not a collection of techniques, but a singular and profound state of mind. My opponent had honed this mindset into a formidable weapon; I had not. It was the moment I realized I was just a beginner and had much to learn.

As it happened, my training in Kenpo came to an end for various reasons about a year later. I was injured in a sparring session, and soon after that, my instructor moved away. I found myself searching for a reputable *dojo* over a period of the next year. I tried classes in various Chinese and Japanese martial arts, staying only a few weeks to a few months in each one. I am sure these were all fine martial arts, but the teachers I met in them were mostly young men who had been practicing for less than ten years.

Many martial artists end up doing this for years. They study for a while under martial arts teachers who only have a partial understanding of their own art. They become impatient or disillusioned and move on to the next martial art. Perhaps, like I did, they believe that whichever teacher can teach them the most devastating side kick, the hardest punch, or the most effective take-down, that's the best teacher. And the ultimate goal is to look the best at what you do. This is only a starting point, but many martial artists never progress beyond it. I wanted something more, but I wasn't at all sure what it was I was looking for.

When the student is ready, the teacher will appear.

One small incident occurred which completely changed my thinking around. I had gone to the Northwest Regionals as a spectator. I wanted to see the black belt division, to size them up. I arrived late in the afternoon and sat in the bleachers near the center ring. I had not been seated more than a few minutes when the tournament director took up the microphone.

"Ladies and gentlemen," he announced. "I have a wonderful surprise for you. We have an honored guest with us today. This is Mr. Kim Sangcook, a master of Hapkido from Korea. He has graciously agreed to do a demonstration of Hapkido for us!"

There were two men standing near the tournament director, both about 30 years old. One was Oriental, one was Caucasian. But neither of these men were in Karate uniforms; in fact, they were both wearing suits and ties. The two men leaned close together, and the non-Oriental appeared to be explaining something. Several people looked around for the martial arts master who was going to be demonstrating.

The oriental man in the three piece suit and tie walked up to the director; he was tight-lipped and obviously angry. He stared into the director's face for just a moment then grabbed a high-ranking black belt nearby who was helping with the tournament. The Oriental man pulled the black belt out into the center of the gym, drew a pack of cigarettes from his vest, and stuck a cigarette into the mouth of the black belt. He stepped back two steps, and then did a flying, spinning turnback heel kick that sent the cigarette flying across the gym, and yet didn't touch the face of the black belt, whose mouth fell open immediately thereafter. The Oriental man straightened his suit and tie on his way over to the director, then stared straight into the director's eyes and pointed a finger at him.

The director's face turned ashen white. "Let's hear it for Master Kim Sangcook!" he stuttered into the microphone. Mr. Kim and his American friend strode across the gym floor and were given a wide and respectful berth as they left the gym. I had never before seen such a self possessed presence of mind under pressure. It had been obvious to everyone the Mr. Kim had no prior warning about putting on a demonstration, but he had taken up the challenge and performed impeccably, almost without effort. I wanted to know more about this Hapkido master, Mr. Kim Sangcook. This man had that special quality

I had been looking for. I could not define it; I could only recognize it. Mr. Kim had proven he could move well but it was more than that. He had an indomitable spirit. He projected a completely unified aura of inner and outer strength, determination, and focus. I instantly knew that Mr. Kim was a formidable warrior, even though I had only seen him do one kick. I vowed that I would try to search him out.

A few days later, I found out the name of the American man who had been with Mr. Kim that day. He was Mr. Kim's senior student, James R. Garrison. Mr. Garrison eventually told me about the art of Hapkido and about Mr. Kim's role in its evolution.

Hapkido is a relatively new martial art. It did not evolve into its present form until the late 1950's. Hapkido was originally a Korean version of Japanese Aikijutsu which was brought from Japan after World War II by Choi Yung Sul. This art was called *Ju Sool Kwan* (Soft Technique Style) until the union of four of Choi's original students with an accomplished Chungdo Kwan stylist named Kim Sangcook. Through this union, the powerful strikes and kicks of Chungdo Kwan were infused into the soft, flowing movements of Ju Sool Kwan, and the dynamic art of modern Hapkido was born.

Presently, three of those original five Hapkido stylists are living in the United States. They are Grandmaster Myung Kwang Sik, Grandmaster Ji Han Jae, and Grandmaster Kim Sangcook. Senior Hapkido practitioners who are in a position to know—including

Grandmasters Myung and Ji—have publicly stated that one of the best Hapkido masters ever to practice that art is Mr. Kim Sangcook, who is quite well known in Korea, but relatively unknown in the United States.

In late October of 1974, I walked into the front door of the original Sangcook Kim Gymnasium in downtown Portland. I sat watching Mr. Kim teach four students, all of them wearing black belts. The students, muscular young men in their twenties, stood in pairs facing one another. One would throw a punch and the other would execute various techniques. Every once in a while, Mr. Kim would have one of the students throw a punch at him so he could demonstrate a technique. Mr. Kim moved with the grace and economy of a master martial artist; but there was something more about his movement that I could not define which intrigued me. The movements were completely real. It didn't matter whether the attacker cooperated with Mr. Kim or not. One moment the attacker would be throwing his best punch, and the next moment, he would be hitting the ground. If the attacker changed the attack, Mr. Kim would smile, and simply alter the defense. The results were always the same.

When Mr. Kim came to the front of the school to speak with me, I asked him, "How do you know which techniques to use?"

Mr. Kim laughed. "Not about technique. It's about mind," he said, pointing to his forehead. When I asked him what he meant, his smile almost disappeared. "First is not the time for questions. First is practice. You have to choose!"

There was nothing else for me to do at that moment. I could either sign up for practice, or I would have to leave and not come back. I stayed, and that first interchange set the tone of my martial training for the next five years.

From 1974 to 1979, I was a student at the original Sangcook Kim Gymnasium in downtown Portland, Oregon under the intense, scary, and often painful tutelage of Mr. Kim, the most accomplished martial artist I have ever known in my forty years of training. Since 1979, I have been a student of Mr. Kim's senior student, Mr. James R. Garrison. Mr. Garrison has practiced numerous martial disciplines for over fifty years, and at 9th degree, has himself reached the grandmaster level. For the past thirty years, Mr. Garrison has been patiently explaining what Mr. Kim told me from the very start; Hapkido is not a set of techniques, it is a frame of mind. It is an incorporation of principles and precepts from the martial arts into the very core of one's life, and being transformed from within by that process. It is a way of relating to the world from a very strong center.

All martial arts involve practicing techniques used in close contact combat: hitting, kicking, grappling, choking, throwing. Through precise and incessant repetition, you learn how to physically impact and manipulate an adversary who is intent on doing the same kinds of things to you. It's a serious, intimidating business; even in the friendly environment of the *dojang* (practice hall), there are occasional bruises and sprains. But after a while, you learn how to protect yourself, and you also learn how to protect the people with whom you practice. Eventually the techniques become automatic. You are attacked a certain way, and you respond in a precise, practiced manner. Stimulus and response, over and over, and then a few times more for good measure. A couple of years go by, and you begin to feel pretty good about your ability to handle these specific situations. You say to yourself, boy, if anybody ever grabs me this way or that way, well, God help him. Then you're awarded the coveted black belt which you put on with deserved pride. You've reached the pinnacle, you've passed the test, you've mastered the art.

All of this is an illusion, of course. Perhaps you can throw a decent side kick, and perhaps you can break two pine boards with a single punch. And perhaps if someone were to grab you in precisely the same manner as you have been grabbed in class, then you could use one of the five hundred techniques your instructor has drilled into you. But real life isn't like that. It's more likely that if you have learned five hundred techniques, you'll be confronted by a 501st situation. The limitation of physical technique is that no martial system can possibly prepare you for all the physical situations. And even if you could be prepared with the applicable techniques for all situations, physical techniques don't always work. Sometimes attackers counter them automatically or even accidentally. Sometimes attackers are just too big or too muscular for your normal training to overcome. Sometimes they are armed, or not alone. There are an infinite number of adversarial situations where martial art technique alone will not provide you with sufficient advantage to prevail. What then?

You have to learn to think strategically, martially. Studying a martial art is a lot like studying a foreign language. You can know an extensive vocabulary in another language, but you won't be able to speak or understand it until you can think in that language in the same manner it is used by its native speakers. When you think in any language, you don't know what words you're going to need until the moment you need them, and then the words come out automatically in the right order. Martial techniques function in exactly this same way. You never know what technique you'll need until the moment it is needed, and then it's either already done, or it's too late. This martial thinking process is essential for techniques to be timely and effective. It is often referred to as *Warrior Mind*.

Warrior mind is the art of thinking strategically in an adversarial confrontation. It is understanding the dynamics of adversarial interaction, and the principles which determine advantage in such situations.

But being a warrior is not just thinking about war. The true warrior does not seek conflict around himself, but seeks peace and balance within himself, as though his own harmony could help to heal the universe. Ultimately, seeking to develop one's warrior nature becomes a personal evolution of the spirit that creates a commonality among all people.

We all have a warrior nature. The warrior within us is that part of us which pursues triumph, which is strengthened by overcoming obstacles, which is challenged by competition, which dares to defy adversity because of conviction or belief. It is also that part of us which strikes out in anger and destroys without reason. It is the best part of us, and the worst as well.

This book is about warrior mindset—how to nurture it, how to control it, how to shape it into our best selves, and how to avoid having it destroy us in the process.

*****

Beach Practice

Chapter 1

True strength comes from within.

About a year after joining the Sangcook Kim School, I found myself in a sparring session with Mr. Kim's senior student, James R. Garrison. I had watched him spar the other students who did not have as much tournament experience as I did; they seemed to be holding their own, but nobody was able to hit Mr. Garrison. I thought, well, I can do better than them! But when it was my turn to spar, I did not have any better luck. Mr. Garrison simply raised the intensity of the interchange, and I felt myself being dominated, driven backwards into a corner. He explained this experience years later, after I became a black belt. It is not a black belt's job to actually contend with lower belts, or the lower belts would quickly become injured and discouraged. It is the task of a black belt to *train* those of lower rank and lesser experience, to function at a level of expertise and intensity just beyond their ability to cope with it. Basically, he had been toying with us.

Mr. Garrison would sometimes play a game with me and with other newer members as well, especially if that student thought he or she was good at sparring. He would point to a corner of the room at the beginning of a match, then, slowly and methodically, he would herd his opponent into that corner until he was trapped there. The game was to see how few kicks or punches he could throw and still manipulate his opponent into the corner. Frequently, he did it without throwing a single punch, yet his opponents invariably thought they had been in a serious sparring match. I really wanted to know how he did that.

After we finished and bowed off the mat, I asked him.

"Mr. Garrison, when we spar, you intimidate me even when you aren't hitting me. How do you do that?"

"It's about taking the initiative," he answered. "You just learn to dominate the action. You take the center. It's all part of Samurai-mind."

"What is Samurai-mind?" I asked.

"It is the warrior mindset. It is the mindset of someone who is totally focused on achieving his objective, so focused that the prospect of adversity, defeat, or even death itself cannot distract him. It is a total dedication to a course of action. The Japanese Samurai had to evolve this frame of mind in order to practice their profession. They were expected to serve their master or their cause to the utmost of their ability, even in the face of certain death. The Japanese have a word for it—*Kokkoro*, indomitable spirit. Mr. Kim calls it *Pil Sung*—Victory Mind. It's just a strong way of looking at things. Martial art is a mental stance as much as it is a physical technique."

"How do I learn the mental part?" I said.

"You practice very hard at the physical part. You keep getting up after you've been knocked down, and eventually you learn how not to get knocked down so easily. You just get tougher. There is no other way. You have to keep practicing for many years, and consistent practice gradually transforms you from within."

"How does that happen?"

"Practice tones the body. Continuously choosing to come back to practice disciplines the mind. Every physical activity has a mental influence. Every mental image has a physical resonance. Your mind is only as strong as your body—and vice versa. Attitude is really more important than technique."

"How can that be?" I asked.

"If you focus on technique, then your attitude becomes dependent on successful application. And if you have in mind a technique which is inappropriate, or which becomes inappropriate because the situation has changed, you will fail and probably become flustered. But if you maintain a positive attitude, a strong mindset that refuses to be a victim to the situation—and you have a general understanding of the principles that make techniques work—then it doesn't matter what techniques you use. They will simply happen when you need them. At least, they will if you have been practicing long enough."

"How long is long enough?" I asked.

Mr. Garrison laughed. "Hapkido is about internalizing your practice into a way of approaching life itself. The principles which make techniques work also make life work. Practice is never finished."

"I don't understand," I said.

"You don't have to understand ahead of time. You just have to practice, and keep on practicing. A life with this kind of focus becomes strong both physically and mentally. Practice every day. Give your heart to it. Eventually, the art emanates from within you, and permeates everything you do. This is the source of true strength," he said.

After thirty years of following this man's guidance, I am beginning to understand this approach to the art, and to life. I call it Warrior Mind; Mr. Garrison simply calls it Hapkido.

A battle is sometimes won by the powerful and the heroic, but more often it goes with he who has prepared to win with the clearest intent.

The word "strength" means many things to different people. To some, strength simply means a great muscular power. To others, being strong might mean having lots of money, or a large organization of associates, or political influence. To still others, strength is a 9mm semi-automatic with extra clips. All of these meanings are correct for the people who hold them—within their own context. But all of these kinds of strength are conditional.

Superior size or muscular power is most often a distinct advantage in a physical confrontation, but what if no hold can be gained to anchor that power? What if your opponent is trained in an art which neutralizes your strength, or uses is against you? And what about having lots of money? Certainly most of us would be amenable to the advantages of being rich. But how would having lots of money help you if you were being attacked by a bully, or a thug? In such a situation, money, political influence, or artistic fame is completely irrelevant. Having lots of friends around you might be helpful, provided you are in good standing with them. Gang members who fall out of favor or who try to quit their own gangs often find themselves under attack by the very people whom they depended on for protection. The 9mm semi-automatic might provide a distinct power advantage—unless you run out of ammunition, or left it in your other jacket at home, or worse yet, you are disarmed, and are now looking down the barrel of your own weapon. How strong do you feel now?

All of these kinds of strength are examples of external strength. External strength depends on conditional advantage, and external conditions can change rapidly beyond one's control. But true strength is not conditional; it cannot be taken away. True strength does not change according to circumstance or location. It is a kind of consciously developed personal vitality that comes from within a person as a result of a long consistency of choices to that end.

You must be deadly serious about training…your opponent must always be present in your mind, whether you sit or stand or walk…
-- Gichin Funakoshi's first rule for the study of Karate-Do

The fountainhead of true strength is the realization that we all have choices, and the course and quality of our lives are a direct result of an accumulation of these choices. Choices are not always obvious, nor are they always simple. Nor do our choices always have the desired effect on external circumstance. But the act of choosing itself strengthens our personal definition. The more often a person can say, "I am who I choose to be," the clearer his or her personal definition becomes. And the more clearly one knows who he is and what he stands for, the more uncompromising he will be when those concepts are challenged. The stronger one's personal definition, the more unwavering one's resolve, the less likely that person will accept the role of "victim of circumstance." Truly strong people seek out ways to become the exact kind of person they desire to be, and they do not compromise that effort.

Regular, consistent practice of any art eventually increases a person's self-discipline, self-awareness, and ultimately, self-respect. This gradual re-definition of the self results in an increase in an individual's feeling of control over his life, and a willingness to accept a certain amount of responsibility for the direction his life is going. For the long-term practice person, his (martial) art ultimately becomes a metaphor for the rest of his circumstance. That is, what works to make his practice better, richer, more meaningful also makes other aspects of his life better, richer, and more meaningful—and *vice versa*. Thus, a commonality of values evolves: personal honesty, respect for others, responsibility for one's actions, confidence in one's intelligence and abilities, cooperation with and trust of one's partners, and positive self-esteem. This is, in short, the evolution of personal integrity.

The strength of one's beliefs imparts resolve to one's actions.

Grandmaster James R. Garrison, ninth-degree Hapkido black belt and vice-president of the World Oriental Martial Arts Federation, was recently asked in an interview what he thought was the most important aspect of martial art training. He was asked how he would complete the following sentence: "Practice your ____." His reply:

> *I would suspect that personal integrity would be the most important. That sentence seems to be set up to read, "practice your basics." But basics are external; they*

are manifestations of the inner person. If someone is a bad person, then that person will have bad basics. If a person is unfocused, then they will have unfocused technique. But if a person practices honesty and respect and makes no compromise of his own integrity, then that person will know how he must approach his basics.

Thus, the key to strengthening one's art is to continuously strengthen and refine one's personal integrity. This is called ***internalizing*** one's practice; that is, directing every aspect of one's being—physical, mental, emotional, and spiritual—toward a single focus. The word "integrity" is after all a variation of the word "integration," which means the act of bringing together all parts of a whole.

The way to maximize one's force-of-being is through learning to conduct one's life as a practice of this holistic unity. This is the most important lesson of any martial art: ***harmony within radiates strength without.***

In a recent interview, Master Garrison had this to say:

"The primary principles of Budo (warrior's way of life) are internal. By that I mean as expressed within the characters of the name Hapkido, or Aikido. The Japanese

translate the "Ai" as the heart principle—love and harmony. They would say that true strength comes from one's alignment with the universe, with nature, with the flow of events. The Koreans are more centered on the self as a controllable universe. The "Hap" character symbolizes wholeness, or unification, referring to all of the aspects of the individual—the external aspects, such as muscular tone, and the internal aspects, such as emotional balance and integrity. The name Hapkido implies that personal strength is actually a blending and merging of all these aspects into a single harmonious force—a kind of force-of-being."
-- from "The Evolution of Hapkido" pub. TaeKwonDo Times Magazine, Nov. 1993.

In order to fully understand the Oriental concept of inner strength, it is essential to understand the concept of **ki,** (*chi* in Chinese). *Ki* is a prominent concept in virtually every facet of Oriental culture, as well as every Oriental martial art, yet which has no direct English translation. Among its many approximate meanings are *strength, energy,* *spirit*, *breath*, *life-force*, and *vitality*. Cosmologically, *ki* represents the vibratory energy generated by the interplay between the two opposing yet complimentary forces of the universe: *Um* (or *yin*)—dark, female, expanding, weak or yielding—and *Yang*—light, male, contracting, strong, dominating. Maximum *ki* is generated by a perfect balance of equal Um and Yang energies, and by an unimpeded flow of these energies as they surge and ebb within the individual. Some say that *ki* is this flow. But however one translates *ki*, the concept implies that personal power is generated by unity of focus and enhanced by a balance of energies. If one's *ki* is to be maximized, no single aspect of one's being can dominate or be dominated by any other. The mental cannot dictate to the physical; the head cannot rule the heart; the right side cannot be stronger than the left; the external cannot overshadow the internal; the emotions cannot negate rationality. ***Harmony is found in convergence, a coming together of opposites to form a balanced whole.***

But in reference to a living being, the whole is more that a sum of its parts. There is an essence, a vital energy, present in the living being that is not found by analysis or dissection. In Eastern cultures, this quintessence of being is also called *ki*. Perhaps the best translation for this use of *ki* would be *spirit*; at least then we can appreciate the diversity of the translations of *ki* when we realize how controversial the word *spirit* has become in Western culture. But *ki*, like *spirit*, is simply the joining energy—that which seeks its balance within a larger whole—that which results from unification.

Many people close themselves off to this potential, emotionally distancing themselves, erecting all sorts of mental (and often physical) barriers between themselves and everything else. In this social and emotional isolation, they are only able to trust themselves and must spend the bulk of their personal energies guarding against that which is "foreign" and "threatening." They do not allow their lives to regenerate their energies, and are soon just coping. Continuously vexed by change seen as interruption, incessantly disappointed by a reality seen as unkind fate; such people plod through their lives in near exhaustion, on the edge of panic. There is no balance of *ki* within their lives; they are like overturned bottles whose contents only flow outward and are quickly depleted. Weakness follows; eventually, sickness becomes inevitable.

How much better is it to connect with something larger than oneself so the outflow of energy is balanced by an influx of energy as well? It is much more sustaining to view ourselves as citizens of a benevolent universe, or as pilgrims on a sacred journey. Then, there is balance; there is a flow of energy between us and something larger than us. Energy expended generates energy as reward, and we resonate within this cycle, drawing from it what we need to evolve into our full potential for vibrant health and strength.

In Eastern cultures, this greater whole is often referred to as the "Way," or "*Tao*" The approximate meaning of the *Tao* is "the endless and uncontainable flows of energy which constitute the universe." But the "Way" is not definable and only implies direction insofar as it is easier and wiser for an individual to surrender to and blend with (harmonize, empathize, join, become) the *Tao* than it is to try to resist (dominate, ignore, reject, force) the *Tao*. The character which represents the *Tao*, is the same as the ending characters of Hapkido and Aikido, as well as innumerable other martial arts. Within the martial context, *-do* also translates as the "Way," in the sense of lesson, study, or path. But some of the *Taoist* meaning also remains. In a traditional martial discipline, the *–do* is said to mean the "wayless Way" or the "endless path." And old Zen *Ko-an*, (or puzzle for contemplation) which probably evolved through the medium of martial arts, states:

"*The way to the temple is the temple.*"

Strength is generated from within by internal and external unity. A person's force-of-being is ensured by, but only as strong as, his personal integrity. Inner strength is maximized by a life which seeks a balance of its internal and its external energies. Also growth toward strength and skill is intensified and accelerated if it is a shared experience. Practice of any art is an act of continuously joining into a learning experience which has no end. It is purposely altering one's state of being to become a part of the collective consciousness of the art during its manifestation. **The**

—do of any art is entirely experiential; that is, how one experiences the art is the art itself.

Therefore, it is essential that the art be carefully controlled by the head instructor. The –do, or "Way" that is shared is entirely an expression of—and a reflection upon—his or her own connection with it. It is the sacred duty of every head instructor to seek continuously for any new knowledge of or insight into his own art, so that his students may also learn how to remain a student by his example. It is the duty of every head instructor to remain courteous and respectful at all times, so that his students may learn cooperation and trust. Deadly technique cannot be leaned in an atmosphere of distrust and disrespect. For this reason, it is the head instructor's duty above all to make absolutely no compromises of his own personal integrity, so his students will have no cause to compromise their respect. The value of experiencing an art can never be greater than the purity with which it is presented. Properly guided, the study of any art thus becomes a continuous and unending rite of purification. Just as the smelting process removes impurities from the raw ore which becomes hardened steel, the continued, consistent practice of an art channels our personal evolution, removing self-doubt and conflict, leaving only hardened and focused ***intent***. And ***intent*** is what separates the hunter from the hunted.

Perhaps reducing one's choices to "the hunter" and "the hunted" is an over-simplification of life's diverse possibilities. But sometimes reality can be very simple and harsh. In a fight, the stronger have a much better chance of survival. Developing dependable, non-conditional strength is the primary intent of the warrior. If you want to be strong, then you must search within yourself to find unwavering intent. You must manifest this intent in every action and every thought. This is your warrior nature. Above all, you must be patient—for the transformation into a warrior is never completed.

Your intent should become a beacon which you use to navigate your life. Then, your intent will manifest itself.

An Example of Inner Strength

Back in the sixties and early seventies, there was a questionable practice called "dojo bashing," and anyone who opened a martial arts school needed to be ready and able to defend it at a moment's notice. When Grandmaster Kim Sangcook first came to the United States, he opened a new dojang in the middle of one of the sleaziest neighborhoods in downtown Portland, Oregon.

One day, three huge, muscular men came sauntering through the front door of the dojang. They all had scraggly beards, and all three were wearing motorcycle jackets and big, black boots, which they did not remove despite the neat line of shoes by the door. Master James Garrison, then a low-ranking black belt, and I, not yet a black belt, looked at each other and knew there was going to be trouble. These strangers were the meanest, cockiest looking guys we had ever seen walk through that front door.

Mr. Kim ambled up to the leader of the three, the one who had come through the door first, and stood with his hands on his hips, right foot slightly but imperceptibly behind, an arm's length away. Mr. Kim stared him square in the eye, but didn't say anything, as his English was still at a simple stage in those days, and none of the three looked Korean.

The leader said, "And what degree black belt are you?" His voice held unmistakable disdain.

Neither Mr. Kim's expression nor his posture changed in the least; he simply kept staring at the man and finally said, "Why?"

A span of time passed that I thought must have been at least a couple of minutes, but which was more likely about fifteen seconds as the two men stared at each other in complete silence, Mr. Kim seeming not to care in the least whether the other man answered or threw a punch. Then the three strangers bowed and left the dojang without another word.

*****

Mr. Garrison on the mat teaching.

Chapter 2

The Mind and the Body are One

My first Hapkido black belt test turned out to be not what I expected. Instead of "Show me this or that technique," it was, "Put on the sparring pads." I remember being paired up with a skinny, wiry little guy who on his best day was a good sixty pounds lighter than I. At first, I was very confident, self-assured of an easy victory. But this little guy was very strong-willed and determined, and no matter what I did, he just kept coming at me. Instead of a polite punch or kick combination, he leapt on top of me, arms and feet grabbing and flailing. No particular attack was discernable; consequently, no particular defense suggested itself. I was reduced to trying to pry his arms and legs from around me, and felt as though I were wrestling a crazed octopus. At one point, I managed to peel off all his limbs at the same time, and I threw him across the room. But Mr. Garrison picked him up and shoved him back in my direction, saying, "We'll keep going until you find what you need."

What I needed? I had bruises and cuts all over my body, I was frazzled and confused, and I was out of breath. I needed a long coffee break, preferably across town. But I wouldn't quit in the middle of a match. Never again. And as the wiry little guy circled me, crouching and ready to spring, my mind calmed and reached a point of singularity. I had come to the conclusion that no particular technique was going to be effective against these *kamakazi* type attacks. I was going to have to hurt him so that he couldn't move anymore. I had reached a point of mental extremity that whatever this guy did, I was going to break his arm, or whatever bone I could get leverage on, and I was calmly resolved to do so. It was as if suddenly things were simpler; his moves appeared slower and clearer to me. At that moment, just when my opponent was about to launch himself, Mr. Garrison stopped the match. "I've been waiting a long time for you to find that state of mind," he said. "We can stop now. No sense anyone getting hurt," he added.

During moments requiring extremes of physical exertion, concentration, and focus, one often finds the mind and body fused into one intense and marvelous reality. In such moments, there is no duality; there is only a focused awareness. The Japanese have a word for it: **mushin**—which literally translates as "no-mind" or the "no-mind mind-set." To achieve this mind-set is a primary goal of every student of the martial arts, no matter which form or style; for without *mushin*, no warrior-art is combat effective. But *mushin* implies much more than a particular state-of-mind; it implies a personal unity-of-being that is distinctly different than the normal Western mind-set. In order to understand the term, it is necessary to examine the Taoist philosophy from which it evolved—a philosophy which has permeated virtually every Oriental culture for three thousand years.

According to Taoist beliefs, duality exists all around us. Pairs of opposing forces swirl and blend into one another, forming dynamic balances of their energies. Light and darkness cycle into one another to form the passage of days. Warm and cold fronts swirl into one another to form our weather. Male and female are equally essential for the continuance of the species. Each half of a duality is a reflection of—a shadow of—its opposite, and has some of its opposite qualities within itself. All dualities eventually balance; extremity cannot exist alone for very long.

The term *mushin*, rooted in this Taoist understanding of the synthesis of opposites, implies a complete harmony of body and mind. *Mushin* implies a mind that is completely empty of the chatter of socialization, politics, or self-evaluation, a mind completely focused on optimizing the outcome of a physical challenge. *Mushin* also implies that the body is equally programmed to remember all by itself how it has been trained to move in order to achieve maximum results. Any professional race-car driver, driving at 200 mph surrounded by other racers only a few feet away can describe "becoming one with his machine." Any pro-basketball player who makes a mid-court three-pointer in the last second of a play-off game can describe the "unconscious play." Any surfer who goes into the "bonsai pipeline" and comes out still standing on his board knows about the "beauty of mindlessness," even without a word to describe it. Just so, the warrior who has no choice but to fight, who is facing an attacker intent on harming him, must achieve this unity of being, this primal awareness, in order to successfully defend himself, maybe even in order to survive. Consequently, *mushin* is often referred to as *warrior-mind*. But *mushin* is actually only an expression of warrior-mind, much like a blossom is an expression of the plant. But unless a plant has already taken root and matured, it will not bloom.

The problem is, so many people want to look like the blossom, yet don't want to be bothered with nurturing the plant. Many martial artists become fixated on "looking good" and learn only the external aspects of their art. They learn how the body moves during many flashy techniques. They assume that if one learns a given number of techniques, one deserves a certain rank. Obtaining rank becomes the goal instead of perfecting the art. But such a martial artist, armed with the rapid-fire learning of dozens, perhaps hundreds of techniques—who finds himself face to face with a real enemy who is trying to harm him—will more than likely discover that the massive dose of adrenalin just released into his bloodstream has seriously interfered with his ability to remember any techniques at all. His mind become befuddled, his body freezes up, and he is easily defeated. The truth is, most fight situations develop so quickly that the person who is attacked usually has no time to prepare himself or to organize a defense. Most fights from beginning to end last less than ten seconds—not nearly enough time for decision-making based on rational analysis. And a mind full of adrenalin is not likely to be very rational or analytical anyway.

A fight is truly a moment beyond understanding. It represents the epitomy of misunderstanding. Unlike sports which have rules to help channel and guide play, unlike games which incorporate turn-taking, unlike social protocol with its niceties of courtesy and manners, a fight is a total breakdown of civilized interaction. Anything can happen at any time, in any order. You can get seriously hurt or even killed in a real fight if you are not properly prepared. And you usually do not have any time for additional planning or preparation. ***What you have to work with in a fight situation is who you are before it starts.***

It is for this reason that the martial arts are taught in a radically different way than other kinds of art. The martial artist must cultivate a *focus-of-being*; that is, the task of the martial artist is to re-create the self so that his martial training, his martial discipline, and his martial philosophy form the very foundation of his existence. A person's martial skills do not approach effectiveness until they are practiced so regularly and so consistently that they become a natural emanation of the inner Self—as natural as breathing, as automatic as speaking one's native tongue. This is the reason martial artists, even those of advanced rank, practice basic moves over and over again each and every class. Such moves are most effective when they have become automatic responses to specific stimulations. The simpler the move and the longer one has practiced it, the more likely it is that move will be a natural form of self-expression when the situation is appropriate for it.

In a crisis, you will not rise to the occasion, but rather, default to your level of training.--B. Cooley, Jr.

An adage that has come to us from the age of the ancient Samurai says, **To be is to act.** This short but profound statement illustrates the proper relationship between the mind as self-definition, and the body as self-expression. In other words, **what you do is determined by who you are, and determines who you are as well.** Consistency in action encourages consistency of character. Character integrity manifests itself in precision of action. Practicing a warrior's art creates warrior mind; exercising warrior mind sharpens the warrior's art. This is the cornerstone of martial effectiveness.

Studies in modern bio-physics tend to substantiate this axiom. In fact, recent research at the quantum level suggests that the body itself has memory. Repetitive movement, such as that which occurs during the practice of a physical art, imprints a "motion memory" within the muscle tissue involved in that movement. The more consistently the movement is practiced, the more intelligent the muscle becomes. Eventually, the muscles involved in well-practiced movement remember how they are supposed to function all by themselves without cognitive awareness. At this stage, the movement has become an expression of that inner intelligence we call the "Self." As the "Self" grows, so does its influence on our personal definition.

But even though physical fitness and trained muscular response may do wonders for one's self-definition, martial arts training cannot stop there. While an opponent is being physically engaged, he is being mentally engaged as well. Unless an opponent's mind is overcome, he will continue to struggle. Conflict will continue until an opponent is made to redefine himself as defeated. The mental discipline and readiness of a warrior is as important as his physical strength and prowess. Physical practice and mental practice must be simultaneous and complimentary. They must work together to transform the warrior from within.

Ultimately, the dance creates the dancer as much as the dancer creates the dance.

Actually, one's mind plays a far greater role in the manifestation of one's physical being than merely supplying self-image. Each moment, the brain is producing hundreds of chemicals called neurotransmitters which flow outward to the farthest digits of the body, each with its own distinct neural message. *(I am feeling young today! I am feeling old today!)* Modern biophysicists are finding new neurotransmitters every few months. Research at the quantum level suggests the possibility that chemicals located within the nucleus of every cell in the body are particularly sensitive to these neurotransmitters. Evidence suggests that physical structures within a cell's nucleus can actually re-form themselves moment by moment to incorporate the messages received by various neurotransmitters.

The ramifications of this are profound. Our thoughts result in the creation of a complex soup of neuropeptides which then flood our bodies with new information. Our bodies are constantly transforming themselves in order to incorporate this new information into their physical reality. **In effect, our every thought affects every cell in our body.** The new paradigm is that the body is less like a sculpture—frozen into its own shape and only eroded by age or acts of God—but rather more like a river. Dr. Deepak Chopra, noted author of <u>Quantum Healing</u> and other books about the mind/body connection, describes the body as *"a river of information and energy that is constantly renewing itself."* A river may appear the same one moment to the next, but the water in any given part is constantly replacing itself. (Be careful what you allow to flow downstream!)

It is as though modern science is finally substantiating the viewpoint of the ancient Vedic sages, that there really is only one being. And that being is undergoing incessant transformation, whether or not we acknowledge it. We are a dynamic swirl of interactive energy seeking its own balance. Our general health and vitality directly affects our outlook, and our outlook will eventually manifest itself within our bodies. Vibrant health encourages a positive attitude. Often the first sign of failing health is a negative attitude. This fluctuating personal energy is called the ***flow of ki***. *Ki* can have either a positive or negative value. There is actually an element of choice involved.

The primary task of the martial artist, then, is to consistently shape and guide his *ki*, or personal energy, toward a positive manifestation. He does this by internalizing the practice of his art. That is, he practices his art with the idea of not only improving his physical technique, but with the goal of transforming his entire being—his physique, his self-definition, his mental imaging, his very spirit. He strives to become a perfect manifestation of the art itself and allows no compromise of that effort. It is this other-directedness that channels his *ki*; it is this unity of focus which makes his *ki* strong.

If the art that is focused on is a warrior art, then the warrior-nature emerges like a seed planted in fertile ground. One nurtures the seed by weeding out any thoughts or actions which might harm it. Eventually one arrives at a level of development where one's self-definition and one's self expression are the same. The art and the artist become One; there is no discord—no hypocrisy. Hapkido Grandmaster Kim Sangcook defines the warrior nature as, **"...a mind completely without doubt. Doubt can lead to hesitation. Hesitation for the warrior can mean death. The warrior, through the practice of his art, strives to erase all such shadows from his mind."** The warrior *is* the art.

This, then, is **Warrior-Mind.** It is a person's intent present in every action and thought. It is practicing, thinking about, and visualizing one's art every moment. It is eating, drinking, and sleeping one's art. It is breathing as a warrior breathes and speaking as a warrior speaks. It is a singular focus manifested each moment of one's existence, and the personal integrity not to compromise that effort. It is perceiving oneself as evolving along a path that one's art dictates, and embracing the personal transformation that occurs with this choice. As the warrior's art shapes and tones the body, the mind is tempered and honed into a mind completely without the turmoil that accompanies inner conflict or self-doubt. Then, if there is conflict, one need not think or remember what to do. Response becomes an automatic emanation of the inner Self. One is already a warrior before the trouble begins.

Developing Warrior-Mind is the most important part of martial art practice. Ultimately there is no other practice.

There are ten major practices that are essential for the development of Warrior-Mind.

1. Practice your art every day without fail.

Attend formal class as often as possible, since it is best to receive information from someone who is more experienced in your art than you are. But even on those days when there is no scheduled class available, you can practice your art. Your body itself carries memory implanted by previous classes. Your body can be your teacher if you learn to listen to it daily. The more consistently you train your body, the more intelligent your inner teacher will become.

2. Develop habits which support practice; eliminate habits which undermine it.

Practice must become a priority. It must become a ritual without which the day is incomplete. Practice is what defines a "practice-person." If a person's energy is directed toward something else, then that person will become someone else. This is especially true of habits that affect one's health. If you are a practice-person, eventually you will have to give up personal habits which undermine your practice. You will quit such activities as smoking cigarettes, drinking alcoholic beverages, and eating "junk" foods; you will arrange your days to get enough calming rest and so that you have no more stressors than you can handle, and still get in your practice. Eventually, practice will become an essential part of the physical and mental balance of your inner self.

3. Internalize your practice.

Mental and emotional practice is as important to the warrior nature as physical practice. Mentally practice your art. Learn to visualize various situations in which your art can be utilized, and then visualize yourself dealing successfully with those situations. Examine your concept of the ultimate warrior, and perceive yourself as becoming an example of this to others. If an attribute of your warrior concept is bravery, for example, then practice being courageous in all your actions. Learn to apply all the attributes, strategies, and philosophy of your art to the rest of your life. Eventually, the metaphors which help you to understand yourself will apply equally to your art and to your life. If courtesy and respect for others are traits you believe a warrior should exemplify, you will find yourself acting courteously and respectfully to everyone you meet, regardless of their position or importance to you. The warrior, by internalizing his practice, emanates who he is from within, and is not dependent on his company or his surroundings for his self-definition.

4. Develop uncompromisable personal integrity.

The average person settles for less than perfect in so many ways. His business is "getting by," or "covering his tracks." His constructs are "good enough," or "whatever." His language is imprecise or even vulgar. His relationships are "tolerable." When we fail to do our best work, our minds learn to settle for less quality than we are capable of. We compromise our efforts, we take reckless shortcuts, we abandon our projects before they are complete. We view the world as a place where this behavior is to be expected from everybody, and we expend a large portion of our energy guarding our personal space against the compromised integrity of others.

The warrior cannot afford to live in this manner. The warrior knows that he must expend his best efforts in all activities. His life may one day depend on the level of integrity with which he has learned to conduct himself. The level of integrity he exhibits in his conduct will determine the manner in which he approaches the practice of his art. Over time, his art will manifest itself only to the level of his involvement with it. If he settles for less that his very best efforts, his art will remain imprecise or flawed. If he makes no compromise in his efforts to achieve his very best, his art will continually evolve toward perfection. Therefore, the warrior has to have a strong sense of personal integrity which he does not compromise in any endeavor. ***The practice of personal integrity is the most important exercise in the development of warrior-mind.***

The philosophy of Hapkido emphasizes non-compromisable integrity in three key areas of behavior. ***Jong-euye*** is *"right behavior."* The warrior always acts within the boundaries of that which he perceives as right conduct. Then, if conflict arises, he knows he is not the cause—only the resolution—and he will not hesitate to act. ***Yea-euye*** is *"courteous behavior."* The warrior is ever respectful of others; he does not look for trouble in order to test his martial skill. He never tempts or goads another into an adversarial position. Such behavior is not only bad manners, but bad strategy. When action becomes necessary, the warrior acts without harsh words or posturing, since these do not insure victory—they only surrender the element of surprise. ***Jen-nay*** is *"patient behavior."* The warrior learns not to compromise the practice of his art because he is tired or too busy. To compromise the art is to compromise the victory to which the art aspires. The warrior is never eager to fight. He will wait if he can, and seek the ground of best advantage. He may find that by waiting, adversarial situations—like all energy imbalances—may resolve themselves. The warrior is never in a hurry. The warrior-art is not measured in minutes or hours; it is a life-long endeavor and is measured in years.

A compromise of one's integrity is the result of either a departure from ethics, a lapse of respect, or a lack of patience.

5. Practice honesty in all matters. Develop honest self-perception.

It is impossible to internalize one's art without developing an honest and ongoing self-examination process. We must get past all the various intrigues we construct for ourselves—the wigs and mascara we wish other to see, the puffed up chests and sucked-in stomachs we wish ourselves to be, the professional selves we are at work, the prospective selves we are on our resumes. The real self, the *inner Self*, is far more than this, but it takes a brutal honesty to open our inner eyes to see. We may not always be pleased with the view. But just as exercise is essential for muscular tone, a consistently honest self-examination process is essential for mind/body connectedness.

In order for us to be honest with ourselves, we must first practice honesty with others. When we deceive others, we deceive ourselves as well; we elevate the image of truth above truth itself. When we are young, image is more important than truth, achievement more important than conduct. It becomes easy to explain away unethical behavior. *"I wanted to win above all else,"* the cheater says. *"I desired this external thing,"* (trophy, promotion, reward). But as we mature, we realize that the most important events in life happen within us. Without personal honesty, we would miss them entirely.

The warrior must be sure of whom he is. He cannot afford to waste time looking for himself among the trophies of the world. He does not alter his self-examination process because of the praise or condemnation of others, nor cloud it with mind-altering substances which obscure the truth. He learns to speak directly with his own heart and to trust this inner Self. A warrior must be able to listen to what his heart tells him and act upon that information without uncertainty or hesitation. The warrior's ability to act decisively depends on his ability to perceive his inner nature clearly and without deception. There may not be time to vacilate or to ponder a dilemma at the last moment. A warrior may have to choose his path for years to come in a single instant, and it is then that he must listen closest to his heart. But his heart will not deceive him if he has approached it with honesty.

6. Learn to restrain your emotions.

It is neither possible nor wise to suppress our emotions. They will build like the pressure in a pressure-cooker until they are beyond containment. It is better to simply acknowledge our emotions, even welcome them but to disassociate them from our actions. Our actions communicate who we are to others and to ourselves as well.

Be careful to choose only those actions which deepen your connection with, or your understanding of, your art. Do not allow strong emotions to overwhelm you and disconnect you from your art, causing you to act in such a way that, later, you are ashamed or embarrassed.

People often say, "I was so angry I lost control!" or, "He made me crazy!" This is being a victim, not a warrior. The warrior says, "Though strong, my anger (or fear) was irrelevant. I acted exactly as I felt necessary." The warrior is proactive, not reactive.

Eventually, one learns to disassociate one's emotions not only from the actions of others, but from their negative emotions as well. It is not necessary to ingest the angst of every rude driver, aggressive salesman, arrogant rebel, or drunken social drop-out; they are working with or failing at their own lessons in their own way. We need only deal with others' actions insofar as they affect our personal space. Once our personal space is secured, we can let go of that interaction entirely.

Why store up the negative energy of others? Grudges only slow you down with unnecessary burdens, like an overloaded truck. Practice forgiveness instead; it detoxifies the river of your body, and smoothes your flow from one moment to the next. And fluid movement through both space and time is an essential skill of the warrior-nature.

7. Believe in yourself; develop "Victory-Mind."

Living a focused life is not enough, by itself, to achieve warrior-mind. One must believe oneself to be living *successfully*. A warrior perceives himself as being on a path that proceeds toward a chosen goal. It does not matter whether he ever actually achieves this goal, for the warrior's path is endless. But he draws his satisfaction—his feelings of personal victory—from simply remaining on the path. As long as he consistently practices his warrior art, he can perceive himself as carefully laying the groundwork necessary for success. This perception boosts his self-confidence and provides a reference point for increasing self-esteem.

This kind of self-esteem, based on a focused effort, is very different from the modern Western cult of self-esteem. So many books, so many social workers and media managers are flooding our culture with the idea that self-esteem can be a non-judgmental self-acceptance completely disconnected from any external guidance or benchmarks. It is like a display of power without a power source. It is like walking down a set of railroad tracks and pretending you are a train (which is fine, unless you happen to meet a real train coming the other way). It is an illusion the warrior can ill afford. The warrior's self-esteem ebbs and flows with his connection to his art. It is greatest when this connection is nearest to his heart. But it is connection with his art that the warrior seeks, for that is the source of his power. The warrior's self-esteem is based on this effort. As long as he tries his best, his esteem can remain high. And because he has given his best efforts, he learns to expect the best results.

The secret of a warrior's courage and tenacity is not found in superior weapons or armor; it is found in his relentless optimism.

The warrior learns to visualize success in all his undertakings. In fact, the transformation from a mere martial arts student into a warrior cannot begin until the concept of failure becomes unacceptable—until the thought of giving up can gain no foot-hold. Nothing undermines the warrior's position more than visualizing failure.

However, victory-mind does not imply unrealistic over-confidence. The warrior plays a never-ending balancing act between optimism and strategy. After all, the primary victory is to survive. A good warrior does not rush headlong into the face of overwhelming odds; neither does he ignore good strategy or sound advice. Rather, he will examine each situation in search of the best outcome. If retreat is his best option, then he will do so with the idea of succeeding at his retreat. Within every situation, the warrior will find choices; among those choices, he will find the choice of maximum yield. In this way, he will take advantage of every situation. The warrior perceives himself either in position to win, or in position to learn.

In the face of so many temptations to compromise his values and divide his energies, the warrior knows that the real victory is victory over the Self. As long as he remains grounded in his art, the warrior remains victorious. As the warrior learns to trust this connection, he learns also to trust his own choices. Eventually, an aura of self-confidence and positive energy develops around him which totally changes his relationship with the world. He relates from a position of strength (and vibrant health as well, since optimism has been proven to boost the immune system) no matter where he may find himself. Every action will emanate his focus, and even soft words will project the power behind them.

At this point, the warrior will begin to perceive a dichotomy of power around him. Events or energies which help him in his choices, which strengthen him or give him knowledge, are perceived as positive. Those that weaken or confuse him are perceived as negative. Eventually, he learns to discern the energy pattern around situations and people as clearly as reading signs. When the warrior encounters a vortex of negative energy—such as a person who is violently angry—he simply avoids that person and averts confrontation ahead of time. Many stories and legends have surrounded great warriors who have displayed this kind of sixth sense, but it is really just the result of practicing victory-mind and maintaining a positive-energy orientation.

8. Learn to empathize with others; develop "collective-mind."

The warrior is not a solitary and unfeeling machine who is adept at killing people, even though the mass media may idolize these lone-wolf "Rambo" types. But the truth is, wolves as a rule hunt in packs, and the lone wolf most often goes hungry or becomes prey itself. It is distinctly advantageous for the warrior to practice interacting with other people and to seek to understand the state-of-mind of everyone nearby—especially those people who are within striking distance. Often, the only warning a person may receive that he is about to be attacked is just a feeling that a person nearby is angry or unbalanced.

Therefore, the warrior is not afraid to reach out and connect with others. In fact, this becomes one aspect of his constant practice. Just as he is aware of positive and negative energies within his own body, the warrior seeks to perceive these energies within others as well. With practice, he may side-step danger before it even develops, or diffuse it by applying an opposite energy. An angry person may be calmed by an act of kindness; a fearful person will often react to a show of power with violence, but react to a show of calmness by becoming calmed himself. In any case, through empathetic connection with others, the warrior will receive the earliest possible warning to remove himself from a dangerous situation.

The best way to develop empathy is to connect on a regular basis with people one can trust. A good martial arts instructor will insist that his senior ranked students are of one mind about practice in order that the newer members of the *dojang* may more easily perceive a unified impression. Not only must self-defense techniques be taught the same by all instructors, but rules of order, courtesy, and respect must be practiced the same as well. In such a controlled environment, aberrant states of mind will stand out like red flags. For example, there is a correct manner and time to bow, and even though there will be many small variations in bowing, what is most noticeable is the student who forgets to bow. It is as important to correct this oversight as it is to correct improper technique. Martial efficiency must evolve within a group setting, and all members of that group must trust one another implicitly in order to practice deadly technique. A rebellious or arrogant mind must either be redirected or expelled.

The warrior practices *selective* empathy. He practices "collective-mind" only with trusted individuals who offer positive attitudes and unwavering courtesy. He does not take inside himself the feelings of untrustworthy or unbalanced people or the emotional propaganda of media group-think. He is simply as aware of them as he needs to be in order to insure his own safety.

9. Practice patience. Develop "beginner's mind."

No one can consider himself the best in a warrior art, since no one is truly invulnerable. Grandmaster Kim Sangcook, widely acknowledged by other Hapkido masters as one of the best ever in that art, once stated it this way:

I have never been beaten. But that does not mean that the fighter who can beat me does not exist. He does; he is out there somewhere. I just haven't met him yet. I practice for him.

The warrior's mind is opened outward, constantly searching for new information which may help him improve his technique or his warrior-nature. Just as students learn from teachers, teachers may also learn from students. The warrior knows that his practice is never finished, but is an endless path of refinement. He views himself as on the beginning of that path, rather than at its end. He knows that if he allows himself to become impatient with learning, or if he were to declare himself "done," or an "expert," then the only times that he would learn anything would be at times of harsh and unpleasant surprise. Remain humble, and you will not have to be humbled by life itself after you have become too arrogant to be wary. This thought will help you remain patient in all endeavors.

10. Learn to expand your awareness. Develop "listening-mind." In his famous *Book of Five Rings*, Miyamoto Musashi wrote nine rules for living the "Way." Three of these rules describe a mind which is constantly on alert, or *"listening"* to one's surroundings:

1. Do not think dishonestly.

2. The Way is in training.

3. Become acquainted with every art.

4. Know the ways of all professions.

5. Distinguish between gain and loss in worldly matters.

6. Develop intuitive judgment and understanding for everything.

7. Perceive those things which cannot be seen.

8. Pay attention even to trifles.

9. Do nothing which is of no use.

Eiji Yoshikawa, in his epic novel *Musashi*, describes an incident in the life of that great swordsman which perfectly illustrates "Listening-mind:"

> *Musashi was invited to a tea ceremony to be held in the garden of a friend who was himself a master swordsman. At the appointed time, one of the other guests, a student of the host, hid himself in the shadows beside the only entrance to the*

> *garden. Thinking to test Musashi's renown with the sword, he stood out of sight, motionless, with his sword drawn. After awhile, his arms became tired; he lowered his sword and turned toward the garden. There sat Musashi, holding his teacup and looking at him with innocence and amusement. Musashi had come into the garden through the trees!*

The warrior's senses are constantly on alert, and no information is ignored. He is aware of the shadows as well as the light, the quiet as well as the sounds. He is aware of the shapes around him, and he tastes the air in between. He knows if the wall behind him is solid, or if it holds a weapons rack ready to clatter to the floor if he bumps it. He is aware of the sudden movement of people around him who may step into his path, and he is ready to change his motions at any time to avoid collision. Eventually, he learns to become aware of the energy patterns which surround people, and he learns to read their intentions like an open book.

The martial artist who is "filled up with himself" and how good he looks is like the proverbial "overfilled cup," and is likely to miss the subtle changes around him, dismissing them as unimportant. The true warrior remains like an empty cup, filled only with awareness, not with ego. The warrior's awareness extends as far into his surroundings as is necessary to give him the earliest possible warning of danger.

Warrior mind is a state of expanded awareness and focused, unwavering intent. Technique is just an expression of this. Practice warrior mind, and technique will flow out of your body like a river out of the mountains.

As you perceive the necessity to act, you will already know how to act; by the time you think of a technique, it will already be done.

*****

Tan-Jun Breathing exercise.

Chapter 3

Breath control expands awareness

1. AWARENESS

I remember a time in the inexperience of my youth when I was pickpocketed in the infamous Navy-town of Olongapo in the Philippines. Fresh off the boat in the first port of call on my way to Viet-Nam, I was dressed in my best white uniform, a skip in my step, a grin on my face, and a wad of bills in my shirt pocket. Suddenly, there were four or five boys about 12 or 13 years old surrounding me, and one of them smeared a foul smelling grease onto one of my newly shined shoes. "Shine?" he said, grinning with insolence. I said something which can't be repeated here, but translates as "no," in most any language; then I grabbed him and wiped my shoe on his pant leg. Instantly I was being pushed in all directions as the kids yelled at me in *Tagolag*, the native dialect. I took a martial stance and was determined that the next kid to push me was going to get hit. But as my awareness spread outward, I noticed that they were already gone, the last one disappearing around the side of a building. And right after that, I noticed that my shirt-pocket button was torn off and my wad of bills was gone, too. It hadn't been about a shoe shine all along, although I had realized that about two seconds too late.

It seems often the most important lessons we learn in life, we learn about that much too late. The whole point of practicing the martial arts is to regain those two seconds. Those two seconds are the ones in which we find ourselves a move behind in the game of life, in which we find out we weren't paying quite enough attention. Those are the two seconds we could die in; and no matter how long you practice your martial technique, too late is, well, too late. There is something we need to practice that is more crucial to survival than technique. ***It is essential that the warrior learns to sharpen and quicken his perception and to sustain that mindset as he goes about his daily life.***

The trouble is, most martial arts instructors base their classes on learning technique. The students are drilled in a particular technique, or combination of techniques, until they can execute those moves automatically when the proper stimulus occurs. The attacker throws a right punch to the face, the defender steps aside, blocks the punch, and counters with a roundhouse to the solar plexus. Everyone knows what to do, and when it is going to happen. And this is a good way to begin at training, as long as the instructor realizes that this stimulus/response approach to training, by itself, is not preparing his students for real life. In the real world, anything can happen at any time.

I remember early in my martial arts training, in my Kenpo years, we practiced blocking punches for hours—hard blocks of hard, serious punches—high and low, hooks, and uppercuts. I used to go home after practice with my arms black and blue from my wrists to my shoulders. And yet early in my full-contact competition career, I got my jaw dislocated after I stepped out of the ring with one foot and the referee stopped the match. I let my guard down for a second, and my opponent came up over the referee's shoulder with a left hook. The technique was illegal, and my opponent got a warning. I got put on a liquid diet for a week. I should have seen it coming, but I just didn't expect it.

It seems the more we expect something, the more unprepared we are if something else happens. This perception delay is the missing ingredient that is present in every real fight and absent in every choreographed one. Simply put, if you don't know what is going to happen ahead of time, you can't react appropriately until after it starts. You must first see an attack, then your brain must identify it. (Attention! Alert! Left hook coming in fast at eleven o'clock!) Then your brain must send out an emergency signal to react, and finally, your hands move into blocking position. Well, actually, unless your hands were already in blocking position, it's probably too late by then: Sock-o and you suddenly find yourself in the slow-motion of shock, spiraling downward…

This stimulus/response delay is called reaction time. Studies done on reaction time have shown that even in athletes given a simple task, reaction time is still a significant factor. The fastest reaction time measured for a single-movement, non-complex task (pushing a button) is still approximately three-tenths of a second (0.30 sec.). A normal reaction time in a healthy individual is approximately 0.50 seconds. And most martial arts defenses are considerably more complex than pushing a button. We must assume at least a half-second delay in any martial technique we attempt. Thus, any aggression that completes itself within that first half-second is all but unstoppable by the poor, defenseless and unsuspecting victim. This is the main reason that "sucker punches" are so effective; there is precious little warning about them.

In the book *Aikido and the Dynamic Sphere*, authors Westbrook and Ratti write:

> ***Every process of defense will consist of these three stages: perception, evaluation-decision, and reaction. The effectiveness of any defense strategy will depend largely upon the time lapse between the first inkling that an attack may be imminent, and your defensive reaction…the strategic aim is to train***

> *and refine your faculties to such an extent that perception, evaluation-decision, and reaction will become almost simultaneous (p. 62).*

It is for this reason that the warrior trains at his basic moves repeatedly, without tiring of the repetition; he is whittling down his reaction time. But training which concentrates entirely on the physics of technique only whittles down the reaction time of the second two of these critical factors—evaluation-decision and the initiation of appropriate action. And while these factors can be reduced through long and diligent training to an almost instantaneous response, we have seen that the biomechanics of our bodies almost guarantees that this will never be fast enough. There is still the matter of—and the time lapse that occurs during—*perception*, the first and most important of the three critical defense factors. The warrior must introduce another direction into his training in order to regain the critical edge; that direction transcends the physical level and enters a dimension of Mind.

The term *perception* implies that there is a particular object, action, or predicament to be perceived. That sounds simple enough; "Just keep yer eyes peeled," John Wayne used to say. But perception is filtered by the mind of the perceiver, and always begs the question, *"What does this mean to me?"* perception implies at least some personal judgment, and is by definition, egocentric. And as long as our own understanding is a part of the perception of our environment, there is a possibility of misunderstanding, of *misperception*. There are many people in this world who make their living creating misperception, as I found out so long ago in Olongapo.

Perception must be further refined to meet a warrior's needs. He must learn to open the doors of perception that is, **the warrior's goal is not merely to perceive, but to be in a continuous state of openness.** He must expand and sharpen his **awareness.** Only by becoming aware of danger early enough can the warrior hope to initiate a defensive reaction soon enough to be effective. In fact, eventually physical technique becomes a secondary focus; the primary focus of the warrior is to incorporate total awareness of his surroundings as an on-going part of his consciousness. He achieves this by incorporating a variety of mental practices into his training. Systematic relaxation, calming and centering meditation, and breath control become a daily ritual, whether or not he attends a formal training session. His intention is to achieve and sustain maximum awareness at all times, not just in class.

Ordinarily, people find themselves experiencing this kind of maximum awareness instinctively only in situations of eminent danger, such as the instant before falling from a great height, or the instant before crashing their car at high speed. It is a state of total involvement with the here-and-now. Some people have described this mental state as feeling as if everything were happening in slow motion, but it's really the compression of everything one is—one's history, personality, and intent—into a single instant. It is the most important moment in one's universe. The Japanese call this mental state **Zanshin**, which in our culture has no direct translation, but *primal awareness* is close. It is a state in which both the body and the mind are totally focused on staying alive. The ultimate goal of martial training is to teach a warrior how to achieve this state of mind early enough to be of use-- before losing one's balance over a great height, before the car goes out of control, before the punch even begins. The most successful warriors are aware of subtle shifts in the energies and emotions around them to such an extent that they become just as aware of an attack as the attackers themselves. In most cases, an attacker will give off subliminal clues in his behavior, his speech, or his emotional intensity that may indicate a decision to become aggressive even before his attack begins.

I have only met one man in my life who is able to achieve this state at will; that man is Grandmaster Kim Sangcook. We sparred many times in the five years I trained with him, and a few times in the more than thirty years I have trained with his senior student, Grandmaster James Garrison. In all that time, I was never able to land either a punch or kick, not even one. Yet Grandmaster Kim could read my intentions like a large-print children's book and hit me at his leisure. Grandmaster Kim recently said this:

"If a student bases a lifetime of training on defense, he has already imagined defeat. If one's life is rooted in action, defense becomes a natural variable in the scheme of things."

This describes Zanshin, a state in which one's *ki*, or total life-force, is extended not only into awareness, but into movement as well. Awareness and movement become one consciousness in which there is no reaction time. By the time one realizes an action is needed, it is already done.

This state of mind is not easy to attain. In daily living, it is only experienced when one's normal expectations are disrupted; it may be that an element of fear is necessary to initiate it. But a warrior needs to learn how to achieve this mental state without fear. This is the function of true martiality in martial arts training. A good teacher will continuously challenge his students to the point of occasionally awakening fear within them for this purpose. He will demand their attention to the point that it must be perceived as dangerous to become distracted. His intention is to teach his students to expect the unexpected, and to have the confidence to trust their intuitive understanding of the environment around them. With years of practice, this kind of training will eventually open the doors of perception, and the student will be able to achieve and sustain an enhanced, primal awareness.

Awareness is a focus of one's energy on the *here and now*. This is somewhat like a mathematical equation; the more energy an individual has, the more energy that individual can focus into awareness. The less energy an individual has, the less aware he is likely to be. A person who is tired, or sick, or whose perception is altered by drugs cannot be as aware of his surroundings as a person whose vitality and mental clarity are high. Also, the less "here and now" the mind is the less aware it is as well. That is to say, the more distracted by his own thoughts—that ongoing voice inside his head which chatters on about future plans, or past triumphs and regrets—even momentary distraction such as an attractive specimen of the opposite sex—the less aware that person will be of subtle but important changes in his immediate environment.

We all laugh at the comedic situation of the man behind the wheel of his car, who, distracted for a moment by a beautiful girl, drives into the truck in front of him which has suddenly stopped. We laugh because in the comedic setting, no one gets hurt. But the warrior, outside of comedic settings, cannot afford such distractions; they may result in serious injury or even death. Therefore, the warrior must constantly train his mind to maximize awareness of his surroundings, and he must maximize the energy available for this task and focus on it appropriately.

We all experience the ebb and flow of energy along our chosen paths—working, studying, or socializing—and its loss wears us down.

We replenish ourselves through a balanced diet and adequate rest. But the warrior cannot be satisfied with the normal ebb and flow of available energy; his goal is to maximize both his energy and his awareness. He must learn how to focus on the immediacy of the moment, and how to let go of any distractions. He must learn how to quiet the mind so that it is not busy with its own importance. He must learn how to relax the body and center its balance so that he is ready to respond to anything, not just one thing. He must learn how to calm and subjugate strong emotions which distort perception. And he must learn how to recharge his personal energy supply through *ki* building meditation. Then, perhaps, he will be able to reclaim those two seconds when he needs them most.

2. BREATH

The most important exercise a warrior can learn—one which will teach him to accomplish all of the above goals—is how to properly control his breathing. Breath control is rarely taught in Western culture, except superficially in some sport activities. This is probably because to the Western mind, breathing is considered a purely physiological function. We assume we know all there is to know about breathing by the time we are five or six years old. We inhale fresh air, and we exhale used air. We believe that pretty much sums it up, and we rarely think more about it. Meanwhile, we sit in postures that cramp our lungs, and we forget to use our abdominal muscles to help us exhale completely, thus trapping stale air in the lower lungs. And then we find ourselves yawning, which can be a sign that our body would like better oxygenation as well as a sign of fatigue.

While it is true that breathing is largely automatic, it is also true that automatic breathing may not be the most efficient way of breathing. Have you ever been so frightened that you stopped breathing for a moment? Have you ever been so angry that your breath became ragged and shallow? There is a direct link between one's emotions and one's breathing—a biochemical connection. Strong emotions stimulate an adrenergic release; that is, the body's most potent hormones, adrenaline and norepinephrine, are released into the bloodstream as a result of any strong emotion. These hormones directly affect the heart and lungs. Both pulse and blood pressure rise, and breathing becomes more rapid in order to supply the heart (and the rest of the muscles) with oxygen in case there is a need for a sudden burst of activity. This is called the "fight or flight syndrome." But if the oxygen is not used—such as a strong emotion experienced in an inactive or indecisive state—the whole body becomes tense. The muscles, with their increased blood flow and oxygenation, may begin to twitch. The muscles which control the expansion of the chest begin to produce shallow and uneven respirations. The blood vessels all over the body constrict; the blood supply to the brain now carries less oxygen, and we may become light-headed, or even faint. Imagine a warrior, face to face with a mortal enemy, who turns pale and faints!

Fortunately for the warrior, (any athlete for that matter) the converse is also true. Just as hormonal surges affect breathing, breathing also influences hormonal release. Therefore, controlling one's breathing can give an individual a certain degree of control over which hormones are flooding his system. And since there is a direct relationship between hormonal release and one's emotional state, control of one's breathing can result in a certain degree of control over one's emotions. Physiologically, this is how it works: the more rapid the breathing pattern, the more adrenergic hormones are released. The slower the breathing pattern, the more cholinergic hormones, such as acetylcholine and dopamine, are released. Cholinergic hormones stimulate the autonomic nervous system, which acts as the body's emergency brake. The heart-rate is slowed, the blood vessels dilate, long-bone muscles relax, and smooth muscle tissue—found around the hollow organs involved with digestion, are stimulated. As a person's breathing slows, he becomes calmer, thinks clearer, has better small muscle coordination, and digests food better. At least until the next big scare.

The warrior, who knows that big scare is coming, learns to slow his breathing pattern by exerting conscious control over his diaphragm muscle. Although there are many muscles involved in the breathing cycle, the diaphragm, a smooth, domed muscle which separates the pleural (chest) cavity from the visceral (abdominal) cavity, is the largest and most important. When a person inhales, the diaphragm contracts, pulling itself away from the chest cavity and pressing down on the viscera in the abdominal cavity beneath it. This contraction increases the size of the chest cavity (aided by the intercostal muscles which lift the ribs upward and outward) and the lungs expand with fresh air to fill the space.

When a person exhales, the diaphragm and the intercostal muscles relax, the ribs move downward and inward, and the diaphragm moves upward into the chest cavity. The air inside the lungs, which has exchanged its oxygen for carbon dioxide and other body wastes, is now forced out of the airway. Of course, this process is continuous and automatic, or we would die. But as it has been shown, many physiologic and environmental factors influence our breathing pattern without our even being aware of it. Air quality, body temperature, airway congestion, and physical activity all alter our breath, in addition to our emotional state. The body will automatically adjust breath rate, posture, airway openings, and muscle tension to increase blood/oxygen to a normal level. One can observe this at any strenuous athletic event; after a competitor has exerted himself, he will struggle to catch his breath—posture sagging, limp muscled, mouth open, nostrils flaring, chest heaving. The warrior cannot afford to be caught "out of breath" in this way; his survival may depend on his ability to optimize his breathing pattern through several peak exertions. Through breath control training, he learns to "pace" his breath.

Breath control centers on exerting conscious control over two groups of muscles involved in breathing—the intercostal muscles and the diaphragm. Normally, these muscles work in conjunction with one another. During inhalation, both contract or flex; during exhalation, both relax. The warrior must learn to disassociate these two muscle groups. He must learn to concentrate on contracting the diaphragm while restricting the contraction of the intercostals. The result is that the ribs move less upward and outward, and the diaphragm presses down onto the abdominal area with greater force. The feeling one gets during exercise is that one is "breathing into his abdomen," even though this is physiologically impossible. But as the diaphragm presses downward, the abdomen becomes rigid and distended as though filling with air, and a feeling of warmth fills the area below the navel. Indeed, many martial arts teachers will lead diaphragmatic breathing exercises by saying, "Breathe into your abdomen," and the term *abdominal breathing* has been used to describe diaphragmatic breathing for thousands of years.

Physiologically, there are four major effects of this exercise: 1. Because abdominal breathing results in slower and deeper breaths, the oxygen/carbon dioxide exchange is significantly improved. 2. Increased muscular tone in the primary muscles involved with breathing increases aerobic capacity. 3. Increased stimulus of the vagus nerve bundle located in the solar plexus results in emotional control, as we have seen. 4. If done properly in conjunction with certain leg stances and arm movements, this form of breathing is reputed to produce a variety of kinds of visceral massage that other forms of movement cannot produce, thus promoting optimum internal organ circulation and general health. In order to achieve maximum benefit, it is recommended that these exercises be learned from an experienced and knowledgeable practitioner.

So far, we have considered abdominal (diaphragmatic) breathing only in terms of its physiological benefits—its enhancement of optimum oxygenation and its calming effect. But there are other reasons—perhaps even more important reasons—the warrior practices this art. In almost all Oriental cultures, breath control is considered not only a physical exercise, but a mental and philosophical discipline as well. Many Eastern cultures connect the breath with the esoteric concept of *ki*, or personal energy. In China, breath control is known as *chi-kung*, or "healing energy." In Japan, breath control is called *haragei*, or "belly art." In India, the yogis call it *pranayama*, or "spirit breath." In Korea, this art is called *tan-jun* breathing, or "breathing from the center." All of these breathing arts are the same in that they all combine the physical discipline of **slow abdominal breathing**, the mental discipline of **quieting and centering the mind**, and the meditative art of ***ki* visualization**.

In the original Sangcook Kim Hapkido School, Mr. Kim led his students in Tan-Jun breathing exercises that were so slow, I used to think that he wasn't paying attention and had forgotten about us. His timing would allow for only about two breaths per minute and would last for six or seven minutes or more. My lungs would be ready to burst and the muscles involved in my breathing often went into spasm. But every time I broke from the rhythm to gasp for breath, Mr. Kim would simply announce to the class, "Stay with the count." I now believe he was leading our Tan-Jun breathing this way on purpose, to teach us to concentrate all our energy on our breathing. If Abdominal (Tan-Jun) breathing is not challenging, then a student will not be motivated to concentrate on it. But once the mental energy is focused, a whole new dimension of training unfolds.

My wife, Lonnie, a yoga instructor for more than 20 years, often tells her students, *"One cannot breathe in the past, nor in the future; one can only breathe in the present moment."* Concentrating on one's own breathing is an excellent method of focusing on the here and now. Abdominal breathing is traditionally done extremely slowly for two reasons. The first is the physiological reason—to produce maximum inflation and deflation of the lungs and insure optimum oxygen/carbon dioxide exchange. The second reason is to capture the total attention of the mental process.

If one's only thought is to keep control of the breathing process and not gasp for breath prematurely, then all the other thoughts one has, that ongoing internal dialogue which echoes through the mind—voices of past victories or regrets, of future plans and dreams, of relationships, duties, promises and needs—all of these thoughts have to take a "back seat" to the immediate need to breathe. The mind becomes quiet with its own concentration on the here and now.

The Yoga tradition calls the inner dialogue "monkey mind," the incessant chatter of our minds leaping from thought to thought like monkeys jumping from branch to branch in a tree.

There is another reason why this mental focus is valuable to the warrior. Each extraneous thought drains energy from the mind as we try to analyze it and categorize it. Moreover, on a subconscious level, each thought rushes through our bodies as a neural message, directing our entire musculoskeletal structure to react with it. Our bodies tense up with directives, trying to be prepared to go in many different directions at once. Our muscles, poised for action, cannot relax. The more active our mental voices, the more filled with subconscious directives the muscles become. Eventually, they will begin to quiver and twitch with anticipation. In this physical state, it is impossible for the muscles to react appropriately to an outside stimulus because they have been preempted to react to a multitude of imaginary stresses. A direct translation from the Japanese Zen tradition calls this mental state "word-drunkenness." We have all seen suspense movies in which the pretty heroine is surprised by some sudden terror and jumps back, gasping, hands frozen ineffectually in air—the perfect victim.

The warrior cannot afford to have his muscles preempted; he must strive to have them ready to react at all times. That is, his muscles must be kept in a well-toned but neutral state—a state of relaxation. Bruce Lee wrote in his book, *Tao of Jeet Kune Do*, "Relaxed muscles react much faster than tensed muscles." It can also be said that you cannot relax the body until you relax the mind. Therefore, the warrior must quiet all the mental voices which tense him up. He must let go of all thoughts that he will act a certain way, or move a certain way, or even think a certain thought. He knows that these are just distractions. The warrior's ongoing preparation, whether for class or for combat, is to empty his mind of extraneous thoughts, relax completely, and focus all mental energy into ongoing awareness of that particular moment.

I remember a moment many years ago in which this kind of ongoing awareness was demonstrated to me in a simple but unforgettable way. I had gone to an Aikido demonstration by Koichi Tohei Shihan at a local university gymnasium. Since I had arrived early, I decided to visit the restroom before the demonstration began. As I turned down a narrow and crowded hallway leading to the restroom, a door opened in front of me. Out stepped Koichi Tohei Shihan directly into my path. He was flanked by black-belted Aikidokas, and his head was turned away from me as he conversed with one of them. They were all walking toward me at a brisk pace. With people on either side of me and behind me as well, there was nowhere for me to step out of the way. Since I was in the middle of the hallway, and Tohei Shihan was also in the middle of the hallway, a collision was imminent. Tohei Sensei's head was still turned around as he talked to someone slightly behind him; I braced myself for a jarring shoulder-to-shoulder collision, but it never happened. Suddenly, Tohei Sensai was past me without touching. He glanced my way, smiling, and continued to talk as though the close call had never happened.

The Japanese word for this state of mind is **mushin**, or *"the mind of no mind."* Mushin is often explained as the state of mind that an athlete achieves during the moment of exertion—a kind of unconscious action in which the body performs its trained movement without interference from the mind. Actually, mushin is a bit more complicated than that. In peaceful physical activities such as sports, the action and the timing are known events. Emptying the mind and focusing on sports play is fairly easy; mushin is achieved by superior players almost automatically once the action begins. But for the warrior, the action and the moment it will happen are not known; there is no activity to focus on ahead of time. For the warrior, mushin is a state of total mental and physical quietness, a state in which all mental energy is focused into external awareness instead of internal dialogue. It is as though the mind were "listening" with all five senses (See "Listening Mind, Chapt. 2). Controlling and guiding of the mental process to focus energy into awareness of the here and now is also called **centering the mind**. Abdominal breathing has been used by warriors of Eastern cultures to calm and center the mind for thousands of years.

Just as the warrior learns to discard all thoughts which distract from the present moment, he also learns to discard thoughts which steal or squander his energy. In fact, there are exercises that Eastern cultures use which can actually enhance one's personal energy. These exercises are called **ki visualization**.

Ki visualization, also known as *ki* meditation, is based on the Oriental concept of *ki*. The term *ki* does not translate well into the English language because it represents a concept for which Western culture has no counterpart. Consequently, *ki* has been translated in a multitude of different ways, including *spirit, soul, energy, vitality*, and also simply as *breath*. In Oriental cultures, it is believed that a body of energy infuses and surrounds the physical body which is roughly the same size and shape. All objects in the physical world have energy-bodies. Inanimate objects such as rocks have energy bodies that are extremely stable and may not change for millions of years. But living beings have energy-bodies that are in a state of constant flux. The energy within this ethereal body is called **ki**. **Ki** ebbs and floods, flows and pools, gets blocked and unblocked in its pathways around the energy-body. The more intense, or "brighter" his (or her) energy-body, the more healthy and vital the person feels. If one's *ki* is blocked in its flow around the energy-body, one may feel a soreness, dizziness, or any number if symptoms in the physical body. The art of acupuncture is used by Chinese physicians to unblock the flow of *ki* in the energy-body, thereby restoring health to the physical body.

While the warrior cannot quickly prepare for combat by such a complicated and exacting art as sticking needles into his body, there is an exercise that he can do which is quick, simple, and quiet. **Ki visualization**, or *ki meditation*, is done in conjunction with abdominal breathing; in fact, this exercise is sometimes called *ki breathing*.

To better understand *ki* breathing, it is necessary to add one more concept to the process of abdominal breathing—the **ki center**. The center of the physical body's mass is, for the normally shaped person, approximately one or two inches below the navel. This is also the traditional center of the energy-body. In Chinese, this center is called the *tan-tien*. In Japanese, it is called the *hara*. In Korean, this point is called the *tan-jun* center. It is the point of origin of the energy body, the point from which one's energy emanates, along energy lines called meridians, to all parts of the energy-body. Because the *tan-jun* point is the center of both the physical body and the energy body, the *tan-jun* point acts as a gateway between the two. It is believed that if we affect the physical *tan-jun* center, we influence the energy body at the same time. This presents us with a remarkable opportunity to restore and revitalize our personal energy with a simple mental exercise.

Remember that thoughts reach out to all parts of the body in the form of chemical neurotransmitters, and that the body reacts physically to these, whether they originated from inside or outside the mind. Also remember that when one practices *tan-jun* breathing, the abdomen becomes slightly warmer because of the compression of the visceral tissue by the diaphragm. *Ki* visualization meditations simply combine these two phenomena. The following is a fairly typical *ki* meditation done in conjunction with breathing:

> **As you begin to inhale slowly into your abdomen, concentrate your mental focus on your tan-jun center, approximately two inches below your navel. As you inhale, you will feel an increase in both pressure and warmth in that area. Now visualize this pressure and warmth as pure, fresh energy in the form of a white ball of light or a bright flame. As your inhalation deepens, visualize that ball of light (or flame) growing larger and brighter. The**

ball of light will grow in size and intensity until, at the peak of your inhalation, it becomes uncontainable. As you begin your exhalation, you will feel the warmth and tightness in your abdomen begin to dissipate; visualize this feeling as energy spreading out from the glowing light at your tan-jun center and reaching into every last corner of your body. As you continue to exhale, you may direct this emanating energy to any particular place, such as an injury or soreness that you wish to heal. Visualize the new, fresh energy scouring out old, used energy, waste and toxins throughout the tissues of the body. As your exhalation reaches its completion, visualize yourself as renewed, revitalized, and well. At the bottom of your exhalation, you pause briefly before your next inhalation and clear your mind completely of any thoughts other than your next breath. You are empty, quiet, and purified.

It takes as few as three slow, abdominal breaths to change the chemical (adrenergic/cholinergic) balance circulating in the blood. Consequently, tan-jun breathing exercises are usually done a minimum of three times per set. A good instructor will not hurry through this part of practice as though this were less important than the more dynamic appearing self defense techniques. Tan-jun breathing is a time of energy enhancement, so that later, during the execution of technique, a student can simply release his stored energy. Thus, a good instructor will pay close attention to his students' posture, stance, and muscular flexion. He may test the upper body and arm muscles to see that excess focus—in the form of excess muscle flexion—is not present, and he may also test the tan-jun point with gentle prodding to insure that it becomes rigid during inhalation.

An instructor should also be aware that students with considerable training in tan-jun breathing will be able to breathe much slower than white belt beginners who have never done this exercise before. A good rule of thumb is that beginners can perform tan-jun breathing comfortably at a rate of approximately four breaths per minute. With a few months of practice, that rate can be slowed to three breaths per minute. Advanced practitioners, such as black belts, can occasionally practice tan-jun breathing at two breaths per minute. And of course, these rates only apply for adult students. Children under the age of 14 have smaller lung capacities and should not be led in tan-jun breathing exercises slower than six breaths per minute for younger and inexperienced children, or four breaths per minute for older and more experienced children.

Tan-jun breathing combined with *ki* meditation is one of the most personal and private moments in any martial arts class. It is not just a physical exercise. A good instructor will encourage his students to make a mental connection as well. Students who cannot complete the exercise without scratching itches, or straightening their uniforms, or looking around the room to see how other students are doing are only cheating themselves. This lack of concentration should be discouraged.

Once students have learned the basic movements involved in tan-jun breathing, the instructor can invite them to explore how their body feels during the movement, and to visualize revitalizing energy flowing into sore spots or injuries they might have. He may also encourage them to alter the length of the inhalations as compared to the exhalations. In the colder winter months, he may lengthen the inhalations in order to generate more internal warmth. In the summer months when students are usually already warm, he may shorten the inhalations and lengthen the exhalations, concentrating on the waste elimination and purification phase. The idea is to get the students personally involved in their tan-jun exercises, because they will only get out of it what they put into it.

Students should also be encouraged to become aware of their breathing not just in class, but throughout their daily activities. Breath awareness is a life skill, not just a martial skill. Learn to become aware of your breathing, especially during physical activity. How do you breathe when you are running? Chopping wood? Rowing a boat? Throwing a ball? Do you become out of breath during this activity? Can you consciously deepen and enhance your breathing using your diaphragm muscle? Do you notice a calming effect?

Another important exercise to incorporate into your daily life is quieting and centering the mind. While you are concentrating on your breathing, try not to think of anything in particular other than what your senses are telling you. What do you see in front of you? What do you "see" behind you? What do you hear, smell, taste, feel? Is there a source of frantic or unstable energy nearby? What can you "sense" about people without listening to their words?

And finally, remember to tell yourself that you are already becoming the way you wish to be. Tell yourself often that you are healthy, strong, confident, and wise. My wife, ever the Yoga teacher, often says to me, *"Be careful what your mind is saying; your body is always listening."* I have found this to be true both on and off the mat.

During my career as a firefighter/paramedic, tan-jun breathing has saved my life on more than one occasion. Early in my career, self-contained breathing gear was fairly new and not completely reliable. These early prototypes were supposed to have a short-air-supply alarm bell, but these bells didn't always work. Sometimes, firefighters simply ran out of air with no warning. We were taught that if it became difficult to inhale, then you had two, maybe three breaths left in your tank. But if you breathed very slowly using primarily your diaphragm, you could make that small amount of air last a minute or more. It's surprising how calm you can remain while exiting a burning building with no air, but I don't recommend this as a regular training exercise!

There is a wonderful example of expanding awareness in the form of an old Zen tale, recounted in the collection <u>Zen Flesh, Zen Bones</u>, compiled by Paul Reps:

The Taste of Banzo's Sword

Matajuro Yagyu was the son of a famous swordsman. His father, believing that his son's practice was too mediocre to anticipate mastership, disowned him. So Matajuro went to Mount Futara and there, finding the famous swordsman Banzo, pleaded to become his student. Banzo said that he would think about it for a while if Matajuro would stay around and help with the daily chores, but he was never to touch a sword, or speak of fencing.

Matajuro cooked for Banzo, washed his dishes, made his bed, cleaned the yard, and cared for the garden, all without any word of swordsmanship. A year passed, then another. Still Matajuro labored on. Thinking of his plight, he had become sad, for he had not even begun to learn the art to which he had devoted his life.

But one day Banzo crept up behind Marajuro and gave him a terrific blow with a wooden sword. The following day, as he was chopping wood, Banzo again sprang upon him unexpectedly. After that, day and night, Matajuro had to endure these unexpected thrusts. Not a moment passed that he did not have to think of the taste of Banzo's sword. That awareness changed the way he walked, the way he sat, even the way he breathed.

One day, as he was cooking rice, Banzo tried to hit him with his wooden sword, but Matajuro was too quick. He stepped aside, parrying with his frying pan, then went about his cooking as if nothing had happened.

Eventually, Matajuro became the greatest swordsman in the land.

The first defense of the warrior is awareness.

* * * * *

Turnback side kick.

Chapter 4

Move from the Center

A few months ago, I experienced an interesting confrontation while working out on the heavy bag at a local fitness center. I was resting and stretching in between punching and kicking sets when a young man in his mid-teens entered the area where the heavy bag was hung. I looked at him with some curiosity, since it was mid-day and mid-week, and he didn't appear to be old enough to be a high school graduate.

The young man was disheveled and unshaven; he was wearing street clothes instead of workout clothes, and his tennis shoes were muddy. His gait had a definite forward list, as though he were falling into his own footsteps. He was wide-eyed and *sanpaku*, a Japanese term meaning the whites of his eyes were visible below the pupils—a sign of deep fatigue and imbalance. The young man looked at the heavy bag and then at my sparring gloves and his face lifted into a high-nosed sneer. He staggered over to the heavy bag and began flailing at it with poorly executed but still powerful roundhouse punches. Then he began kicking at the bag. He would stagger back several steps, run at the bag, and launch himself into a kind of awkward flying roundhouse kick. When he hit the bag, he would bounce off, lose his balance, and have to take a few steps to regain it. Several times he fell down. After each kick, he would look my way and sneer with insolence, then walk with his staggering gait back to his starting place. I just smiled back, waiting for my turn with the bag.

As I watched him kick, though, my mind practiced its own frequent exercise. I asked myself, if this person and I were to have a fight, how would I defend myself? I observed a person who was much younger and who kicked very hard. The youth appeared to move about as though his mind were altered by drugs. My educated guess from working 25 years as a paramedic was that he was on some sort of stimulant, such as methamphetamine. That meant that not only would his muscles be tight and powerful, but he would not feel pain as acutely as a normal person. Controlling a drug-crazed person with pain-inducing techniques is nearly impossible. If we were to fight, I would have to break one or more of his bones…

But as I watched the youth kicking and falling down, another strategy occurred to me—an easier one. I might not be stronger; I might not even be faster. But I was sure that I had better balance. If we had to fight, all I would have to do would be to stay out of his reach.

I would offer him a target and then move out of the way at the last possible instant, like a bullfighter with a cape. He would keep falling down, and sooner or later he would injure himself. I would let the floor beat him up. That's why I was smiling sincerely, and probably why it was a frustrating experience for him. After a while, he made an obscene gesture with one finger and staggered away. I guess I was too unappreciative of his martial prowess, and he needed to seek out a more admiring audience.

There are quite a number of unbalanced people out there in the real world. Almost every night, the evening new carries at least one story about someone who has gone off the deep end of the social spectrum. Whether these people are unbalanced by illegal drugs or toxic environment, poor diet, abusive relationships, or job stress, the aftermath is usually the same; some innocent bystander has to deal with their lack of control. This chapter is about how to remain balanced both physically and mentally, and how to use this to your advantage.

The word *balance* is multi-dimensional. It is a word which denotes a certain physical state, but connotes a mental and emotional state as well. When we say a person is balanced, we are most often referring to a physical act, such as a circus performer balanced on a high wire. But when we say that a person is unbalanced, we most often mean that person is not in a normal mental or emotional state. The warrior must have a clear understanding of balance in all of its meanings. First we will examine balance as a physical state, and then we will examine mental groundedness. Finally, we will examine the use of balance in an adversarial situation, as a tactical advantage.

PHYSICAL BALANCE

Most people understand balance as something we maintain in order to not fall down. We stand tall as adults, proud of the fact that we can navigate through the normal hazards of the day and not fall. Beyond this involvement, the normal person doesn't give balance much thought.

Let's consider walking. The average person walks with straight legs, from heel to toe. His leg swings forward, propelled in large part by gravity, until the toe points upward, and his entire weight crunches down on the forward heel. The person's momentum carries his weight forward onto the rest of that foot, and the rear foot is drawn forward into the next step. During more than half of this cycle, the average walker is out of control, *falling* into the next step.

The warrior must be trained from the very beginning to move differently. He must be trained to walk with the legs bent and the back straight, on the balls of the feet. He must learn to walk so that at no point during the stepping cycle is he out of control, "falling" into the next step. He must be able to change direction at any time during his step. This demands a highly trained sense of the relationship between balance and movement. **Maintaining balance in all movement is the warrior's most fundamental physical skill. All his power, speed, and focus originate with and depend on good balance.**

Almost the first physical act a new martial art student learns (after bowing!) is how to get into a "horse stance." It is interesting to note that the horse stance (feet wide apart, knees bent and widened, hips forward and back straight) is a beginning basic in nearly every martial system in the world. Yet very few of the world's martial arts teach fighting while crouched in the horse stance. Then why is it taught so universally? Because this stance teaches the student a heightened awareness of his primary physical asset: balance.

In every martial arts class I have ever attended, I have practiced horse stance/middle punch. And in almost every class, the instructor has told someone in the class, "Use your legs!" or, "Move your hips!" or, "Square your shoulders!" And with minor adjustments hardly visible to the untrained eye, a student's balance is corrected, and his power increased dramatically.

What the instructor is trying to teach during these horse stance drills is a two-fold concept. **The first concept of balance is being grounded.** When walking, the average person is interested only in moving from point to point while expending the minimum amount of energy to not fall down. Consequently, when the unexpected interrupts that process—an unseen obstruction in the path, a dip or hole in the sidewalk, or a leg trip or sweep—the average person with his tenuous connection to the ground beneath him falls down and is surprised by the whole event. This is not being grounded.

If you trip over a stick in your path, don't blame the stick.

The martial artist must practice a more connected relationship with the ground. Not only is he interested in maintaining balance and not falling down, but he knows that the strength of any technique originates from the ground, through his legs and hips. The horse stance is the perfect exercise to begin this important lesson.

While standing in a horse stance, a person can throw a punch with absolutely no movement in the hips or legs. But, without hip or leg movement, the shoulder of the punching arm will have to move forward with the fist. The more the shoulder moves, the more power is transmitted into the punch. The trouble with this is twofold. First, the power of such a punch is limited to the arm and shoulder and does not have the whole body weight or power behind it. Second, the shoulder movement itself causes imbalance. The farther the punching shoulder moves forward, the more off-balance the puncher becomes. A trained opponent will take advantage of this by leading the puncher into further imbalance. (See chapter 6 for more information about leading.)

Punching correctly must involve the legs and hips. The legs push into the punch, lengthening the distance between the ground and the center-of-mass, (the *Tan-Jun* center), adding the energy of the most powerful muscles in the body to the punch—the quadriceps of the upper leg. The hips rotate around the *Tan-Jun* transferring the energy generated in the legs to the upper body. Consequently, the shoulders do not have to generate energy, and don't have to move as much. Energy is transferred from the *Tan-Jun* through the shoulders into the punching arm. At the last instant of the punch, the instant of contact, the shoulders and hips move in unison into a position of maximum balance, or groundedness. This is a sudden slight reversal of movement resulting in squared shoulders, squared hips, and equal distribution of weight on both legs. Thus, being grounded is not a static stance; it is a dynamic and ongoing awareness. **Being well grounded means that a person is able to move in any direction instantly without having to adjust his stance and without losing his balance. A person's relationship with the ground defines his power.** This is why a martial artist's legs are always bent, ready to spring into action and transfer their power into movement. One of the excellent teachers I have had a seminar with, James Muro, a California based Kenpo stylist, describes bent-leg stances as "like a coiled spring."

The second concept of balance is centered movement. In previous chapters, we have learned of the Eastern concept of *Ki*, or vital personal energy. We have also learned that the center of this body of energy is located at a point two inches or so below our navel, at the *Tan-Jun center*, which is also our center of physical mass. When we move about, our weight must be equally distributed on our legs with this point at the center. Also, our shoulders must be straight above this point or we become off-balance and our stance is weakened. In an adversarial confrontation, the person who loses his balance first will have the same disadvantage as the person who is hit first: he will probably lose the fight.

A warrior must remain conscious of and in touch with his center at all times. Both his balance and his power depend on it. In the previous discussion of horse-stance/middle punch, it was stated that the hips must commit to the punch. What the hips are actually doing is moving around the Tan-Jun point in such a way as to project in the same direction (and at the same time) as the punch. This hip rotation and projection of the Tan-Jun point movement works exactly in the same manner for punches, kicks, blocks, and even grappling moves. The warrior must learn how to move his body in such a way as to put his total weight into each movement without overextending his balance beyond the stance he has chosen to support that movement.

When I was a beginner in the martial arts, one of my instructors would walk among the students while we stood in the horse-stance and push on us very hard without warning. Those who weren't concentrating on their center would bend in the middle and have to stagger several steps in order not to fall down. Those who were well-centered would accept the energy of the push into their *Tan-Jun* point. If the push was strong enough to move them, they simply took a step away from it, maintaining their balance the whole time. I remember that during kicking practice, this same instructor would walk among us, and at the moment a kick extended outward, he would push against our bodies in the opposite direction. Many of the students would lose their balance and fall down. At the time I thought he was just a bully and enjoyed upsetting us, but now I realize he was trying to teach us to project power while maintaining balance.

Learning the basic front kick is a great way to understand this principle. Most martial art classes practice repetitive kicking drills, all standing in a line and all doing kicks in unison. This is a good drill, as long as the instructor knows the difference between a kick into the air and a kick into a solid object. When students kick into the air, the body unconsciously remains in balance with itself. When the kicking leg moves forward, the upper body moves backward. When the kicking leg moves back, the upper body moves forward again. As long as the foot doesn't make contact with anything, this motion looks graceful, balanced, and powerful. The trouble is, the weight of the kicker is being divided and is moving in two directions at the same time. This becomes all too evident when such a kicker kicks the heavy bag and bounces off, having to take two or three steps backwards in order to regain balance, while the heavy bag barely moves at all.

The warrior must first learn to coordinate the hips and the upper body so that at the instant of full extension, his full weight is moving forward into the kick. A push against the chest of a properly balanced kicker will not result in imbalance, but will be completely absorbed and neutralized.

Of course, if the total weight of the kicker is moving forward at the moment of the kick, unless something else happens, the kicker will fall forward. Many of my instructors have said that while falling down is to be expected occasionally in practice, it is better to fall forward into a kick than to fall backward away from it. But it's best not to lose one's balance at all. That's why the warrior must also learn the art of **retraction**. The *Tan-Jun* point is projected into the target and retracted out of the target as one smooth two-part motion. The kicker's entire weight is thus coordinated with the entire kicking sequence, and whether the person kicks into the air or into a solid target, he is not off balance during any of the motion.

In order for the entire body weight to be coordinated into each movement and still maintain balance, three basic principles of balance must be followed. **First, the warrior must remain aware of his *Tan-Jun* center at all times**. This means that for his body weight to remain centered at that point, any movement must have a simultaneous opposite and equal reaction. Equal amounts of energy circle around the Tan-Jun center, and movement itself is the result of a *controlled net difference* in these energies. Movement becomes more relaxed and natural, as well as more powerful as the body moves as a single unit. Isolated, shortened movements not only cause imbalance and diminished power, but often result in unnatural body alignment, and can be very hard on joints and ligaments.

Aikido Master Koichi Tohei calls this "keeping the One-Point." By extending this principle into movement, keeping the one point during movement may be called, **One-Point Movement.** It is a way to put one's total body weight into each movement without losing balance. This takes many years of practice, but eventually the warrior learns to move this way without even having to think about it. It is as though the warrior becomes a vibrant sphere of energy which he can project and withdraw at will. His body is just a physical manifestation of this, like a shadow of the primary reality. Those who have mastered the art of one-point movement seem to glide over the ground gracefully and naturally, as though riding on a liquid wave of energy. The only jerks or stops in their movement are at moments of chosen focus, such as the full extension of a kick or punch.

In the previous chapter, we discussed the fact that reaction time is faster if the body's muscles are in a relaxed state. This is also true of movement in general. Imbalance places uneven stress on muscles, causing them to tense up involuntarily. **The second principle of balanced movement is that the better one is balanced, the more his muscles can remain relaxed and ready to respond.**

The body remains in this relaxed state until the moment of focus. But at the moment of focus, muscles are tightened, forming a sudden strong link between the *Tan-Jun* center and the striking surface. At that instant, any movement in the Tan-Jun is instantly transferred into the striking surface. At that instant, a two inch movement of the Tan-Jun center projects the striking surface two inches into the target with the entire body weight behind it. It is like a sudden strong burst of energy radiation. Energy is generated by the legs, gathered into the Tan-Jun, and propelled outward into the focus of the warrior's movement so quickly, it is like a shock wave rippling outward from an explosion. Hapkido Grandmaster Sangcook Kim calls this focused movement **Soon Bal Yak**, or, *energy explosion*—maximum power projected into all movement, yet the warrior remains relaxed.

The third principle of balanced movement is *Soon Bal Yak*—the total body is involved in generating power into a single focus. *Soon Bal Yak* is equally useful during sparring, weapon use, or grappling techniques. During a yielding or blending movement *(yin)*, the body is relaxed, and energy is free-flowing around the Tan-Jun. But during the application of power *(yang)*, the warrior moves as though there were an invisible steel rod connecting his *Tan-Jun* to the point of focus, whether it be his hands, feet, elbow, or the point of a weapon. Energy is transferred through this connection so that his entire body weight is committed to the move. Thus, when an opponent grabs a warrior's wrist, he is not dealing with an isolated limb; he is dealing with the warrior's entire body weight at that point, if and when the warrior wishes it.

Soon Bal Yak, or focused movement, is often accompanied by a **kihap**, or spirit yell. This is an exhalation that is initiated from the diaphragm and impeded (controlled) by the vocal chords to produce a deep, powerful yell at the instant of focus. (It is interesting to note that in traditional Taoist philosophy, the exhalation is the *yang* half of the respiratory cycle.) The kihap serves as a mental focus point, so at the instant of *Soon Bal Yak*, the effort is the result of both total physical commitment and total mental intent, coordinated into a single instant of time. This is a warrior's recipe for maximum power.

My first martial arts instructor, a Kenpo stylist with extensive study in Chinese White Crane Gung Fu, was a man of questionable character who seemed to enjoy hurting people. His own personal practice seemed to be how little he could move and still cause major structural damage to his opponent. This man had the hardest inside and outside blocks of any martial artist I have ever met. He would make these short little hand movements, and it felt like being hit with the full swing of a baseball bat. I once asked him how he generated so much power into such small movements, and he simply answered, 'I just direct my *chi* into them."

Then he slowly moved his hand to within two inches of my chest, and with a loud yell, he knocked me across the room with a sudden palm blow from that distance. My chest hurt for days.

Many years later, after Bruce Lee had made this one of his famous personal specialties, a man came into the original Sangcook Kim Hapkido School and asked Mr. Kim, "Do you know Bruce Lee's two-inch punch?" Mr. Kim looked puzzled, and turned to James Garrison. "What does this man mean?" Mr. Kim asked. "*All* punches are two inches!"

Ahh, the secret is out. The secret is that there is no deep Oriental secret. There is only keeping the center, balancing it into one-point movement, and *Soon-Bal-Yak*—projecting the whole body into a single focus with a single coordinated flexion, like a shock-wave of energy rippling out from the *Tan-Jun* center. I am still practicing this. My teacher is still practicing this. His teacher, the man who invented the term, still practices this every day.

Being Mentally Grounded

There is an old Japanese saying: *"Where the mind goes, the ki* (or chi) *follows."* Since we know that *ki*, the ethereal energy that surrounds a physical body, is influenced both physically and mentally, we must consider how balance and movement are influenced by the will of the mind.

I vividly remember the first adversarial confrontation I was ever involved in. It was not quite a fight, but it significantly altered the direction my life would take. It was during my freshman year of high school, a particularly embarrassing, stress-filled and fear-fraught period of my life. I was the tallest, skinniest, and likely the most awkward 14 year old boy in our class of more than four hundred.

It happened during P.E. class, in which our *torture-du-jour* was flag football. Because I was not particularly athletic, I ended up as one of the linemen, as a sort of stumbling block for the opposing team. At the snap of the ball, the player opposite me, a shorter but much stockier kid with a mean smirk on his face, elbow-blocked me as hard as he could right in the collarbone. I thought it was an accident, and so I crouched back into my position. The smirking smiler elbowed me again on the next play, this time square in the throat. While I wheezed and gasped for breath, he laughed so hard he actually slapped his knee a couple of times.

The quarterback saw what had happened and pulled me off the line into the backfield. But as we crouched down for the next play, I could see the look in the smirker's eyes. He had enjoyed hurting me, and it was obvious that he would be coming straight for me again. I was so afraid that I was trembling, but somehow my quaking fear and embarrassment transformed itself into indignant anger. How dare he do this to me? Even though he was bigger and stronger, I suddenly became determined that he would not hit me again. Whatever happened to me was unimportant. What was important was that this creep had to go *down!*

When the ball snapped past me, I ignored it. I knew the real game afoot. Sure enough, the smirking creep came sprinting toward me with a grin of high confidence on his face, his right elbow already raised forward and braced by his left hand. I moved automatically to my left, out of the way at the last possible instant. What happened next was almost an accident. I don't know what guided my hands, but my left led his elbow forward and down, and my right hand hooked his neck. He did a complete summersault in mid-air and landed on his back with a heavy thud. It knocked his breath and his confidence completely out of him, although I was as astonished as he was.

But that moment got me to thinking. Maybe I could learn to move like that on purpose! And thus began a lifelong fascination with the martial arts. The significance of this memory for me is not about the successful technique, which I learned some thirty years later to have been a very crude form of the Aikido throw *Kaiten-Nage*. The point is that I remember the exact moment that fear became determination and the clarity of mind that swept over me. Every thought, every speculation, every emotion ebbed from my mind as I concentrated on not getting elbowed in the throat again. Since I didn't have any martial training yet, there was no pre-conceived plan of defense to fumble with. My mind was empty, my senses alert, my body relaxed and ready. I was as grounded in defense as I have ever been, and have spent more than 40 years contemplating the purity of that one brief moment.

My point is that being grounded is as much a mental stance as a physical one. Just as being physically grounded involves connecting one's physical center with the ground; being mentally grounded involves connecting the body and mind into one experience. I believe this is what Mr. Kim meant when he said, *"The warrior's life is rooted in action."*

Mental groundedness begins with **mental centering**, or eliminating distractions in order to be completely attentive to the present moment. That is, quieting the inner dialogue, calming the emotions, relaxing the muscles, letting go of self-involvement, and most important, breath control. The objective is to create a state of mentally "just being" in the here-and-now without having to think about it. It is a state of mind which practices complete non-attachment. There is no past, no future, no emotion, no conscious activity, not even any thought pattern. All mental energy is directed into connecting to the moment, and to the world around oneself. All senses are alert and clear. *O-Sensei* Morihei Ueshiba used to describe this state as *"Being One with the ground, the opponent, nature and the self."* Mental groundedness adds another dimension. While being mentally centered is to **be in the moment** without having to think about it, being mentally grounded is being able to *act in the moment* without having to think about it.

The warrior's primary goal is to maximize his chances of survival. He must learn to recognize danger, evaluate it, and respond to it in a single instant without distraction. This seamless response is only possible with a mind that is rooted in action. Mental groundedness begins with mental centering, but involved further refinement for this kind of automatic appropriate response.

Being mentally grounded means that the warrior must stay connected with his art every moment, in every activity. However, this does not mean thinking about the art in a conscious way. It would be dangerous for the warrior to have his mind filled with snippets of martial technique, history and philosophy. It would be very distracting, and he might not notice a very important stimulus, such as an incoming punch. Being mentally grounded means that the warrior, because of his ongoing practice of correct repetition, combined with visualization of successful action, alters his behavior and awareness *automatically* to take the best advantage of his circumstances without having to think about it. His practice is a form of creating a situation to which he reacts ahead of time. Then, when the real situation happens, it is more a form of recognition than a situation that needs analysis. The longer and more consistently he practices, the more his understanding of the world around him is filtered through his understanding of his art. Thus, the better he remains connected with his art, the more he is aware of and connected to the world around him.

I remember an incident that underscores this point. A few years ago, before I retired from my career as a firefighter/paramedic, I happened upon a serious auto accident while off duty. A van had broadsided the passenger door of a small car. A woman in the passenger seat was severely injured. I automatically went to the car to see if I could help. I found the car surrounded by people, but no one was examining or helping the injured woman. I looked in and found her slumped onto the dashboard, covered with blood, and not breathing. I reached in and established an airway by lifting her head and neck into a neutral position, and she began breathing on her own. It was a very simple procedure that anyone can do and everyone should know. It was the "A" in the A-B-C's of cardiopulmonary resuscitation: Airway. I remember being somewhat perplexed and annoyed that although several people had arrived at the wreck before me, everyone seemed agitated and confused, and no one had bothered to help the victim. As soon as the paramedics arrived, I gave a patient assessment, left my name as a witness, and went on my way.

About a month later, I received a phone call from a local television station. They were putting together a talk show line-up of people who had done heroic deeds, and they asked me to be a guest. Although I didn't think what I did was heroic, I accepted. I appeared on an afternoon talk show with two other guys who had done these amazingly heroic "good Samaritan" acts at great risk to themselves. I was embarrassed to be the only professional rescue person on the guest panel. But I was impressed when the host of the show asked all three of us, "What makes a hero? What makes someone do a heroic act?"

The younger of the two, a man wise beyond his twenty-something years, said:

> *"It's kind of automatic. I've always told myself that I'm the kind of guy who will stop and help others in need. Then, when something happened and help was needed, I didn't have to think about it. I just did it."*

This is being mentally grounded. I had stopped and helped exactly because I was a professional. I had rehearsed that exact scenario hundreds of times in two decades of training so that when the moment happened, the help would be automatic, and the movement would be precise. The two men who were with me on that television show both had *pre-defined* themselves as people who would help others, and when those situations arose, their behavior was predetermined.

How you respond under stress depends on your training to respond under those conditions, and on who you have told yourself you are.

Permission to Act

Many beginners get discouraged learning basic movements, not because the movements are difficult, but because their minds have to sift through and carefully evaluate each phase of the technique before allowing the body to proceed. They do not trust their bodies to respond on their own. In class, these poor souls can be seen moving by the count, frowning, and after each move, they will often shake their head as though they were giving themselves a bad grade for that move. One of the most difficult primary lessons for these people is that they need to learn how to give themselves ***permission to act spontaneously, free of this ongoing self-evaluation.***

Within the first two seconds of an adversarial situation, almost anything can happen to the average person, and he probably will not have had sufficient time to analyze the situation and react appropriately. The warrior must be able to react instantly; his life may depend on it. So he lives in such a way as to whittle down as much of that time span as he can.

How much of those two seconds is spent deciding how to act? Can the warrior afford to squander even a fraction of a second in a quandary? No. He must develop the continual habit of visualizing situations for which the action is necessary and specific. Then, should such a situation actually happen to him, he will have already analyzed it and decided ahead of time what he will do. He in effect says to himself, *"Under these circumstances, this is how I will react."* The more one practices a reaction, the less surprised he will be by its provocation, and thus the clearer and more spontaneous his permission to act becomes.

Furthermore, the warrior must practice in such a way as to not only sharpen what he knows, but to prepare himself for that which he does not know. He must be prepared for the unexpected, the unknown, the unlikely, the fluke of fate which could change his life forever. Thus the careful, balanced movements of practice become a part of his everyday movement, and every moment becomes training. Practice becomes a part of his ongoing consciousness and defines who he is.

One's belief system is constantly manifesting itself into one's life. If one's beliefs, one's intent, and one's behavior are not carefully examined and constantly revised, then the result is that one's efforts are haphazard and without focus. Such a person does not learn from his mistakes, nor make progress toward any goal. His decisions will be tentative and his actions will be hesitant. The warrior must be more deliberate than this. Through continuous practice, he learns to cultivate a mental focus through which all his experiences and actions are interpreted. This focus is his intent to survive on his own terms.

The whole point of being mentally grounded is to act with deliberation, with certainty. The warrior lives his life and practices his art for the singular purpose of eliminating doubt and hesitation from his behavior. A warrior's survival is best insured by unwavering intent, completely free of any doubt. ***Mental groundedness is the physical training to act precisely combined with the mental empowerment to act instantly.***

When training, one should practice as though the situation were real. When real, one should move as though the situation were only training.

Such deliberate living defines the ethical life. But it doesn't necessarily mean that this person is a nice guy. Ethical behavior simply means that one has decided to live or act a certain way so as not to be overcome by surprise or remorse. Whether or not that way coincides with societal norms is a separate issue. It is an unfortunate reality that a person can be a good fighter and a bad person at the same time. Bullies and street thugs prove this all the time. They make up for lack of training by blustering through and flailing away almost blindly until their enemy is overcome. Teach a person like this a few precise martial moves, and you have created a formidable social problem—a person with the knowledge to injure others and without social ethics to keep him from doing so.

It is much more difficult to train polite, respectful, and courteous martial artists to fight with ferocity and tenaciousness. They must learn to abandon the very restraint that protects them from each other in the training hall. The warrior's training must be in earnest; he must practice as though his moves were meant to accomplish their real task, so that the ethics which restrain him from hurting his partner/opponent are a conscious choice, for that moment, each time. Then he is practicing the martial consciousness as well as the movement, and the ethics he learns in practice will not confuse and disable him in a real fight.

We must always remember that a real fight is a situation totally without ethical restraint. It represents a complete breakdown of social structure. ***The warrior's survival is not an ethical problem. It is a tactical problem.*** He must understand that his permission to act is entirely outside the world of social ethics. It is based solely on his continuous practice of applying his art to various scenarios both in training and in real life. In this sense, his permission to act is premeditated, even though the action itself may be spontaneous. ***The warrior's permission to act becomes his freedom to act totally outside the boundaries of social custom, if he feels such behavior is necessary.*** It is precisely this capability that sets the warrior apart from other members of society. He exudes an aura of this potential in his demeanor, his walk, his posture, and his voice. He is a dangerous man, and this aura emanates from him. Even with soft words and without threats, other people will respect him because they will sense somehow that this person is not to be trifled with.

But the paradox is that the warrior is set apart from the street thug precisely because the warrior must have a well-defined set of ethics in order to practice his art. A martial art is an active, physical study. Ethical behavior is mandatory in any martial art study for class protection. Students can only practice deadly techniques on one another insofar as they trust one another to obey strict rules of conduct. The more closely students adhere to these rules of conduct, the more implicitly they will learn to trust each other, and the more realistic the self-defense techniques can become. Thus, refining the rules of courtesy and respect are actually refining the student's groundedness. Ethical refinement teaches the student emotional calmness, mental clarity, unwavering intent—all qualities necessary to clarify and quicken his permission to act.

One cannot learn marital arts alone, from books, magazines or videotapes. These media may reveal techniques in great detail, but they do not alter behavior. They do not heighten awareness of others. They do not exhort honesty, nor compel courtesy, nor motivate respect. They do not encourage an ongoing self-examination, and the student's character remains unchanged. If one does not learn the technique within the perspective of a martial system, as one of a thoroughly organized and thoroughly examined set of life-choices, one does not learn to take responsibility for his actions. One's life does not change internally, and one's permission to act remains confused and vague. Learning technique alone is nothing more than an egotistical indulgence.

Zen without the accompanying physical exercise is nothing but empty discussion. Martial arts without truly realizing the "mind" is nothing but beastly behavior.

-- from the Chozen-Ji Canon

I remember watching two advanced black belts a few years ago during *Ho Shin Sul* (self defense training) practice. They were grappling so intensely that the entire room full of students stopped to watch them. They would throw each other to the ground, only to be countered and savagely thrown themselves. Drops of sweat and saliva were thrown from them in all directions. Finally, the instructor stopped them, saying, "That's enough! I can't tell if you are practicing or really fighting!" One of the black belts rolled up off the floor, smiled, and said, "That was fun! It was like a glimpse through a doorway into complete chaos!" This kind of training would not have been possible had these two black belts not been friends and had complete trust in one another.

This, then, is mental groundedness: it is a mind centered in movement, its inner voice quiet and all senses alert. It is a mind that has given the body permission to act all on its own and trusts the body's intelligence to move gracefully and precisely. It is a lifetime of practice focused into a single moment of intent. It is a complete union of physical and mental experience. It is the freedom to act the instant the need to act is perceived, so by the time the action is thought about, it is already done. ***The body's movement becomes the mind's voice.***

Movement and Balance as Tactical Tools

There are two adversarial situations in which awareness of one's center creates a distinct tactical advantage. The first is the art of falling. The warrior who is adept at falling has a great advantage over an opponent who does not know how to fall. Since more real fights end up as a tussle on the ground, a good fighter must know how to fall in any direction and in any position without getting hurt, automatically, without even having to think about it. After hours and hours of practice, a student begins to develop a relationship with the ground—that is, he becomes automatically aware of his body position with respect to the ground. The warrior does not lose his balance. If he is thrown, he simply moves his center downward, rotating his body around his *Tan-Jun* in such a way as to land in a protected position.

There are two vital aspects of falling that separate the experienced faller from the novice. The first is that the novice tends to reach out to the ground to break the fall with his hands extended and arms straight.

This action, although completely natural, is extremely dangerous. There is no fall in which this does not put the wrist, elbow, and shoulder in jeopardy. The experienced faller learns to trust his center, and time his arm motions to slap the ground at the exact moment his center hits, and with the arms in the exact position for safe body alignment. One of the most common injuries in the *dojang* (practice hall) is a dislocated shoulder from incorrect or unsafe falling practices.

Another aspect of falling that is vital to safety is the use of the *kihap* (focus yell). One must kihap during the instant of body contact with the ground to protect one's lungs. Our lungs are composed of millions of delicate, thin-walled membranes called alveoli, which are like tiny balloons. When a person falls, the chest wall often contracts suddenly and violently at the moment of body contact with the ground. If a person is holding his breath, the air in his lungs has nowhere to go, and tremendous pressure is exerted on these delicate membranes. There is great potential for alveolar rupture and subsequent pneumothorax, a quite painful and dangerous condition in which air leaks from the lungs into the chest cavity.

To minimize this potential, the faller simply exhales during the final instant of the fall. Then the air in his lungs has an escape route as the chest wall contracts. The experienced faller learns to kihap with every fall.

For the warrior, a fall may place him in a temporary position of disadvantage, but it does not mean he has lost control, or that he has lost the fight. When his balance is taken from him, he simply chooses to fall consciously, coordinating his efforts from his center, slapping and kihaping at the moment of contact with the ground. In this way, it can be said that he is going forward into the fall instead of resisting it. He is, in essence, *attacking the ground.* The idea is to practice falling to such an extent that one is not the least bit intimidated by falling. With this approach, if the warrior falls quickly enough and gracefully enough, he may sometimes gain the advantage over an opponent who is overconfident, who is overly dependent on the fall to injure or unnerve him.

The second use of balance as a tactical tool is called **taking the center.** This is not an isolated martial principle, however. It is the result of closely coordinated, inter-related martial principles, such as the use of proper angles, the art of yielding and blending with an opponent's energy, the art of proper entry, and a finely tuned sense of timing. (All of these principles will be discussed in subsequent chapters.)

Taking the center is simply a method of setting up a throw. There are countless techniques which can be used to unbalance an opponent, but all of them require the *tori*, the one who is attacked, to remain in control of his balance while he is unbalancing his opponent. He must not only remain in control of his own balance, but his own center of balance must become the center of balance for both himself and his opponent.

Whenever a person is unbalanced, it may be said that he "loses his center." That is, his center of balance becomes different than his center of mass. This difference is called a void. The more momentum that the center of balance has away from the center of mass, the larger this void becomes. Unless this difference is corrected, *ie* brought together again, that person will fall down.

All throws work on the same sequential principles: first, one leads an opponent into an unbalanced position, then prevents that person from correcting the imbalance. He does this by placing his body into a position to act as a barrier to that correction. This is called "stepping into the void." Then, while maintaining his own balance, he continues to add to his opponent's imbalance causing the opponent to rotate around his own center of balance. In this way, the warrior becomes the center of balance for both himself and his opponent. This is what is meant by *taking the center.*

Master James Garrison sometimes uses the analogy of a triangular table to describe this. A table with three legs cannot stand on only two of them. The *tori* becomes the third leg of the support that his opponent needs to remain standing, then he simply removes it. Gravity does the actual work of throwing.

There is one more aspect of taking the center that must be discussed; that is the art of unbalancing an opponent mentally. If a warrior is able to maintain his own balance both physically and mentally by remaining grounded in his art as we have discussed, then his intent can radiate from him like a bright beacon. It may even be so intense as to unnerve his opponent.

I remember many years ago when our martial arts academy first began to practice with the *bokken,* or wooden sword. Our teacher invited a well-known and respected Aikido sensei to our club to help us with out sword basics. After thoroughly impressing upon us that the *bokken* was to be treated exactly the same as a real sword, the Aikido sensei picked an *uke* for a demonstration: me. He told the class to watch us as he faced me with his weapon at ready. He told us that he was going to generate a maximum amount of internal energy *(ki)* and then he was going to project this energy up and over the top of me and crush me like a steamroller rolling over an apple. He told me to take a defensive stance, which I did. As the sensei took his own stance in front of me, I could hear his *kihap* (spirit yell) reverberating through his entire body so clearly, my sensation was that it began to reverberate through my body as well. The look in his eyes at that moment communicated to me that it didn't matter whether his sword was made of steel or wood; I was going to get hit, and there was absolutely nothing I could do about it. That feeling was so intense that I almost dropped my bokken, and had to step backward to gain my composure. He had injected my entire being with profound doubt. Yet when I looked at him again, he had not physically moved! I will never forget that moment.

Unbalancing an opponent is one of the side benefits of developing a strong *kihap*. The primary function of the *kihap* is to focus both physical and mental energy at a single moment in time. But as the warrior becomes adept at this focus, his *kihap* also projects unwavering intent and indomitable spirit. Unless his opponent is a formidable warrior himself, he will likely be intimidated and unnerved by a good, strong *kihap*.

There are other ways of unbalancing an opponent mentally as well. I remember an incident at a tournament many years ago that was humorous at the time, but which illustrated a unique and rather profound tactic. Two competitors faced off for a full contact tie breaker round, known as sudden death. The two young men were roughly equal in both size and ability, and they had competed through two full rounds and an additional tie-breaker round with no clear advantage to either one of them. At the command to begin, one of them assumed his fighting stance, but the other young man did not. Instead, he began to hop up and down, his hands still at his side. He rolled his eyes back, tilted his head from side to side, and began clucking like a chicken for all to hear. Several people thought he might be having some sort of medical problem, and rose to their feet to help him. His opponent seemed momentarily puzzled by this bizarre behavior, and lowered his guard as he pondered what the make of it. At that moment, the young man who had been jumping threw a simple front kick and dropped his opponent, winning the match.

The bizarre behavior had caused his opponent to think too much, obscuring his awareness and slowing his reflexes. We all laughed at the time, but the tactic had been successful. I understand that this defense has been used a few times since then in the same tournament, but without success; word gets around!

The object is not to have five hundred victories in five hundred battles. The object is to have five hundred victories and no battles.
-- Sun Tsu, The Art of War

REVIEW

Maintaining balance is a warrior's most important defensive skill. All the power he can generate depends on this ability. The center of balance is the **tan-jun center**, which is both the center of mass and the origin of energy. All energy and movement must originate and be projected from this center. This is called **one-point movement**. One-point movement is projected into a single focus away from the center by executing a sudden flexion of muscles which create a line of energy from the *Tan-Jun* to the point of focus. This happens so rapidly that it is like the shock wave of an explosion. This movement is called **Soon-Bal-Yak**.

Being grounded is not only a physical stance but a mental one as well. **Mental groundedness** begins with mental centering, or being in the moment without having to think about it. To mental centering we add our constant training through repetition and visualization, and our self definition which predisposes us to act a certain way under certain conditions, so that we can act in the moment automatically and appropriately, without having to think about it.

There are two tactical uses of balance in a conflict—controlled falling and taking the center. An opponent's center can be taken mentally as well as physically—directly by overpowering the opponent with indomitable spirit, or indirectly by deceptively infusing doubt or inappropriate contemplation.

In all cases, we have learned that all energy and movement, all intent and focus, begins with and depends on continuous connection with one's center.

"Never give an opponent your balance." –James R. Garrison

*****

Taking advantage of distance; kick has greater reach than punch.

Chapter 5

All energy is directed toward attaining one's objective.

The Water Principle

I remember an incident that happened several years ago to my brothers and me which reminds me of this principle of Warrior Mind. My oldest brother, Bob, my middle brother, Bill, a friend named Roger, and myself were sailing a 29 foot Cascade sailboat from Port Angeles, Washington down the coast to Astoria, Oregon. The distance was more than two hundred miles, and required us to spend the night at sea. We spent the night anchored in Neah Bay, the last port inside the Straits of Juan De Fuca.

The next morning before we left the harbor, Bob and Roger wanted to call their wives and let them know of our progress and projected arrival time. We hoisted the anchor and pulled into the same gas dock we had done business with the night before. But before we could get tied up, the gas dock attendant came running out of the office, shaking his fist and cursing at us.

"Get away from my goddam dock!" he yelled. "I don't want any sailboats here. You never buy more than a dollar of gas, and you use up all my water," he continued to yell at the top of his lungs.

My brother Bob had been the first one to step to the dock, and stood holding the bow line in his hand. "We just want to make a phone call," he said calmly. "We won't be here more than ten minutes, and we'll cast off if any other boat wants to land at your dock." He continued to secure the bow line.

The attendant stepped closer to him and raised both his fists up. "Get out of here! I'll call the police! Get the hell out of here!" the attendant yelled repeatedly.

I had the stern line in my hand. I thought there might be a fight, so I handed the line to Roger, but before I had gotten more than two steps closer to the two of them, I saw my brother drop the bow line and move into a left-side-forward fighting stance. His hands were ready, but still down at his sides.

"Now, you listen," Bob spoke in a more forceful tone than I had ever heard him speak before. His voice compelled me to stop and listen. "We were here last night and bought a lot more than a dollar's worth of gas. Now we're going to make that phone call and you've got three choices. You can call the cops, but we'll likely be long gone by the time they get here. You can back off and shut up, or you can start swinging. Start with me." Bob was staring hard into the man's eyes.

The attendant stopped in his tracks. He hesitated for just a few seconds, then backed up a step, turned on his heels and stalked into his office. "You got five minutes," he said over his shoulder.

Later, as we cruised out of the harbor, I asked Bob about the incident. "What were you thinking?" I said.

"I was thinking about his nose," Bob answered immediately.

"His nose?" I asked

"Yeah. I was just focused on his nose. If he had done anything else but back up, I was going to punch him in the nose. And if I missed, I was going to keep on punching until I hit it."

"I'm glad you didn't have to fight," I said.

"We did fight," Bob said.

My brother is not a bully, nor a practiced fighter. Most of the time, he is an easy-going, reflective person. But when challenged, he was able to reach down inside himself and find his warrior nature—that part of himself that focuses in on a challenge and faces it head on. That may not always be the best way, and I certainly do not advocate aggressiveness as a lifestyle. But sometimes the potential for a violent confrontation rises up in our path like a beast of prey. We may find ourselves in danger despite our best efforts to lead a peaceful life. Sometimes a person has no time to weigh his options or reflect upon the correctness of his actions. He may have no choice but to deal with the situation he finds himself in right then. The person who hesitates in shock or reflection will most likely find himself already in a position of clear disadvantage.

An important strategic martial principle is to **give no advantage to the enemy. Take the initiative away from them as soon as possible.** What this means is that once an adversarial situation begins, one must quickly choose a course of action, or outcome objective, and apply all the energy and resources at one's command to succeed in that effort. There is no advantage in making a half-hearted effort or achieving half a victory. And there are clearly some disadvantages. More than a few fights are lost by fighters who are winning, but pause to rest or reflect on the situation, thereby allowing their opponents to recover sufficiently to renew the attack. Once a fight begins, the warrior does not turn away from it. There is no stepping backward. There is no yielding, no mercy. It's just business—the business of survival.

The spirit of this principle is exemplified in Miyamoto Musashi's **_A Book of Five Rings_**. The third chapter (or ring) is about overcoming the enemy. Musashi writes, *"We must defeat [the enemy] at the start of his attack, in the spirit of treading him down with the feet, so that he cannot rise again to the attack…fix your eye on the enemy's collapse, and chase him, attacking so that you do not let him recover…"*

And again: *"Whenever you cross swords with an enemy, you must not think of cutting him [this way or that way]; just think of cutting him and killing him."*

This chapter of Musashi's book is entitled *Fire*, an appropriate symbol for the most aggressive passage written by Japan's most famous swordsman, a man reputed to have cut down 60 men in sword combat. The point Musashi has made here is that the whole objective in a combat situation is to *win*. There is no other goal. A warrior must reach into his soul and find the strength, the intent, the resolve, and the courage to face the adversary and overcome him as quickly and as completely as possible. Without hesitation. Without tentativeness. Without emotion. Once the fight begins, the warrior's imperative is to become the bigger fire.

This presents the ultimate paradox for the warrior. He must train diligently to become the best possible fighter, yet fighting itself does not exemplify his better nature, his higher Self. Contention is the least productive of social behaviors, and fighting is the most destructive form of contention. Actually, fighting represents complete social interactive failure. And how can the warrior aspire to failure? Thus the warrior who trains in the fighting arts must develop some form of personal doctrine which can serve as a foundation for his character, a central statement of belief which nurtures his higher nature, yet also allows him to respond with physical force if necessary in his own defense. His life becomes rather like water running downhill; if unimpeded and peaceful, his life will continue to flow towards becoming the admirable and self-respecting human being he has chosen to be. Upon encountering resistance, his energy will incessantly flow around the obstruction in his path until it is either bypassed or overcome. But his central nature, like water, never really departs from its original course. ***Becoming like water is the most important dynamic principle of Warrior Mind.***

Consider water's physical properties. Water has the same consistency and the same properties of movement no matter how large or small the amount, and no matter where it is found. It exerts a uniform gravitational pressure against that which contains or obstructs its flow downhill. Water placed into a large bowl instantly conforms to the shape of the bowl which contains it, exerting exactly the same pressure against all sides of the bowl, no matter what shape the bowl is. Quiet as the water is in a bowl, overturn the bowl and the water will instantly rush out in a splashing cascade. The energy to do this is always there, even when completely still in the upright bowl. ***Quiet water is stored energy. Rushing water is released energy. Yet the water itself remains unchanged.***

The lesson here for the warrior is about the application of his own personal energy against an external force acting upon him, such as an attacking opponent. When an adversary charges in with great energy and momentum, the warrior must give way. He must learn to flow away from the center of contention and relate to his opponent's position from other angles. But when the adversary has little momentum—when he is in a defensive stance, or in a recovery phase from a previous move—then like a wave rolling onto a gently sloped shore, the warrior rolls up and over the top of him. The trick is to know the difference between these two tactics, to feel the energy of the opponent and assess its strength accurately. This must be done continuously throughout a physical confrontation, as the dynamics of a fight change moment to moment. Yet at no time does his energy disengage. It is ready to flow outward, like water finding a crack in a dam, the instant a void or flaw in the opponent's defense is found.

The pressure on the opponent is constant, yet ever sensitive to change. It is never resting, never pausing to reflect upon the situation. That time is past. Once a fight starts, ethics and philosophy are irrelevant. The longer a fight continues, the greater chance a warrior has to get injured. Therefore, whatever level of force the warrior chooses, it is never defensive. It is purely offensive. The force the warrior applies is not merely applied to deflect or thwart an attack. This does not resolve the situation which caused it. The warrior's force, once applied, is intended to achieve a chosen objective, and is not lessened or withdrawn until the objective is reached. The challenge for the warrior is to quickly form that objective.

If a student bases a lifetime of training on defense, then he has already imagined defeat.

-- Grandmaster Kim Sangcook

This requires a mental process, an evaluation and decision, based not only on the dynamics of the immediate situation, but also on the foundations of his character—that is, on the personal doctrine with which he has defined his life. The real paradox is that the water principle, as applied to personal energy, is as much mental as it is physical.

This chapter is about clarifying that paradox, about the unification of one's personal energy, both physical and mental, into a single expression, a single direction. First we'll discuss the importance of mental aspiration, and the difference between a central doctrine, which is like the ocean toward which water incessantly runs, and escalating strategies, which are like water meeting increasingly formidable obstacles in its path. Finally, we'll discuss the water principle as a fighting tactic.

The Importance of a Central Doctrine

All human disciplines aspire to enrich the lives of their adherents in some way by encouraging them to accept some form of central doctrine. The central doctrine, whatever it may be, is usually designed to clarify and strengthen the adherent's definition of himself, or help guide the adherent's behavior towards both benevolence and effectiveness. All human endeavors that require discipline, resolve, and patience transform practitioners internally—that is, mentally and emotionally as well as physically. Traditional martial arts are not different in this regard.

A doctrine is defined as a principle or set of principles intended to establish a commonality of belief for a particular group. The more specialized the group, the more specific the belief. For instance, the doctrine of a baseball team might be something like, *Always practice teamwork, never drop the ball.* This is a fine belief for a ball player, but not much help to a minister or business man. The larger the group, the more general, the more universal, its doctrine becomes.

The purpose of accepting a central doctrine is to have a guiding principle in our lives from which we can assess our progress in transforming ourselves from what we are into what we wish to become. It is our social responsibility as well as to our personal benefit to aspire to become as disciplined and as self-actualized as we can. Our continuous efforts to conform to our central beliefs are an example of the water principle at work in our own lives both physically and mentally. Furthermore, the more universal our central beliefs, the more harmonious our lives will be with all around us. This is not only the definition of an ethical life, but the beginning of a spiritual life.

"You are here for no other purpose than to realize your inner divinity and manifest your innate enlightenment."

-- Morihei Ueshiba, founder of Aikido

The word *spirit*—as in team spirit or martial spirit—surfaces often in writings about martial arts, yoga, religion, philosophy, even in sports. It is not an easily defined word. But to simplify the concept for usefulness in the context of the warrior arts, I am using the word in much the same way as Dr. Deepak Chopra has used the word in his writings and lectures on Ayurvedic wisdom. Dr. Chopra often says, *"The spiritual energy is the connecting energy."* This means that how you relate to things other than yourself—especially to other people—defines your spirit. The more you connect with others, the larger and stronger your spirit. The goal of spiritual growth, then, is to connect with the most people the most often—ultimately, all people, all of the time.

"The goal of all martial study is to enrich and nurture the spirit."
James R. Garrison, 9th dan, Hapkido

The warrior's doctrine is no different. In order to mature spiritually as well as physically and mentally, the warrior must embrace a doctrine of universal relevance, a doctrine of relating to other people in the same overall benevolent manner, even when in an adversarial situation. Aikido Sensei Terry Dobson, one of the few Westerners to have studied under Aikido's founder Morihei Ueshiba, wrote a wonderful doctrinal statement in his book, <u>Aikido in Daily Life</u>: *"The restoration of harmony is the goal of all conflict."* Expanding on this theme, we as warriors might agree to something like this:

> ***The goal of all martial training is to promote one's well-being with the most peace and benevolence possible, and with the least harm to others.***

However the warrior's central doctrine is worded, it provides him with an overall focus, an ongoing aspiration that, the better he becomes at his art, the more enriched and fulfilled his life will become.

It is a sad fact, though, that there are many people who study diligently at the martial arts who have no inclination at all to develop any enlightened doctrine, other than "winning is the only thing better than looking good." And these people can be formidable fighters. There are a disturbing number of these externally oriented martial artists competing in tournaments all across our country, indeed, all around the world. You can see them strutting about in their fancy multi-colored uniforms, patches on every flat surface, yelling and gesturing, out of control of every aspect of the tournament scene. "The judging was bad," they shout. "I lost because my opponent cheated!" "I won, I'm king of the world!"

The truth is, tournaments are a valuable learning experience. It takes a strong will to step into the ring with a stranger who wants to kick your butt to the moon. But tournaments are all about external value—winning the trophy, risking all to experience praise. And it's an artificial format anyway.

O-sensei Ueshiba used to say, *"Ten years in an art, then the student begins to become the art."* Those who stay in the martial arts for thirty or forty years must be deriving some benefit other than its external rewards, of which there are few. Health, fitness, humility, austerity, self-discipline, social perspective, spiritual enlightenment—these are all internal values.

"The sole purpose of our existence on earth is to take the matter with which God has graced us, and transform it into spirit."
-- St. Francis of Assisi

A peaceful and benevolent central doctrine is admirable, and as long as our surroundings remain peaceful, harmonious, and predictable, all is well and good. But in the real world, things aren't like that some of the time. The fact is, our situation can change in a heartbeat. The warrior's training is designed to have him never be caught off guard.

There are two vital considerations that the warrior must keep in mind at all times. The first is that the warrior's awareness must be fine tuned to give him the earliest warning of impending danger. The second is that while his central doctrine may not change, his strategies for adhering to it will change, according to the situation.

Escalating Awareness

In his book *"Secrets of Modern Professional Warriors: SEAL Team Combat Course,"* martial artist and former Navy SEAL Frank Cucci writes about the four levels of readiness.

"**White:** The level of awareness most people walk around in as they go about their daily lives…largely oblivious to their surroundings. This awareness level is one of simply not paying attention. Whatever's out there, it's not going to happen to them. These people are the most easily victimized.

Yellow: The level of awareness in which you live with a heightened awareness of what's going on around you. This level acknowledges the fact that it may not be a totally friendly world out there at times, and it's best to keep an eye out.

Orange: When you feel that something around you isn't right, or something might happen that won't be conducive to your overall health; you realize that some action is necessary to deal with this specific situation.

Red: The state in which that move or action takes place. It's action *now*."

Warrior mind is the physical and mental practice of preparing for that moment of action, that split-second of moving from Orange to Red. It is training in recognizing that moment, formulating a response strategy, and choosing the tactics to carry it out successfully. Every aspect of our lives influences our readiness for that moment. Is our awareness high enough to give us early warning? Is our mental process clear and uninfluenced by toxins? Are we calm enough to choose our course of action rationally and not emotionally? Are we physically fit enough to carry out our action plan? The warrior must practice a disciplined life both on and off the mat. How can he say he is ready for action if his regular daily diet, exercise, stress level, and rest have not prepared him? There is no in-between training; life itself is training. Toxicity and fatigue of mind and body erodes one's clarity of intent, not matter what the endeavor.

To aid in the evaluation of our condition of readiness, consider the Three "C's" of the moment of action: **calmness, confidence, and commitment.**

CALMNESS. It is vitally important for the warrior to remain in control of his emotions. Runaway emotions, as fear becomes panic, or anger becomes rage, destroy his ability to judge a situation with any kind of clarity or perspective. He may act inappropriately, ineffectively, or prematurely. Moreover, strong emotions, and the adrenalin surge which accompanies them, drastically reduce muscle control. Many assailants attempt to frighten a potential victim by appearing suddenly out of nowhere, or by affecting a bizarre appearance, or by making threatening gestures for this exact purpose. Learning how to remain calm under stress takes the advantage away from the assailant, and may deter him entirely from his intent. Emotional control and breath control are intricately linked, as discussed in greater detail in chapter 3.

CONFIDENCE. Martial arts training—at least the physical part of it—is not enough. One can practice a thousand techniques, only to be confronted by the thousand-and-first situation. One must develop *Pil Sung*, the Korean term for "Victory Mind," (See chapter 2). This is a state of confidence and indomitable spirit that meets all challenges head on, and even welcomes them. There can be no backing away from an attack; the moment of avoidance has slipped past. As Frank Cucci writes in the SEAL manual:

> *"Be decisive. Ready to go. Don't hesitate. You've got to cultivate the aggressive side of your personality. You have to have the attitude that people do not have the right to prey on you. Be proud. Be indignant. They*

can't do this to you!"

This is a mind-set of going about one's daily life with awareness, focus of intent, and optimism. Once you choose a path for yourself, you work diligently toward seeing your efforts through to a positive conclusion, and you have high confidence that you will succeed. This mind-set must be practiced constantly in one's everyday activities. Then, when an adversarial confrontation arises, your self-confidence will be firmly established, and you will not be easily intimidated.

COMMITMENT. *All other things being roughly equal, the person who brings the most energy to bear on a confrontation usually wins.* There can be no halfway defenses. In fact, there is really no such thing as an effective, purely defensive move. Blocking a punch does not deter an opponent from throwing another. One must meet an attack head-on, with more energy than the adversary expects, sooner than he expects, and with more aggression than he expects. Commitment must be total and unreserved. The intent is to overwhelm the adversary with so much energy, intent, and devastation of his perceived position that he is forced to redefine the situation as a bad investment of his time.

There are two parts to this level of commitment: there must be a thorough familiarity with our own permission to act, and a thorough understanding of strategy. Our permission to act is intricately linked to our personal doctrine, our understanding of ourselves as ethical beings. As long as we can view ourselves as adhering to this doctrine, our permission to act is automatic. Therefore, we must have a preconceived set of responses that supports our overall belief system.

It must be pointed out that not all of us may be ethical beings. The adversary you face when the decision to act becomes mandatory may not give ethical behavior any thought at all, ever. He may just be a predator in search of new prey, or so angry or strung out that he may act automatically and think about it later. Such people think that ethics means feeling sorry if they are caught.

Remember, a fight is a struggle for survival. It is not an ethical problem; it is a tactical problem. This presents the warrior with the dilemma mentioned earlier: how can the warrior lead a purposeful *ie* ethical life and still give himself instantaneous permission to act in a potentially violent manner? This question must be resolved in the warrior's mind before he can act effectively. The only way this can be achieved is to have in place a thoroughly examined set of escalating action strategies. Then, to remain ethical, he simply has to remain within those action boundaries. Strategies have an ethical base. Tactics are success oriented and are not ethically based. We will examine this escalating scale of strategic responses, and the tactics that support them. But before we start, we must remember one vitally important axiom. An adversarial confrontation will demand the level of commitment of the aggressor, and no lesser commitment on the part of the defender can possibly be effective or successful. The defender can be ready and willing to de-escalate a confrontation and should do so if the situation allows it. But he must never exhibit less energy or less commitment than his opponent. **One can only negotiate from a position of strength.**

ESCALATING STRATEGIES

The overall strategic imperative in Hapkido (and in most other traditional martial arts as well) is to resolve adversarial confrontation with the least amount of violence and/or damage. Response strategies are prioritized to that end.

The first strategy, of course, is *avoidance.* If we are alert enough, perhaps we can sense the potential for violence in a situation early enough to simply detour around it. One does not have to be a coward to want to avoid trouble. It's simply a matter of energy conservation. As Mr. Kim so colorfully put it one day, "If you are walking down the sidewalk, and you see a pile of ["dog leavings"] in front of you, you walk around it. That doesn't mean you're afraid of it." This is the preferred strategy; avoid adversarial situations, if possible. It's best to avoid locations or gatherings that contain the potential for violent behavior, and to keep one's awareness extended outward to detect the earliest hint of social instability.

But, of course, it's not always possible to avoid confrontation. The second strategy, failing avoidance, is *diplomacy.* One always remains polite and reasonable, no matter how an adversary acts. That way, we maximize our chances of resolving the conflict by non-violent means—by discussion, compromise, diffusion or agreement. The spiritual path is to seek ways that you may have in common with people, not ways in which they are different. Aikido Sensei Terry Dobson wrote in <u>Aikido in Daily Life</u>, *"The best resolution of conflict is one in which everyone is a winner."* He wrote a widely published story that illustrates this point, entitled, "A Kind Word Turneth Away Wrath": (for the sake of brevity, I am paraphrasing here.)

> ***Not long after I received my black belt in Aikido, I was traveling by train in a large city in Japan. It was quite crowded, and I had to remain standing. A man got on the train soon after I did, and started pushing people out of his way. The man was disheveled and unshaven, and speaking very loudly and rudely to all around him. I was feeling very confident in those days, and edged my way toward him. If there were trouble, I intended to take him down as quickly if possible, and as I listened to him shouting and cursing, began to care less and less whether I would hurt him in the process.***

Just then a little old man seated next to the disheveled passenger spoke in a calm and sympathetic manner to him: "You are not mad at these fine people! Come and tell me, why are you so angry?"

The man began talking rapidly, and told of losing his wife, and his job of many years in the same month, and how he had not been able to cope with this, and he had been drinking too much. Within minutes, the disheveled man was kneeling, crying, with his head on the old man's lap!

Sensei Doson ends his essay this way: "I saw that what I had been prepared to accomplish with bone and muscle had been accomplished with a smile and a few kind words. I recognized that I had seen Aikido used in action, and that the essence of it was reconciliation, as the founder had said. I felt dumb and brutal and gross. I knew I would have to practice with an entirely different spirit. And I knew it would be a long time before I could speak with knowledge about

Aikido or the resolution of conflict."

[from the book, <u>Aikido and the New Warrior</u>, by Richard Strozzi Heckler, North Atlantic Books, 1985; pp. 65-69.]

Remaining calm, polite, and reasonable will accomplish much toward conflict resolution all by itself. But, of course, this won't always be successful. However, if an adversarial situation continues to escalate, if you have acted calmly and reasonably up until that point, it will be apparent to anyone witnessing the situation that you did not contribute to the escalation of the incident. This could be a vital asset should the incident be a cause for litigation. In this day and age, it's important to remember that you not only have to protect yourself physically, but legally as well.

The third strategy, failing to avoid trouble and/or diffuse it, is one that is not always possible in a fight situation. It involves some sort of **admonition or warning.** This is a statement to the effect that there is a line between acceptable and unacceptable behavior. The warrior draws this line, and states as clearly as possible under the circumstances, that there will be immediate consequences for anyone crossing that line into unacceptable behavior. The statement does not have to be rude, or loud, or even verbal. It just has to confirm in everyone's mind that your adversary knows that he is crossing a line into unacceptable behavior, and is doing so on purpose, regardless of any consequences.

A friend of mine named Jim Sullens was one of the first acquaintances that Hapkido Grandmaster Kim Sangcook made when he immigrated to the U.S. from Korea in the early 1970's. Mr. Sullens tells this story:

> *"One day we were out driving and stopped at a rest stop along the highway to use the facilities. While we were finishing up in the men's restroom, two big guys came in. One of them pulled a balisong-style folding knife and did some slashes in the air, smiling menacingly. I was petrified, but Mr. Kim just continued to ignore the man, and finished washing his hands. When he was done, he walked to the hand drying machine, which was a metal box mounted on the wall about four feet above the floor, with a push button about two inches in diameter. Because his hands were wet, he simply turned on the machine with a perfectly executed roundhouse kick to the start button, just hard enough with the toe of his shoe to activate it. Then he began drying his hands, only glancing once over his shoulder at the man with the knife as if to*

say, *There would be consequences you can't even imagine. The man closed up the balisong, put it into his pocket, and the two men left without saying a word."*

An admonition is not a threat, or a put down, or a form of macho posturing. It is actually more mental than it is physical. It is a clarification of intent. It is making someone understand that you view a situation a certain way, and that you have the intent, the courage, and the ability to take charge of the situation and cause it to unfold in a certain way. A way that *you choose*, regardless of how the other person (or people) feel about it. This attitude, that one is in control of one's own immediate environment, one's own circumstances, is precisely the mental state that separates the warrior from the victim. The prime characteristic of a potential victim is that he defines himself as one. He sees no action alternatives that result in a favorable situation, so he just gives up. The warrior never ceases his efforts to bring about the most desirable resolution of conflict, even if all the alternatives are bleak. In fact, this is when the warrior is at his strongest and most alert.

The warrior may lose the battle, but he never loses himself in the battle.

His intent and his resolve—his spirit—remain indomitable. The admonition is simply the warrior's form of politeness. He makes his indomitable spirit visible as a warning.

Reactions to impending conflict are best left unstated, however. This is a legal tactic as well as a confrontational tactic. If you threaten someone with a specific action, not only will your moves become slightly more predictable, but you are showing both intent and premeditation, and if witnessed, will not be a point in your favor in a court of law. The strongest admonitions are those that are calm and polite, yet firm and unyielding, and always allow for a graceful retreat of the adversary.

Guarding Your Distance

It is vitally important to recognize the moment a physical conflict begins. Most fights begin before one of the fighters realizes he's in a fight. One moment, he was in a "spirited discussion," and the next moment, BAM! and he's missing three or four front teeth. How does this happen? It happens when we let someone we don't know well enough to trust get too close to us.

There is a line between people that we all are instinctually aware of, even if only subliminally. It is a line that we are not comfortable with people crossing unless they are invited inside its perimeter by us, by choice. When an unbalanced person exhibits anger or aggression toward us, we may view it as unpleasant or unsettling, but the situation doesn't really get personally threatening until that person approaches to within a certain distance from us. This is generally accepted as the distance between two people who are standing face to face with their arms outstretched, fingertips just touching. It is the distance at which a person only has to take one step to reach us. Inside that distance, a person can strike us, and we will not have time to react quickly enough to stop his attack. A line around us at this distance circumscribes our defensible perimeter. ***We must guard this defense perimeter with our full and constant awareness. There can be no exceptions.*** Anyone we do not trust who comes closer than this has entered into our personal space, *our fight zone*, and we are at Mr. Frank Cucci's "Condition Red." A physical confrontation has already begun!

It is relatively easy to spot a person who is angry or acting aggressively; however, not all social predators act so predictably. Their goal may be to get close enough to you to control or harm you before you are on to their plans. They might act very polite, cordial, perhaps soliciting your aid in some seemingly innocent act. They may even appear to be disabled and need your help. In an interview, serial rapist/killer Ted Bundy described how he sometimes wore a fake plaster cast around one ankle to appear "needy" to his intended victims. If you don't know a person, especially if you are alone with them, it's best not to let them beguile you into letting them inside your defense perimeter *under any circumstances.* I am not describing or endorsing paranoia. I am simply agreeing with Frank Cucci's "Condition Yellow." Keep an eye out for the unexpected, and be aware that the closer it happens to you, the less time you have to react to it. You can still be helpful. Just don't place yourself in an indefensible position.

An **admonition** is called for in these two cases: to indicate that another person's behavior is unacceptable, or to indicate that someone we don't know or trust is approaching too close, *whether or not their behavior is acceptable.* If the latter is the case, you should tell the other person clearly that you are uncomfortable with their approach, and that if they come any closer, you will interpret that as a threat, and will act accordingly. You might hold up your hands, palm outward toward the approaching person, indicating that you do not want them to come any closer. This is a non-threatening gesture, and it also places the arms and hands more closely into a defensive position. You might even take a step away from the person to regain your defensive perimeter; but if you do so, step away at a sharp angle to their approach if possible. This takes the momentum out of their straight-line approach, and also makes their intentions clearer if they have to change directions to approach you.

If avoidance is impossible and diplomacy is ineffectual, and if there is no time for any form of admonition—or the adversary simply ignores it—then a physical confrontation is already in progress. The time for action is **now!**

This is the moment when people are in the most danger of losing sight of their personal doctrine, of getting caught up in the frenzy of the situation and losing control. It is a moment they may later regret, if they have not mentally prepared for it. It is a dark side to warrior nature that because we know how to hurt people, sometimes we want to. But we cannot give ourselves *carte blanche* to hurt someone just because a confrontation has begun, even if we are sorely tempted. Those who practice martial arts and give in to this urge have only shown that their training is woefully incomplete. I know this from personal experience. I too have a "train story." But unlike Terry Dobson's, mine ended with a less benign resolution.

In the summer of 1967, I had just turned twenty-one, and had the urge for adventure. I hitch hiked to Vancouver B.C. and then took the train across Canada to the World Fair in Montreal. On the second night, about midnight, I had settled into my seat for sleep when I was awakened by someone banging open the door at the rear of the car. I looked up to see who could be so inconsiderate of an entire passenger car full of people trying to sleep. I saw a man perhaps a few years older than I, nicely dressed, but with his shirt pulled out of his pants and his tie askew. He was tottering on his feet, bumping into people in their seats as he walked up the aisle. The man began to sing a lewd song very loudly, and as he bumped into people, he would lean into their faces and belch. Several people put their fingers to their lips to shush him, but he would not be shushed, and he began to curse at people who did so.

I had been studying the art of Kenpo for about four years, and thought myself to be pretty tough. Here was an opportunity to use my art. I got out of my seat, determined to either shush this person—clearly the will of the people—or throw him out the rear door. I walked up to him and blocked his way. I said, "Keep quiet man. People are trying to sleep!"

He looked at me sideways, his eyes going up and down my height. Even though I was a good six inches taller than him, his mouth formed a sneering smile. "Maybe I don't want to!" he said. "Maybe I'll just sing louder!" He started his song again, louder than before.

I had thought that he would take the first hint and quiet down. Now he was making me angry. I took another step closer, leaned into his face, and said with my most determined karate-face, clenched-teeth grimace, "Pipe down or I will throw you off the train!"

He didn't back away even an inch. Instead, suddenly there was the flash of a stiletto blade opening just a few inches from my throat. "I don't think so, asshole," he said through a mean smile, waving the knife's blade back and forth in front of my face as he struggled with his balance.

I was alarmed by the knife, but I was more angry than anything else. I was angry at him for pulling a knife, and angry at myself for not seeing him do it. Before I knew I had even moved, his knife arm was across my shoulder, and I pulled down against his elbow with both hands. There was a snap, the man howled in pain, and the knife dropped to the floor. But I didn't stop there. I flattened his nose with my elbow, and he dropped like a sack of potatoes. Several people gasped, and a woman screamed.

Just then, two train conductors entered from the front. After a few minutes of questions, they hauled the man off. I'll never forget his last look over his shoulder at me. He was wide-eyed and slack-mouthed, his right arm dangling, and his nose bleeding. When he silently mouthed the word *"Why?"* he reminded me of a puppy that someone had kicked for no reason.

No one congratulated me on my fine victory over a very drunk man. Actually, when I sat down, people nearby got up and moved away. I was deeply embarrassed by the whole incident, and vowed to study the martial arts to the point that I could control such a situation without having to hurt anyone.

Physical Response

At the moment a physical confrontation becomes unavoidable, it has already begun. Despite our best intentions, we are about as far from our central doctrine as we are ever likely to be. Yet actually, we are not far from it at all. We still want peace and harmony in the world, we just have to survive the next few seconds. We are like the water flowing towards the sea, coming to a large boulder in its path. How we react largely depends on our character and our training. ***At that moment, who we are determines our entry into the confrontation.***

We still have two choices of action left to consider. A physical confrontation is already in progress. We can't avoid it; attempts to diffuse the situation have failed, our admonition has been ignored, and our defensive perimeter is being penetrated. We must either attempt to **control** the person so that they will not be in a position to injure us, or we can attempt to **injure** them first so that they will be unable to continue their attack.

The less calm the defender is, and the less confident he is, the more likely he will resort to injurious technique. But if a trained martial artist holds to his central doctrine, he is morally obligated to resolve conflicts with the least amount of violence and the greatest amount of benevolence possible. He is then obligated to perfect his control techniques so that he can be confident enough of them to actually use them to avoid injuring his attacker.

Injuring someone is easy. Six months of Tae-Kwon-Do classes will teach someone how to break a rib, smash a nose, or dislocate a knee. But that should not be the ultimate goal of learning self-defense. One should practice to the point that one *doesn't have to*. We should prefer to control an adversary, unless it is unreasonable to expect success.

If one intends benevolence, then to strike out in anger is to injure the inner Self.

Control or Injury?

Your decision to control your opponent if possible without intentionally hurting him should be based on your tactical assessment of the danger your opponent presents you. These are some of the observations you should quickly assess:

1. Is the person bigger/stronger that you? (Younger? Less injured?) Generally, a smaller person is legally permitted to use more deadly force against a larger attacker. This is also true for a woman against a man, a child against an adult, a person past middle age against someone in their prime. Also, if you are disadvantaged or injured, you are justified in using greater force against an attacker, even if they don't know you are.

2. Is the person armed with a weapon? Are they exhibiting the intent to use it to harm you? Is it a concealed weapon that the attacker has extracted from his clothing such as a gun or knife, indicating a pre-existing permission to act on their part? Or is it a convenient object picked up and being wielded as a weapon, such as a stick, a rock or a chair? This indicates a spontaneous act, possibly an act motivated by fear or anger. It can indicate both a lack of commitment and a lack of confidence on the part of the attacker whose intent may be possibly diffused by calming him down—but remember, it's still a weapon he's holding!

3. Is the person alone? If your attacker has friends to back him up, even if they have not moved toward your defensive perimeter, you are justified in using greater force. The logic of this is that you can't afford to focus all your attention on only one member of a hostile group. You risk losing track of its other members, who may attack you from a blind angle. If you can put the first attacker down in the first few seconds, not only will the others not have had the chance to "blindside" you, but the sight of their most aggressive ally going down may shake their confidence.

4. Is the person acting irrationally? Most control techniques work by inflicting pain on the attacker. However, if the attacker is extremely agitated or strung out on drugs, they will not feel pain as quickly or as acutely as a normal person. You are at grave risk of being injured by them while you are attempting to apply a pain inducing technique that they cannot feel. In my twenty-five years as a paramedic, I have seen many pain-inducing control techniques applied by paramedics and police officers fail, and the attempt to control ends up on the ground as a seething pile of perpetrator and police officers.

5. Is your level of training sufficient for what you are attempting? Confidence in control techniques must come from regular, consistent training in applying them. The higher your level of expertise, the higher the standard of control to which you will be held morally and legally accountable. A yellow belt who injures an attacker is less liable than a black belt who fails to control an attacker without injuring him

Situation A. You have gone to a local tavern with an old friend to have a beer and catch up on each other's lives. It's a week-end evening, and the tavern is crowded with patrons, some of whom are noisy and exhibiting out-of-control, raucous behavior. A man about your size backs up into your table, spilling your drink. Instead of apologizing, he curses at you and says in a loud, slurred voice to move your table out of the way. You help him off of your table, explaining that it's not your table, and it's probably right where the tavern owner wants it. He takes offense, and explains for all to hear how he is now going to rearrange your face. He steps toward you, just at the edge of your fight zone, and his right fist raises up, balled into a fist, and starts its flat arc toward your face. *What do you do?*

The attacker in this scenario is alone, unarmed, and somewhat drunk. This presents a trained person with a situation appropriate to attempt control.

Control Tactics

Generally speaking, it's best not to attempt to control an attacker by force. That's a quick path to meeting contention with contention, and will likely result in a static, strength against strength stand-off. Rather, one should focus on controlling the four dynamics of entry: **distance, angle of entry, timing of contact, and energy of contact.**

Distance: Guarding your defensive perimeter and controlling the fighting distance are two different tactics. Guarding your defense perimeter is a tactic when you are unsure of the other person's intention. In that case, it's reasonable to take a step away from the other person to give yourself more time and information to assess their approach. Once you have assessed that the other person is choosing an adversarial role, stepping backward away from them becomes a tactical error. It only gives him more time and momentum to catch up to you, and he can come forward faster than you can go backward. It is better to close the distance quickly so that you make contact with them at your own choice of timing—perhaps even before they expect it. The only reason one might choose to step backwards is to do so in order to improve one's angle of defense; and even then one's energy is still engaged, still moving forward into the conflict. (This is called ***paradoxical movement,*** and will be discussed in more detail in chapter 6.)

Angle of Entry: Generally speaking, the energy of violent contention is linear; the energy of control is circular. We must choose our outcome objective as early as possible. ***The desire to control an opponent changes the way we enter into a confrontation in order to make control possible.***

"In the technique, the doctrine is revealed." –Walter Todd Shihan, Aikido

---

This is the most evident in the angle we establish in relation to the line of attack. The angrier and the more focused the adversary is on harming you, the more linear his attack energy becomes. For instance, if he is trying to punch you in the nose, his arm usually will inscribe a flat arc through the air directly toward your face. Most "hard" martial arts such as Shotokan or Kenpo primarily teach blocking the arm out of the way and punching or kicking the opponent back along the same attack line. Most "softer" martial arts such as Aikido or Hapkido, which seek to control rather than injure, teach simply stepping off the line of attack. Then you can relate to the opponent along a line of energy that *you* create, rather than relating to him through the line of energy that he has created. (More about defensive angles in chapter 7).

Timing of Contact: as an adversary moves toward you with intention to injure you, his mind will automatically calculate the aim and focus of his movement. For instance, the man from above who is trying to punch you will automatically throw his weight into his punching arm, and automatically brace himself for the instant of contact. His senses expect to feel your face and weight against his fist at the instant he intends it. His balance will anticipate this resistance. He will subconsciously depend on this resistance to stop his momentum. By stepping out of the way and avoiding his chosen instant of contact, you interrupt the attacker's timing. There is a moment—perhaps as long as a second—that the attacker must recover his balance and redirect his momentum in order to continue his attack. This moment is called a ***void***. It is the moment when an attacker is the most vulnerable. Counter-attacking within this vulnerable recovery period is called, *"Operating within the void."* (Discussed in more detail in chapter 8.)

Energy of Contact: A rule of thumb about entering energy is, ***move in such a way as to have your energy penetrate your opponent's space. Do not allow him to penetrate yours.*** This means that if you control the distance, the angle, and the timing of your entry into the physical contact, you also control the energy of contact. The idea is to have the moment of contact result in a distinct advantage to you instead of to your opponent. For example, let's look at the puncher in situation A. if the puncher has put his full weight into his punch but misses you, he will be off balance. If you apply light lateral pressure against his shoulder or upper arm at that instant, you may cause him to lose balance completely.

Control techniques work by accomplishing two objectives: either you must take control of the adversary's balance, or you must inflict enough pain to have them submit to your control. But in the latter case, you must be in control of his balance initially so that he is in a poor position to resist your technique. The whole idea of controlling your fighting distance, your entry angle, and your entry timing is to minimize resistance to your entering energy. Then, the precise, surgical application of a small amount of energy in a direction that the adversary is not expecting can unbalance him completely. (See chapter 6: art of **blending**, or learning how to guide the opponent's energy into such a position of imbalance.)

The art of controlling an attacker's energy to your own advantages takes many years to develop. However, the first step in that direction is actually mental. One must practice the mindset of the water principle: *Apply constant physical and mental energy towards one's chosen outcome objective, and do not be dissuaded.* **"Do not step back"** *is as much a mental proscription as it is a physical one!*

Let's get back to our friend, the tavern drunk, for a moment. Now let's change the scenario:

Situation B. You sidestep the man's punch and walk away. You visit with your friend a few minutes, and then decide to leave the tavern. As you step out the side door, you are confronted by two men. One is the drunk from the tavern. The other, obviously a friend of his, is a big, lean, sober man, and he has a length of iron pipe in his right hand. The drunk steps into your fight zone, points a figure at your face, smiles meanly and begins to tell you in grisly detail exactly what he and his friend are going to do to you. The man with the pipe takes a step closer, but hasn't reached your fight zone yet. *What do you do?*

This is now an entirely different situation, one in which it is inappropriate to attempt control techniques. You are faced with multiple opponents, one who is armed. Avoidance is impossible, and attempts to dissuade these men will probably be interpreted by them as intimidation or weakness. There is absolutely no "peace and harmony" in this situation. You know that someone is going to get injured. Your only choice appears to be to have the injured party not be yourself. You can make no progress toward any benevolent central doctrine if you don't survive.

Your best strategy is to take the nearest adversary out of action as soon as possible. You have arrived at that conclusion coolly and logically, and chosen it as your outcome objective. Your entry into the physical conflict begins with that intent. The four dynamics of entry are still of paramount importance, but your relationship to your adversary changes them.

"Self defense is not about technique. It's about relationship."
—James R. Garrison

Distance: The distance you establish to your adversary depends on your fighting style, and on your observation of the adversary's posture. Roughly speaking, there are three fighting ranges. **Long range fighting** is when fighters are at kicking distance; **medium range fighting** is when fighters are at punching distance; and **short range fighting** is at contact, or grappling distance. Is your fighting style primarily a kicking style? If so, your advantage will be to establish an optimal distance for your best kick. Are you a grappler? If this is the case, you might want to close the distance as quickly as possible. But before you do, you should take a look at how your adversary is standing. Are his legs wide apart? This would indicate that he's used to long range movement in a fight and is probably a good kicker. You may want to close the distance on this person as soon as possible, and stay inside of his optimum kicking distance. Are his legs closer together, but his left shoulder turned toward you? This may indicate a person who is in a trained defensive stance, and because his legs are closer together, may indicate someone trained in boxing. You probably would be wise to stay back in your own kicking range—or close with him and throw him on his head—but you should stay out of his medium range. Is your adversary's body crouched and his legs bent? This might indicate a person ready to spring forward with his whole body, and probably a person trained in a grappling art such as wrestling. Completely closing the distance on this kind of adversary would be a mistake. It would be better to stay on an angle disadvantageous to him, and keep your distance. The idea is to establish a distance from which you have the advantage, and from which your best techniques will be the most effective and most devastating. Maintaining this distance, your energy washing up against your opponent's energy, is like a dance. It is a perfect example of the water principle as a fighting tactic. No matter which techniques you decide to use, launching them from your optimum distance will give you a distinct tactical advantage.

Angle of Entry: As stated above, your intent to control your opponent will be optimized by the use of wider angles and more circular movement in your technique. If you intend from the outset to injure your opponent, your angles will generally become narrower and your movement more linear, but because of the water principle, both of these factors change in relationship to the opponent's forward energy.

The Diamond Principle

All balanced body movement is circular at its center. But maximum power is linear. The resolution of this paradox lies in our understanding of the Tan-Jun center (see chapter 4). When we intend to maximize our power, our energy swirls around our Tan-Jun center in a small, tight circle just before we direct it outward toward a target. This is the only way to project our entire body weight into any move. The more power we intend, the tighter and smaller this circle becomes. Once our weight has generated its maximum momentum, the rest of the movement becomes a straight line into the target.

"The smaller the circle of movement, the more powerful the technique."

--Professor Wally Jay, founder of Small Circle Jujitsu

If you are attacked and you choose to respond with the intent to injure, your best option is to move off the line of the attacker's approach, and back into his centerline with your own counter-attack in one smooth two-part flow. The pivot point, the point at which you change your energy flow from divergent to convergent, is the moment of circular movement in the Tan-Jun center. If this movement were larger, it would resemble a horizontal wave, moving away from the attacking force and forward into the target with the same flow; but the circle is so small and intense, it is not apparent. Whether you move to the inside of your opponent's arm or to the outside of it depends on other factors and tactics, but these two options form the two sides of a diamond (see chapter 7). The shape of the diamond depends on the forward energy of the attack. The more forward momentum the attacker has, the wider the diamond becomes; the less forward energy the attacker has, the narrower the diamond. This is the water principle in its most aggressive form. Almost all fighting systems have many basic techniques in which the diamond pattern is quite evident.

The intent to injure completely changes your relationship with your adversary from the first moment of the confrontation. There should be no confusion in your mind about what you want to accomplish.

In the original Sangcook Kim Dojang, we used to intermix punching and grappling techniques, until Grandmaster Kim watched us one day. One of our black belts took down his attacker with a shoulder throw; and then, while the man was on his back, the black belt threw a reverse punch to the attacker's face. Mr. Kim asked why he did that. *"The whole point of throwing someone down is so that you don't have to hit them,"* Mr. Kim said. *"If you're going to hit someone anyway, you might as well hit him first, while they are standing up. More efficient."* I believe the point of his statement was that one should be very clear about one's intentions.

"Mastering technique is fine, but mastering strategy is better. Hapkido teaches us to use our brains first." –James R. Garrison

---

Taking Life

As a final and extreme measure, a warrior may be forced to kill. He must only do so as a last resort, only to save his own life or the life of another person. The better trained he is, the more his chances improve to control and defeat his opponent short of taking his life. The true warrior looks upon the act of killing as a failure to properly manifest his warrior art. He may be forced to kill by extreme circumstances. If so, he must do so without hesitation, but he remains reluctant. For an ethical person, such an act causes remorse, not pride.

So many action movies depict the hero as someone who kills with a deft touch, maims multiple inept attackers with his quick and deadly hands, wields all manner of deadly weapons, and leaves behind him piles of dead or severely wounded bodies. The hero is shown moving along his way without so much as a backward glance or grimace. What kind of role model is this? Does the plot justify such action from an ethical viewpoint? Sadly, not much of the time. Isn't the point of **Budo** *(warrior's way)* to seek the most benevolent path? Action movies which depict capricious violence set a woeful behavioral standard. Do we really want a society of kids who idolize and imitate sadistic sociopaths? Martial arts and ethics are inseparable.

Review

In this chapter, we have discussed the ***water principle***—flowing without interruption toward our chosen objective. Sometimes our path is unobstructed, and we flow directly toward our goal. Other times, we meet obstacles in out path, and our challenge becomes how to flow around them. But our path does not change, because it is ***internal***. In order to have an ongoing permission to act, we must create an ethical construct from which we control and direct our behavior, called a ***central doctrine***. This becomes the ethical foundation of our ***escalating action strategies***. These include ***avoidance, diplomacy and diffusion***, giving an ***admonition***, guarding our ***defense perimeter***, attempting to ***control***, and as a last resort, deciding to ***injure***. ***Tactics*** which support these strategies are success oriented and not ethically based. Tactics change constantly, as a situation changes. ***A warrior must learn to become like water and flow with the dynamics of the situation. Above all, he must learn to constantly flow toward his chosen objective with every*** *decision, so at the moment of action, he is physically and mentally already in motion.*

"My definition of self defense is to nourish all those things in our lives which are to our ultimate spiritual benefit, and to discard all of those things which can do us ultimate spiritual harm."
-- Shannon Kawika Phelps, 10th dan (from <u>Demon Chaser</u>, Temple Bell, Ltd.)

*****

Seonage throw.

Chapter 6

Do Not Resist Force; Blend with it.

"Softness triumphs over hardness, feebleness over strength. What is more malleable is always superior over that which is immovable. This is the principle of controlling things by going along with them, of mastery through adaptation."

-- Lao-Tsu

I have a large, S-curved scar on my right knee. It is an old scar, from much younger and less wiser days, a pointless fighting injury, the end result of out-of-control attitude and angst. I was in my mid-twenties, fresh out of the Navy and home from Vietnam, a confused, disillusioned college kid with a chip on my shoulder, a few years of martial arts training, and a drinking problem. I found myself back in college because the G.I. Bill paid me to be there, but I had no ambitions other than to take easy classes, eat pizza, smoke cigarettes, and hang out with my friends. In between these indulgences, I would practice Chinese Kenpo, in which I had earned a black belt despite my lifestyle.

I remember that my martial arts practice in those days was entirely based on technique and the speed of delivery. I didn't care about the history or traditions of martial art, or its philosophy, or even martial manners. Martial art was about beating the other guy so senseless that he couldn't move. That was all it was to me. And I went through those days with clenched teeth, tightened muscles, and rude words for anyone who dared be in my way.

One day at "Kenpo class"—a small group of "rotating dojo" roughnecks and Kenpo dropouts who practiced in basements, garages, and abandoned warehouses—we were doing six-second sparring rounds. We would attack each other ferociously and try to overwhelm our opponent in the first few seconds of the match. Any bout that went longer than six seconds was stopped. Our club held classes in an area of town that seemed to attract a larger percentage of hoods, gang members, and misfits, kind of like myself in those days. In six-second sparring, there wasn't much control. Everybody expected a few bumps and bruises, and nobody seemed to care. When it was my turn to spar, I'd kick and punch full power, and so would the others. Sometimes,

I'd get hit; sometimes I'd hit them first. I just didn't give a damn, and I liked hurting people.

But that day, when it was my turn, I faced off with a wiry little guy who was very fast and very mean. I remember being determined to just knock his head in. But when I lunged forward, he calmly stepped aside and side-kicked my leg. I went down like a bag of potatoes, every single medial ligament torn in my right knee. As I lay on the floor holding my knee and gritting my teeth, I said, "Why the hell did you do that?"

I remember him laughing at me. He said, "Like you weren't trying to hurt me? I've been watching you fight. You set the pace, man. You brought it on yourself!"

That was my last day of Kenpo practice. Three months later, after surgery and learning to walk again, I began to search for a new style of martial art. And a new approach to them as well—one based on physical fitness, mental clarity, and respect.

That period of my life represents a low point to me in terms of my physical health, mental awareness, and ethical involvement. I was living hour to hour, day to day, without any over-all strategy for my life, without involvement or respect for other people, chronically restless, cynical, contentious. It took a broken knee to cause me to take a good hard look at myself, and I didn't much like what I saw. Although I made many major adjustments to my lifestyle in the next few months, such as changing my diet, acquiring an actual job, and getting married, it was many years before I gained a certain perspective on that event. My sparring partner had been right that day; I had brought it on myself. I had been one of the most arrogant and contentious characters around, and hadn't even had the insight at the time to recognize it.

Fortunately, I eventually found instructors who were patient enough with me to teach me that the warrior's craft is much more than macho blustering, flexing, and inflicting pain. It's more about *finessing*-- achieving one's goal without struggling, without abrasion, without any apparent effort-- by using one's mind.

This chapter is about the principle of non-resistance, of giving way to power, and the art of taking advantage of the void that creates. This art is one of the most useful lessons a warrior can master, and yet it's also probably the most difficult. This is because the lesson cannot begin without achieving a certain state of mind. ***Before one can learn the physical art of non-resistance, one has to achieve the mental state of non-contentiousness.***

The essence of "soft-style" martial arts such as Hapkido and Aikido is the principle of non-resistance. One simply does not meet an opponent's force head-on with one's own force. It's an ineffective use of power, not to mention a lot of unnecessary work. And maybe even dangerous— what if the opponent is stronger? I've stopped enough punches and kicks with various parts of my anatomy to realize the foolhardiness of that approach. Yet I still feel the urge, when an adversarial confrontation arises, to bull my way into the center of it and just start swinging. And indeed, this is how most fights escalate—two people totally lose control of themselves, go berserk, and start flailing away blindly, almost unconsciously, at one another. And when the fight is over, it's often difficult to determine who the winner is. Both fighters remain agitated and out of control, and both usually have multiple injuries. Moreover, it's often the case that the fighters don't have a very clear picture of why they began fighting in the first place. I've responded to emergency scenes as a paramedic countless times, and I've often heard fighters answer the question, "Why were you fighting?" with statements such as, *"I don't know…the guy made me mad, and I just saw red." "Something came over me." "I just lost control and wasn't thinking." "I just wanted to hurt him; I don't know why!"*

These are not statements made by someone who is in control of his life, someone who has examined his internal Self and chosen a philosophical path. This is the mindset of someone who has already out of control before the fight started. It's the mindset of someone who has a contentious nature and may not even be aware of it.

There is a direct relationship between our inner balance, our overall health, our mental clarity, and the way we relate to our environment and the people in it. The mind and body are one existence, one awareness. It is not possible to have the body be in a state of disease, health imbalance, or unresolved stress, and have the mental process not be effected.

Every lifestyle choice that adversely affects the body affects the mental process as well. Poor diet, alcohol, cigarettes, mind-altering drugs, toxic relationships, the stresses of exhaustion or danger—all cause physical and chemical imbalances throughout the body. It's no wonder that such lifestyle choices are accompanied by mental anguish, depression, cynicism, or an ongoing feeling of desperation. People habitualized to any or all of these life choices are often ill at ease, jumpy, short-tempered, and contentious without even being aware of it. Put two of these types together, and an adversarial confrontation is inevitable.

A contentious nature is often a sign of internal imbalance; how can one be at peace with the world if one is in conflict within himself? It is a warrior's continuous task to examine his inner nature for any sign of contention, to understand its cause, and to eliminate it if possible. Contention destroys "listening mind." It disconnects people from one another. It stops receptivity, erodes emotional calmness, and makes any diplomatic resolution of conflict more difficult.

Contentiousness is harmful to the spirit. Seek ways in which you are the same as others, not ways in which you differ.

In addition to being philosophically objectionable, contentiousness is a strategic error as well. The more contentious the moment becomes, the more dangerous it becomes. It is to the warrior's advantage to avoid conflict if possible. But mental non-confrontation precedes physical non-confrontation. The warrior must look within to insure that he himself is not the source of the conflict. He insures this by his ongoing choices—by continuously optimizing his health, minimizing his stress load, clarifying his self definition, and practicing his art. His focused and purposeful life results in self respect and self acceptance. This is the beginning of peace of mind, the prerequisite of non-contentiousness.

Peace of mind is rooted in affection and compassion.
-- the Dalai Lama, ***The Art of Happiness***

Non-contentiousness is a mindset of projecting peace and benevolence outward from the center of the Self to the rest of the world. Non-contentiousness is an ongoing practice, much the same as the practice of martial techniques. In order to become skilled at it, you must learn to project benevolence and good will *even in a challenging environment.* The only way to do this is to be so consistent in your attitude toward others that it becomes a permanent part of your personal definition, and radiates from you like a beacon. These are a few methods for cultivating a non-contentious mind:

1. ***Practice unwavering respect.*** Seek only to give aid, to educate, to comfort, not to control, belittle, or punish.

2. ***Develop an empathetic mind.*** Practice understanding and forgiveness—it will help you anticipate another person's intent.

3. ***Practice non-attachment.*** Learn to accept situations rather than to attempt to control them. Allow yourself to flow with the situation and not get too heavily invested in a certain outcome.

4. ***Let go of your edges.*** An over-inflated ego interferes with perception and limits the expansion of awareness. Learn to become other-than-self oriented. Some lessons (such as martial arts) are best learned by developing "group consciousness."

5. ***Remember that true victory is remaining on the Way.*** That which is truly important is internal. Our own victory is achieving a peace of mind which may not be readily apparent to others, but this does not matter.

Our perceptions of the people we make contact with will be affected by our prevailing attitude. Moreover, the way in which people perceive us almost entirely depends on the way we relate to them. Maintaining a calm and peaceful demeanor will often forestall an altercation. An old Zen tale illustrates this nicely:

> *A traveler stopped in at an inn on the outskirts of a town. He inquired of the innkeeper, "What kind of people live in this town? I am moving here soon, and wondered what I'm likely to find." The innkeeper responded with, "Well, what kind of people live in the town you are from?" The traveler answered, "Oh, that town was filled with petty, backstabbing, rude and dishonest people! That's why I'm moving!" "Well," the innkeeper replied, "That's just the kind of people you'll find live here!" Upon hearing that, the traveler frowned and left the inn. Awhile later, another traveler entered the inn. He too asked the innkeeper, "What kind of people live in this town? I'm moving here and wondered what to expect." "Well," the innkeeper replied, "What kind of people live in the town where you came from?" "Oh," the second traveler replied, "They are kind, generous and happy folks. I've never known better!" "Well," the innkeeper replied, "That's just the kind of people you'll find live here!"*
>
> from Zen **Flash, Zen Bones,** edited by Paul Reps

One of the most difficult lessons a warrior must learn is that contention is a state of mind. Contention is the result of mental disconnection. It begins the moment we stop listening, stop empathizing, stop trying to understand others. It is the mind-set of resistance. Contention destroys our calmness, tightens our muscles, and erodes our intent for peace and harmony. And unfortunately, contention will do this even if it does not originate within us. It only takes one contentious mind to cause a disconnection. And since few of us are saints or Buddha incarnations, contentious situations invariably pop into our lives, probably at inopportune times, and then we have to decide what to do about it.

Several years ago, Hapkido Grandmaster James R. Garrison attended an Aikido instructors' seminar in Seattle, Washington. In the afternoon of a hot summer Saturday, the temperature inside the dojo, a large converted warehouse with only one row of small windows open to the fresh air, was approaching 90 degrees. Nobody seemed to mind, so he continued to practice with the Aikidoists, prominent instructors from up and down the entire west coast.

In the hottest part of the day, a car drove up and parked outside the dojo. Several Japanese teenagers climbed out and began yelling at the Aikidokas (students of Aikido) inside the dojo. Along with their insults and profanity, they challenged anyone inside to come out and fight them. From their hard punches and deep stances, Master Garrison guessed they were probably students of a hard-style Japanese karate. Through the open windows, the teenagers' taunts were loud and impossible to ignore.

Now, it is not Master Garrison's nature to back away from a fight. He had decided, at the very least, to go out and shoo them away like so many flies. But just as he was putting on his shoes, some of the Aikidokas simply closed all the windows. The teens' voices were significantly muted. However, now there was no fresh air, and the temperature inside the dojo began to rise.

Master Garrison reflected on the Way of Aikido, which is the way of peace and harmony, the way of non-contention. Any good Hapkidoist would have just stepped outside and punched the first teen out, then come back and opened the windows for some fresh air. But the Aikidokas were all practicing blissfully, ignoring the jeering teens outside and sweating away in the sweltering heat of the dojo, which was then surly above 100 degrees. But, Master Garrison reflected, this was not his seminar. If the Aikidokas preferred to suffer in the heat to avoid a confrontation, then he felt it would be proper to follow their example. Although personally, he wanted to just go beat the teens up, his lesson would be how to be less contentious and more peaceful, like the other Aikidokas. He did not go outside, and after awhile, the teens gave a few obscene gestures and drove off, the windows were re-opened, and the Aikido seminar continued as though nothing had happened. Master Garrison thought that his lesson in patience and forbearance had been a good exercise in the harmonious spirit of Aikido.

About a year later, Master Garrison was at another Aikido conference, this time in southern California. At a meeting, he told the story of his experience in Seattle, and how he had learned to control his temper and contemplate the meaning of inner peace. Some of the Aikidokas who had been in Seattle at the time were present, and began laughing.

When he asked why they were laughing, one of them said, "We were all afraid of the teenagers. If we had known you wanted to go outside and beat them up, we would have *sicced* you on them!" Everyone had a good laugh.

This story points out a major difference between the philosophies of Aikido and Hapkido. Aikidokas are taught to harmonize with the environment around them. They do this by blending their movements with the movements of others, by listening, by empathizing, by subjugating their own feelings and ego to the collective reality of their surroundings. Hapkidoists seek harmony within themselves. Hapkidoists seek a physical, mental, and spiritual oneness, a focus of not being in contention within oneself. This unity helps to sustain a benevolent nature toward others as a part of one's personal definition, *but not as a subjugation of the self to the environment.* Contention or non-contention thus becomes a personal, conscious choice. The choice itself, then, is a deliberate statement of intent rather than a subconscious state of mind.

We should remember that not all contention is bad. Sports competition is a healthy form of contention; but here, the intent is to enjoy a challenge, and no ill will is meant towards one's competitor. The contention a police officer feels toward a suspect who is resisting arrest is necessary; but here, the goal is the safety and well-being of society. Contention with someone who is trying to hurt you is obviously necessary and should be recognized early enough to defend yourself. But each of these forms of contention is accepted as a given result of one's intent to achieve a socially desirable goal. It is one's intentions that must be kept very clear.

In the last chapter, we discussed the importance of a central doctrine—a statement we use to define our character and guide our personal behavior. The ethical person lives a guided life. That is, he chooses to act in a purposeful manner, according to his beliefs. Sometimes he will find himself in contention with others because of those beliefs. In such a case, he can either remain steadfast in his beliefs and deal with the resulting conflict as diplomatically as possible, or simply change his beliefs. But sometimes, conflict just happens, and has no relevance or connection with one's beliefs. In this case, he must decide if the contention is justified or even wise. The warrior consciously picks his battles.

He does this by asking himself three questions. The first is,

Do I understand the nature of the conflict?

The nature of the conflict is determined by its source. Is the source of conflict internal or external? The warrior must ask himself if he is projecting his own internal conflict onto his surroundings and the people he is dealing with. Is he himself the cause of the contentious situation? There are three considerations which will help clarify this question in his mind. The first is, ***"Am I calm?"*** Anger erodes rational thinking. Anger also erodes compassion and benevolent intent. Often, it is difficult to tell whether one's feeling of contentiousness preceded one's anger, or the other way around. The true nature of conflict cannot be recognized by an agitated mind.

The prevailing idea is not to be <u>where</u> the opponents expect you to be; the real trick is not to be <u>who</u> they expect you to be.

The second consideration is, ***"Am I acting egocentrically?"*** One of the most common causes of contention is that one person begins to think that he is more important, more insightful, more privileged, more right than someone else. The warrior must learn to let go of his personal feelings and put his ego aside so that he can truly listen to a viewpoint which may be very different from his own. Part of the virtue of "listening mind" is the ability to examine conflict from all sides, and to empathize with different opinions than one's own in order to understand the nature of conflict.

The third consideration necessary for understanding the nature of a conflict is, ***"Have I lost my perspective?"*** By perspective, I mean one's intent to remain faithful to one's central doctrine of benevolence toward others. Feelings of contentiousness will erode out inner intent without our even being aware of it. We may just want to strike out in anger, but we cannot allow ourselves to give in to that urge. We must always govern our actions so that we operate from a position of forgiveness and compassion. This is very difficult to do in a potentially violent situation. But we must remember that our intent is not to be the cause of the conflict, but to be its resolution. Always seek the most harmonious resolution, the solution that's best for everyone, if possible. If such a resolution is not possible, then one must sustain compassion for the one who is (or is about to become) the injured party. Otherwise, one might inflict more injury than is necessary to achieve victory.

The second question necessary for the warrior to ask himself before he chooses to engage in conflict is,

Is action / intervention necessary?

My wife often reminds me when we are deeply involved in a discussion that I have a tendency to believe that it's my duty to answer every question and solve every problem. She reminds me this is not the case. Sometimes she just likes to talk about a dilemma she might find herself in and doesn't expect me to solve it for her. Sometimes, I want to solve a problem or settle a conflict just so I can feel good about my power to do so. But sometimes, conflict is just a part of the way things are, like the balance between warm and cold fronts in the jet stream, or the exchange of ideas in a political debate. Sometimes, it really isn't about *you*. Sometimes it's best to accept some situations, and let them resolve themselves through their own impetus, in their own time. Sometimes we can agree to disagree. The warrior learns to relinquish control of a situation when his control is neither needed nor desired. Author Joe Hyams writes in his book <u>Zen in the Martial Arts</u> a quote from his teacher, Kenpo Grandmaster Ed Parker:

"The only reason men fight is because they are insecure; one man needs to prove that he is better or stronger than another. The man who is secure within himself has no need to prove anything with force, so he can walk away from a fight with dignity and pride. He is the true martial artist—a man so strong inside that he has no need to demonstrate power. The point of achieving proficiency in any martial art is to be able to walk away from a fight rather than to [have to] win it."

The third question the warrior must ask himself before he chooses a battle is a two-part question:

What is to be gained? Is it worth the risk?

Many people engage in conflict to "prove a point," whatever that means. It's usually obvious afterward that no one has been forced to change his beliefs the least little bit. How ironic; attempting to prove a point by violence is usually pointless! Is it really worth risking injury to insist that you are the top dog, alpha-male, coolest, hippest, most correct, most important person in the group? If you have a clear self-image and a little bit of self confidence, it won't matter in the least what other people think of you or your issues.

There is a line from an old movie I remember; the movie is "Road House," in which Patrick Swayze stars as a night-club bouncer. A man comes up to him and says, "People say you're not so tough. They say you're all talk." Swayze just smiles and answers as he turns away, "Opinions vary."

If nothing useful is to be gained, then no risk is justified. Moreover, the concept of "winning" itself becomes suspect. The fact that a social situation is defined in terms of "winning" and "losing" indicates that the people involved are predisposed to contention. If there is no contention, there is no winning or losing!

"The art of peace is the principle of non-resistance. Because it is non-resistant, it is victorious from the beginning. The art of peace is invincible because it contends with nothing." --Morihei Ueshiba O-Sensei, <u>The Art of Peace</u>

There are many cases where it may be more advantageous to "lose" a confrontation in order to bring about a more desirable resolution. We only have to keep in mind our desire for peacefulness, respect, and goodwill to remind us that true victory is for us to remain on that path. Every time we yield the right-of-way to someone who is in a greater rush than we are, we are practicing this principle. Every time we choose not to be angered or frustrated by a difference of opinion, we are practicing this principle by simply maintaining a non-contentious mind. It is not necessary to take inside our psyches every insult, every social slight, every act of aggression or neglect in which we represent a speed-bump in someone else's fast lane. It's usually not personal to us anyway. It's better to simply remember who we are, be satisfied that we have a fairly accurate handle on our personal definition, and that others can insult us only if we allow it by believing them. Our only legitimate concern is whether we are endangered by someone else's actions. If this is the case—or better still, *if this might be potentially the case*—then we can simply focus our awareness on the situation without the distractions of emotional involvement or prejudice.

Many older boys feel strong peer pressure to follow an unwritten and non-descript "code of manhood" which might include hiding one's feelings, brash and dangerous stunts, violent behavior, substance abuse, and poor scholastic achievement in order to not be perceived by others the same age as "unmacho" or "nerdy." Ironically, they only succeed in appearing rude and immature. What a release for the warrior when he finally realizes that none of this behavior is necessary.

Grandmaster James Garrison tells this story about one of his many trips to the Far East with Grandmaster Kim Sangcook. One evening, Master Garrison, his wife, and Grandmaster Kim were walking down a narrow, dimly lit street in downtown Hong Kong, involved in an animated discussion about the day's events. Suddenly, there was a group of six or seven teenaged boys in front of them, all similarly dressed in leather jackets and black jeans. The young men continued to walk down the middle of the street, just as though Master Garrison's group wasn't there or hadn't been seen. When they reached the threesome, the young man in front walked between Master Garrison and Grandmaster Kim, bumping both their shoulders out of his way as he passed through. Grandmaster Kim turned to get a look at the young man, and the whole group of teenagers turned to face him. The young man who had bumped him glared at Grandmaster Kim, said something in Chinese, and took a flamboyant martial stance, hands circling high in the air. Grandmaster Garrison knew there was going to be trouble. He handed a bag of purchases to his wife, along with his wristwatch, to free up his hands. But Grandmaster Kim did not take a martial stance. He simply stood with his hands at his sides and looked at the lead teenager, who was crouched into a low Kung-Fu stance of some sort, curling his hands in an insolent universal gesture meant to say, "Come here and see what happens." Grandmaster Garrison could see absolutely no fear in Grandmaster Kim's demeanor, yet no aggression either. This standoff lasted what seemed to Grandmaster Garrison to be two or three minutes, but was actually probably about 15 or 20 seconds. Then the leader simply waved his arm in dismissal at Grandmaster Kim, and all of the young men walked away snickering. Grandmaster Garrison took a big sigh of relief, but Grandmaster Kim shrugged his shoulders and chuckled. "Just boys," he said, then began walking again as through nothing had happened.

The Art of Non-Resistance

The mighty oak, resisting,

Is uprooted by the storm;

The lowly reed simply bends,

And survives another day.

-- Taoist Proverb

Judo (Jujitsu) Master Henry Seishiro Okazaki wrote, "Only by cultivating a receptive state of mind, without preconceived thoughts, can one master the secret art of reacting spontaneously and naturally without hesitation and without purposeless resistance."

-- from "The Esoteric Principles of Judo" (unpublished paper)

The idea that we can overcome force by not resisting it is a concept that has been difficult for me to grasp. It has taken years for me to explore its ramifications. Even so, every now and again I lose track of it, and have to be reminded by my teachers to regain my perspective. There are some of us that just have to learn life's lessons the hard way. The first time I met James Garrison was an example of this I will never forget.

It was in the spring of 1974, and I was looking around for a martial arts group to practice with. My knee had heeled quickly. I was running five miles a day, and swimming a mile after running, in the best shape of my life. I had tried out various martial arts, including Japanese Karate, Chinese Wing Chun, Tai Chi, and Korean Tae Kwon Do without finding a teacher I completely respected, nor an art that suited all my needs. I was looking for a more sophisticated, more philosophical approach, a martial practice through which my life would evolve, not just my martial technique.

With this approach in mind, I attended an evening Aikido class taught in a local junior high school. I took my only gi, an old white karate uniform that I had attempted to dye black so it would look like a Kenpo style uniform, but it had turned out dull grey instead, including the belt. I stepped onto the mat without bowing (I was still completely ignorant of formal martial manners then) in my weird grey gi and belt, and noticed that a few of the other students were staring at me. The sensei, Master Garrison, was wearing a crisp white top over a black *hakama*, a formal dress-like robe that seemed to flow as he moved about. His senior student, Little Bill Wheeler, a man with long, dark hair and a beard who was much smaller than I, was also wearing a white top and a black *hakama*. The two of them were talking quietly together, and occasionally looking over at me.

The next thing I knew, I was paired with Little Bill. He told me to throw a punch at him. My first punch was a bit tentative. I didn't want to hurt anybody. But then he told me to really punch hard, right at his chin. I didn't like being told my punch wasn't very good, so I was determined to hit him if I could. I was a Kenpo black belt, after all. (Or at least a *grey* belt.) But when I threw my best punch, suddenly I was on my back with my arm in the most painful arm-lock I had ever experienced. I hadn't made any contact, or even felt a block; and yet I was totally immobilized. Little Bill patiently taught me the fine art of slapping at my side or thigh when I had had enough. I had been in the martial arts for ten years and didn't know how to yield gracefully.

Well, I was determined that it had been an accident or a stroke of luck on his part; so on the next attack, I lunged at Little Bill with an anger and a fury I didn't realize was in me, and again ended up on my back with my arm bent into an extremely painful angle. I tried several more times to get a hold of him or hit him, without success. Finally, Little Bill looked down at me and said, *"Stop fighting me! The more you try to force me, the more energy you give me to work with. I'm afraid you're going to hurt yourself!"*

I never once got a solid hit on him; yet I went home bruised up from my frequent meetings with the floor, not to mention the extreme pain my arms and wrists had endured. I was sore for days. Little Bill had beaten me by simply yielding to my energy.

Later, I learned that Master Garrison and Little Bill had not known what to think of the guy in the weird gi, but they had noticed my lack of manners. Master Garrison had told Bill Wheeler, "Pair up with him, and see what he knows. And see that he feels some pain." Well, I felt so much pain I never went back to that particular class. I never wore my grey gi again either. But I was intrigued. A much smaller man had completely dominated me, and never once did I get an opportunity to resist. It was like trying to grab onto smoke. I was determined to investigate this new approach to martial arts, and began looking for a school which taught throwing. A few months later, I discovered the Sangcook Kim School of Hapkido.

Years passed before I fully understood what had happened. Little Bill had simply ridden my force and spurred me on into my own imbalance. I understand the experience now as a kind of gift exchange. I gave Little Bill the gift of energy to redirect to my disadvantage, and he gave me the gift of *connection*—that is, he consciously chose to protect me from becoming too badly damaged. I threw myself at him with such agitation and fury that he could have dropped me onto my head any number of ways, but he didn't. He remained receptive to the experience of our interchange, constantly in touch with my energy, and guided it into the best resolution for both of us, gentling my falls. This has been a prime example to me of how a warrior should act.

Once we have achieved a mindset of non-contentiousness and empathy, we also achieve the physical prerequisites necessary to practice the tactics of non-resistance: relaxed muscles, calm emotions, and a flowing mind. We must remember that the art of non-resistance depends on our connection—*our relationship*—with our opponent. Martial arts in Japan have developed a special set of words to describe this relationship in order to avoid the contentiousness inherent in such words as "opponent," "attacker," and "adversary." In Japanese, the term *"Uke"* refers to the person who attacks another student in training; but the word translates more accurately to *"one who provides the gift of learning."* The student who defends himself is called *"Tori,"* or, *"one who receives the gift of learning."* The action between the two, the *uke* and *tori*, can become fast and furious, but the relationship of mutual respect and concern for one another's welfare does not change. The more advanced a warrior's training, the more his relationship with other people he comes in contact with resembles this relationship between the *uke* and *tori*, even if the relationship is contentious. Other people present us with opportunities to express our good intentions. Our choices of resolution can thus become the gifts of empathy and compassion. We choose not to injure people beyond our need to protect ourselves from further attack.

Aikido Sensei Terry Dobson used to tell his students that when he is attacked, it is a gift of energy wrapped in violence. "I simply accept the gift without the package."

Let's assume you are in a situation that has a potential for physical conflict. We have previously discussed the prerequisites that you need to be prepared for this moment: cultivating an indomitable spirit; engaging in regular practice in order to develop a flexible mind and intelligent muscles; the importance of calmness, breath control, and relaxation; developing physical and mental groundedness; choosing a strategy with unwavering intent, and most important, a non-contentious mind. Now you are ready to apply the art of non-resistance.

There are four steps in the art of non-resistance. They are:

1. **Get out of the way.**
2. **Blend with *uke*'s momentum.**
3. **Lead *uke* into imbalance**
4. **Obstruct *uke*'s balance correction**

1. Get out of the way

More martial arts teach beginners to block an incoming attack. The very first techniques learned are the inside block, the outside block, the upper and lower blocks, and so on. But all blocks are contentious by their very nature—impeding force with an opposing force. As martial training evolves, smooth and balanced movement takes on an increasingly important role in avoiding an attack. One simply learns not to be in the path of the force. And if one isn't in the path of the attack, then blocking becomes less imperative. The hands and arms are freed from the absolute need to stop the blow or push; because, even when completed, the blow or push will connect with nothing. Once the defender is out of the way, there is no longer any reason to impede the attack.

This allows the early training of thousands of various hard blocking movements to evolve into something new and different. The blocks can become simultaneous punches that can connect with an opponent at the same instant he would have hit you—or they can become gentle, circular, soft, allowing the attacking movement to continue on its original course. The hands still move, but now the intent is different. The intent has already progressed to the next stage of the conflict; the intent is to continuously improve one's tactical position.

> *Words that describe action are different that the actions themselves. "Soft" does not really mean soft, but nonresistant, smooth and precise; nothing about the intent behind the movement itself is soft. And "circular" does not mean traveling in a circle, for the motion would end up where it started and thus have no purpose. "Circular" moves are actually spirals, in which a small amount of progress is made in the direction of one's intent.*

This initial engagement to improve one's position is called **the entry.** (See critical forces of entry, chapter 5.) One should achieve entry into what is now a fight with three goals firmly in mind. The first, obviously, is to not get hit. The second goal of entry is to be in good position to hit back. The third goal is to be on an angle with the opponent which allows you better access to his center than he has to yours. Then he has to readjust his position in order to continue his attack, but you do not. (More about the advantages of correct angles in chapter 7.)

In the last chapter, the principle of continuous pressure on the opponent was discussed. Entry, then, is a continuous process, even while apparently giving way. When one gives ground, yields to greater force, one moves in such a way as to improve his position—and thus improve his entry. This is called ***paradoxical movement.*** But since the warrior learns to move in whatever direction will improve his position, all non-resistant tactics are paradoxical. It is important to recognize that non-resistance tactics are not completely non-resistant. By employing them, we are resisting getting hit. We are resisting becoming dominated or controlled. We are resisting our opponent's intent by not yielding to it. The only thing we are not resisting is his force. And by not resisting the force of the attack, we can turn it to our own advantage.

2. Blend with opponent's momentum

Blending with an *uke's* (attacker's) momentum is a split second defense in which the *tori* (defender) adjusts his balance so that both *uke* and *tori* are flowing in the same direction for a brief moment. The characteristic movement of blending is a sudden shift of the hips to align both movements from the center, the *tan-jun* point. In other words, the defender gets out of the way of the attack, and then aligns his energy to flow in the same direction, at the same time, as the attacker.

There are three main reasons for you to blend your momentum with your attacker. The first is that it creates a moment of confusion for the attacker. The moment he expected to make contact with you never happens. An attacker braces for this moment of contact. He expects the resistance of a ribcage or a face at the end of his grasp, and subconsciously programs his muscles to flex into it. When his muscles are denied this experience, there is a split-second of disorientation, of imbalance ripe with opportunity for the defender to exploit.

The second reason to blend your momentum with an attacker's is so you and your attacker are both moving in the same direction. This allows you to remain in balance and in touch with your attacker's energy. By remaining in touch with his energy and momentum, you are also staying in touch with his intent. If his intent changes, his energy will change. You will become aware of it instantly because you are in touch with him; and, since you have good balance, you can adjust your response instantly as well. Remember that you are continuously seeking to enter your opponent's space in a way that is to your advantage. By blending with his energy instead of resisting it, your own energy is freed up to seek that advantage one step ahead of your opponent.

Seek to enter your opponent's space; do not let him enter your space.

The third reason to blend your movement with the momentum of the attacker has to do with the movement itself. In order to blend, you must move from your center—i.e. align your hips with the direction of the flow. That is, your hips turn towards and into the direction of the movement. If you as the defender maintain your balance during this blending movement, your hips will be in perfect position to change direction quickly and forcefully. Blending constitutes the first half of "rolling hips," discussed in chapter 4—the principle of generating maximum power in movement. It's rather like drawing back a bowstring, or cocking the trigger of a gun. The second half of the rolling hips is simply your movement evolving into an injection of power into your defensive choice.

3. Lead opponent into imbalance

Blending is done with a completely open and receptive mind. You cannot be completely certain just how your opponent is going to attack—what opportunities or difficulties his energy is going to present to you. But once you have gotten out of the way and blended your movement with your opponent's, then a path to your advantage and dominance will present itself. It takes many years to become instantly aware of all of these pathways, these opportunities, but I'll attempt to outline the major ones. After you have blended with your opponent, you should seek these conditions:

-- *Your opponent is fully extended*
-- *Your opponent's momentum has moved off his own strong angle*
-- *Your opponent has presented a void which is open for attack*
-- *Your opponent is distracted*

All of these conditions have one aspect in common; if you direct your energy further into these conditions while you and your opponent's energies are aligned, your advantage will increase.

Your opponent is fully extended

If *uke* throws a punch at *tori* and misses, chances are he will have to retract his arm before he continues his attack. This is especially true of an attacker who kicks; he will have to retract his leg to maintain his balance. If *tori* has blended with the attack, then, while *uke*'s arm or leg is in full extension, he can add a small amount of his own energy to *uke*'s momentum before it begins to retract. This will result in **overextension**. *Uke*'s power dissipates at full extension. *Uke*'s balance dissipates with overextension.

Your opponent's momentum has moved off his own strong angle

Uke's attack energy usually becomes very focused, very linear. An attacker will automatically adjust his power and momentum to maximize his impact into a chosen target. This is his *attack angle*. His attack angle is his strongest point of balance, but it is a narrow focus. That is, at the moment of his attack, *uke* is easily unbalanced with a small amount of secondary pressure in another direction. If *tori* has blended with *uke*'s attack, he will be just as aware of the attack angle as *uke*, and can easily apply lateral pressure to lead *uke* off of his own attack angle, where he will become unbalanced.

Remember, balance is the "great equalizer." When a person has control of his balance, his size and weight make a big difference. When a person is off balance, his size and weight make no difference. He will either have to regain his balance, or he will fall down. Taking an opponent's balance away from him is the single most advantageous tactic a warrior can learn.

Mr. Garrison has a picture hanging in his office of one of his teachers at the Kodokan. Master Kotani Sensei is in the middle of a throw, his *uke* high in the air, and the Master is holding onto his *uke* with only two fingers.

Your opponent has presented a void which is open for attack

An attack is a major shift in energy. If you could see energy, what you would see during a strong punch is that there is a surge of energy away from the body, extending down the arm toward he intended target, and because we only have a given amount of energy around us at any one time, you might also see a thinning of energy around the rest of the body. That's a fairly esoteric approach; let's put in another way. When *uke* punches, his attention is drawn into his arm and away from the rest of his body. It *tori* has stepped aside and blended with *uke*'s movement, then he will be relating to *uke* from a different angle and a different perspective. At the moment of the punch, *uke* may be thinking so much about his fist that he forgets to protect other areas of his body, such as his ribcage, which may be exposed to counterattack. In military terms, this is called *"flanking the enemy."* In martial terms, this is called *"seeking the void."* Until *uke* recovers his energy and rebalances his defenses, he may be exposing multiple targets of his own.

Viewing a void, or exposure, as a target is a more contentious approach than simply seeking to unbalance an attacker. In chapter 5, we discussed various reasons that might justify this approach—the attacker is bigger than we are, or armed with a weapon, or not alone, etc. But there is another consideration. *Hitting your attacker may be the most effective way to unbalance him.* Remember, you have already moved off the attack angle, so any strike you initiate will be at a sharp angle to your attacker's balance. Striking is just another method of applying secondary force, and has the added benefit of disabling as well as unbalancing. This is one of the key distinguishing characteristics of Hapkido. All throws have moments within their execution when striking the attacker is an option, and the strike becomes an integral part of the throw.

Your opponent is distracted

In *Precepts of the Martial Artist*, Walter Muryasz writes about moving an attacker where you want him by leading his *attention*. "The true lead draws the opponent into the space where you want him. To give him what he wants also draws him into that space, but only if you are aware of what he wants. It is the mind you are leading—its intent, conditioning and perceptions."

-- from the book, *Leading from Within*, by Robert Pater

My first martial arts teacher, one of the Tracy brothers of Tracy's Kenpo, used to be very good at staying just out of his opponent's reach. During sparring, he would crouch backward, away from his opponent, so that it appeared that he was farther away than he really was. The moment this was a most effective distraction was just after his opponent had punched. He would lean away, just out of reach; and then, as his opponent's arm was retracting, he was able to lean forward and punch over the retracting arm without taking a step. His timing was deadly. Before you could throw a second punch, he rolled right up over the top of you. And in those days, the mid 1960's, contact was full power. We wore mouthpieces, but it's still a wonder I have all my teeth.

Another example of leading the attention is presenting a false target. This is done by making yourself appear vulnerable during a movement which has two parts. The first part of your movement draws attention to some target area you are purposely exposing to your opponent until he fixes his attention on it. The second part of your movement is a planned response to his now predictable attack.

I remember falling prey to this gambit early in my sparring career. I was in a match for first place of the black belt heavyweight division of a regional tournament. My opponent was shorter that I, but well muscled and stocky. I had the longer reach, but he was cagy and a fast kicker. The score was two to two. The next point would win the match. We stood facing each other, catching out breath, crouched into our fighting stances.

Then my opponent started weaving his hand back and forth in front of me. It was a bit like watching him change stances, and a bit like watching a snake dance. I didn't know what he was attempting, but it aggravated me, so I reached out and knocked it away. Instantly, he roundhouse kicked me square in the ribs, a good, clean shot under my outstretched arm. He had been waiting for me to do just that—reach out and expose my ribcage. He had made my next move—and my next vulnerability—predictable. The match was over; his distraction had won him first place.

4. Obstruct opponent's balance correction

Once you have blended with your opponent's energy and led him into imbalance, you must exploit your advantage, and not allow him to regain his balance. Unless your opponent is an adept wrestler, he will not want to fall down. (And even if he is a wrestler, he will not want to go down out of control.) Chances are, if your opponent is off balance, his highest priority on either a conscious or subconscious level is going to be to regain his balance. This almost always means taking an extra step.

Because you have had a hand in the direction your opponent has lost his balance, the step he will take to regain his balance becomes predictable. That predictability gives you a tremendous advantage. All you have to do to cause him to lose his balance entirely is to prevent him from taking that step. Virtually all Judo throws work in exactly this way.

Review

In this chapter, we have discussed the relationship between the non-contentious mind and the art of non-resistance. *In order to succeed at mastering the art of non-resistance, you must first cultivate a non-contentious mind.* This includes practicing unwavering respect, developing empathy and forgiveness, practicing non-attachment and non-aggressiveness, and keeping your ego in perspective by learning to become other-than-self oriented. You must formulate and remember your self definition of personal power, and balance it with benevolence toward others at all times. These are prerequisites for the warrior's virtue called *"Listening mind."*

The art of non-resistance has four parts. They are: **Get out of the way. Blend with the opponent's momentum. Lead opponent into his own imbalance. Obstruct his balance correction.**

Remember, if you have strong character and clear intent, you may be able to lead an adversary by dominating his mental path. If you do not have strong character and clear intent, you are in danger of being dominated and led away from your own path.

"The true warrior is never at war; he is at peace, <u>especially when he is at war.</u>" – Morihei Ueshiba O-sensei, <u>The Art of Peace.</u>

*****

Slipping inside a left jab to counterpunch.

Chapter 7

Seek the Angle of Best Advantage

Grandmaster James Garrison has often told this tale of how he first met Mr. Kim, his long-time teacher and friend.

"I can remember that day very clearly. It was a Saturday, a hot, late spring day. I was in fairly good condition in those days. I had at that time been in the martial arts community for about 18 years. I had run several miles that morning and had just finished about two hours of full-contact sparring with our small practice group. A student of mine, a black belt himself, and I were returning from that practice when we spotted this new dojang on Washington Street at 13th Avenue, in downtown Portland. This Korean guy was just finishing lettering the window with the word *Hapkido.*

We decided to pay him a visit, but it was more than that. The people in our full contact practice group were pretty self confident in those days. We thought we were pretty hot stuff. We'd visited other clubs in town just to have a little fun. You know—you go in, choose the top few guys, throw them around a little bit, thumb your nose, and leave. We wanted to check this new Korean guy out. But also, we wanted him to know we were in town, and we were "it."

But we were respectful, we didn't just challenge him. We went into his dojang, and the minute I saw him, a chill went up my spine. There was something about him that instantly bowled me over. I can only refer to it as this tremendous force-of-being, a totally confident calmness. Mr. Kim didn't speak much English, so much of our conversation took place on the phone, with his sister on the other end translating for both of us. Mr. Kim asked about my training; he was very polite. I told him about my rank in Judo, Aikido, and Jujitsu. Then he said, "Show me Jujitsu." So, I took hold of his wrist, and it was like grabbing onto a rock. I was trying to throw him, and he wasn't exactly resisting, but absolutely nothing was happening. Then he said, "Not like that"; and all of a sudden, I was airborne. "More like that," he said. I was kind of shaken up, but I still thought maybe I had been off-balance or something. I think Mr. Kim must have sensed that, because he motioned for me to punch him. I threw a punch and the next thing I knew, I was flying through the air again. Then Mr. Kim got this look on his face that turned the sweat on my back to ice. I remember him coming close—within punching range—and he said, "No, you really try to punch me." I should have been getting the message, but I was so angry and frustrated that I really wanted to punch him out. I was going to put him in the hospital if I could. I threw my best punch straight at his face, and it made absolutely no difference. There was this huge military type metal desk in the front of the dojang, and I went flying over the top of that desk, and barely touched it. Nothing in my experience had prepared me for that. I was totally at the mercy of this one little Korean. Between my black belt friend and I, we had handled everything from multiple angry karatekas to a bunch of bikers with no problem. Now, there I was, propped upside-down in the corner of the room, and my friend was plastered against the wall with eyes the size of teacup saucers. Here was a man that, if he chose, was to be feared. I had never felt that emotion before from anyone, nor have I felt it from anyone quite so clearly since.

At that point, there wasn't anything to do but get up, bow, and very politely ask, "Can I be your student?" He said, "Twenty-five dollars a month." I only had thirty dollars in my account, but right then and there I wrote him a check for twenty-five dollars. And that's how I became Mr. Kim's first student in the U.S."

-- from the interview, ***"The Evolution of Hapkido"*** pub. TaeKwonDo Times Magazine, Nov. 1993

Mr. Garrison has added further perspective on that meeting. In a discussion about fighting angles, he told me this:

"Understanding the angles of fighting is essential, but it is also essential to understand that the angles of advantage are not all physical. The mental and psychological angles of advantage are just as important. In my first encounter with Mr. Kim, he created a tremendous advantage by offering his wrist in such a way to suggest I do kotogaeshi (wrist throw). Then by his own foot placement and by projecting power into his wrist in a certain way, he made it impossible for me to succeed. With his dominance of the situation, he made my response predictable, giving himself a distinct advantage. And then, as I became more and more flustered, he was able to direct the action to my disadvantage. His technique was impeccable, but it was more than that from the very start. He injected doubt into my thought process, and exploited it fully. He had instituted an angle of psychological advantage before I was ever aware it had happened. It was one of the most significant martial arts lessons of my life."

The warrior's mind contains no doubt. –Grandmaster Kim Sangcook

---

It's important to remember that once an adversarial situation becomes unavoidable, an ethical dilemma always presents itself. Remember our central doctrine from chapter 5: ***The goal of all martial training is to promote one's well-being with the most peace and benevolence possible, and with the least harm to others.*** That's a very lofty goal, and may be difficult to remember and adhere to in the frenzy of a heated situation. But if the confrontation turns physical, winning becomes imperative. Our life or the lives of others may depend on it. We must exploit every advantage and must not hesitate to do so, wondering whether our behavior is ethical, or whether the end justifies the means. The key to solving this dilemma lies in being very clear about what end we wish to accomplish.

If you maintain your integrity, justifiable behavior will naturally result. Do not lose sight of your goal in order to attain it.

An ethically guided life helps clarify our goals and helps resolve such dilemmas by practicing our strategic choices ahead of time. We tell ourselves, *"In this kind of situation, I will act in this manner."* Then, even if we have not experienced a particular situation before, at least we are practiced at quickly choosing a realistic behavioral strategy. Such choices must be practiced constantly throughout all aspects of our life, as strategic thinking is a continuously evolving consciousness.

In all forms of strategy, it is necessary to maintain the combat stance in everyday life and to make your everyday stance your combat stance. *– Musashi*

Once you have clarified your goal, your imperative changes, evolves. You must seek to maximize your advantage and minimize your risk. What remains to decide in the heat of the moment is entirely tactical.

This chapter is about finding and exploiting your best advantage in an adversarial situation.

There are three types of exploitable advantage in an adversarial confrontation: *psychological, environmental,* and *angular.* A *psychological advantage* results when your opponent can be made to lose his concentration, his emotional equilibrium, or his confidence. An *environmental advantage* is some factor of your surroundings or the situation that can be exploited to your benefit. An *angular advantage* is a physical, measurable angle in relationship to an opponent's line of attack. Most confrontations present one or more of these potential advantages, and the warrior should seek all three if possible.

There are two books that do an admirable job listing several of these factors.
Sun Tsu's The Art of War is a classic of military strategy which is still read by military officers to this day. Sun Tsu was a Chinese military general in the fourth century, B.C. who wrote his brief essays on war for Holu, the king of Wu. The thirteen chapters of The Art of War were meant to outline strategies that would be useful to generals commanding large armies, but the principles

are so universal that they can be applied to the individual as well. Miyomoto Musashi's <u>The Book of Five Rings</u> was written by Japan's most famous samurai warrior after retiring from a lifetime of sword battles, in which he was reputed to have killed at least sixty men in sword combat. He finished <u>Go Rin No Sho</u> (Book of Five Rings) and addressed it to his pupil, Teruo Nobuyuki, a few weeks before his death in 1645 A.D. Musashi's complete dominance of the world of swordsmanship during his lifetime is discussed as more than just strategy; it is a way of thinking some have come to refer to as,
Samurai Mind.

Seeking a Psychological Advantage

Let's assume you have met the criteria of warrior mind so far. You have established your practice as a way of life. You have trained your body to be intelligent, and your mind to be strong. You have learned to control your breathing, remain calm, and expand your awareness. You have learned to honor your *tan-jun* center and to originate all movement from there. You have learned to apply the water principle to your chosen path and goals, and you have cultivated a non-contentious nature. This still does not guarantee that there will be no adversarial confrontations in your life. Sooner or later, someone with a chip on their shoulder and a slush-fund of unresolved emotional turmoil will get in your face and want to have their way with you.

Let's also assume that you have tried to avoid this situation without success, and that your attempts to diffuse the other person's objections to your position—or even your very existence on the planet—have met with failure, rebuke or derision. Now is the time for some form of **admonition**—some form of a warning that the other person's perception of the situation differs from yours, and that you have both the means and the intent to back it up.

The most common form of admonition is a threat, a statement meant to intimidate your opponent and dissuade him from action. However, threatening someone is actually a sign of weakness meant to bolster the speaker's courage. If your opponent is an experienced fighter, he will view a threat as the blustering of a defensive mind, a sign of fear that it usually is. The difference between an admonition and a threat is your absolute clarity of intent. Never say anything you don't intend to back up with action.

The best form of admonition is a simple statement or gesture that conveys pure indomitable spirit, and an iron will—that you are absolutely going to do whatever it takes to gain and keep control of the situation.

Speaking from the heart is your best psychological advantage. Such focused determination more than likely will create some hesitation in your adversary. If enough doubt can be injected into your adversary's mind to cause him to redefine his position and question the outcome of further escalation, he may choose to disengage from his adversarial position before he has even started his attack. The earlier you can inject doubt and hesitation into your opponent's mind, the greater your psychological advantage will be. This should be your initial defensive tactic.

People who find themselves in an ongoing violent situation often will establish an ongoing form of admonition, i.e. ***intimidation***, meant to unnerve their adversaries for exactly this reason. They may develop a bizarre appearance, or bizarre behavior, or carry visible weapons.

A friend of mine, a police officer who works a rough section of the city, told me about a gang member who used to wear a large ring with a sharp edge. Because he was in a violent gang and got into fights fairly often, this man developed the habit of marking his adversaries by cutting their faces with his ring. Because the mark was always visible, word quickly circulated that the gang member was a bad dude to get into a fight with. Consequently, the man found he had to fight less and less; nobody wanted to tangle with him because of the intimidation factor he had established.

I was recently told of another example of effective intimidation which occurred during the war in Vietnam. One of my original Hapkido colleagues was a man of small stature but with great *kokorro* (indomitable spirit). He had one of the most dangerous jobs in the Vietnam War: he was a tunnel scout. It was his job to go into the underground passages used by the Viet Cong and capture or kill anyone in them. And not many of the Viet Cong encountered in tunnels were captured. My friend had business cards printed up in both Vietnamese and English with his name on them, and every time he had to kill an enemy soldier, he placed a card on the body. It wasn't long before all of the Viet Cong knew his name. When he entered a new tunnel, he used to shout out his name as he advanced. The results were that most of the Viet Cong soldiers would panic and scurry out secondary exits, where they were captured or killed without him having to have any contact with them. And as far as he or any of his friends knew, he became the only U.S. soldier in Vietnam with a price on his head established by the North Vietnamese Army.

The point of these stories is that gaining a psychological advantage can be crucial to staying alive, and these acts of intimidation may have been appropriate in gang life and in war. But for the rest of us, intimidation is probably not a good tactic. Most of us live in a more sophisticated social environment, where an intimidating appearance and antisocial behavior will get us ostracized, censured, fired, divorced, and probably arrested. There are more subtle ways to unnerve an adversary without becoming a social outcast.

To win one hundred victories in one hundred battles is not the acme of skill. To subdue the enemy without fighting is the acme of skill. —Sun Tsu, III, (3)

It is impossible to list all the ways in which you can gain a psychological advantage, but I will try to list a few to give an idea of the possibilities. There are eight main methods of creating psychological advantage. The first group are mental stances that should be practiced at all times, so that as an adversarial confrontation begins, you will already be adept at them. They are: **correctness, patience, invulnerability, and tenacity.** The second group are active mental tactics that may present themselves as possibilities at the moment an encounter begins. They are: **goading, baiting, deception, and surprise.**

Correctness

A principle that is found in all martial arts is correct and honorable behavior. The first principle of Hapkido philosophy is ***Jong-euye***, which roughly translates as *"righteousness."* The warrior consistently acts within the boundaries of that which he perceives as proper conduct. The strategic value of proper conduct is that this mind-set results in natural self confidence and determination. Then, if conflict arises, he knows he is not the cause—only the resolution—and he will not hesitate to act. It must be stressed that the opportunity to establish this kind of psychological advantage is not an accidental or haphazard occurrence. It is the result of a long-time practice of disciplined behavior. But, if your behavior is unassailable, then the point of contention is always focused on the other person, and you will always have the initiative to gently make that person aware of the error of their ways.

"Those who excel at war first cultivate their own humanity and justice and maintain their laws and institutions. By these means, they make their government invincible."

-- Sun Tsu, IV, (15)

Faced with such strong self-confidence, an adversary is forced to reconsider his position, and thus creates the first chink in his own psychological armor: self doubt. However, you should not automatically depend on this advantage, as your adversary may also believe himself to be completely "in the right" —or he may be antisocial or predatory, and just not care about concepts of right and wrong.

Patience

If you are not in danger, do not fight. – Sun Tsu, XII, (17)

Patience is another universal martial virtue. The warrior is never eager to fight. He will wait if he can, and seek the ground of best advantage. He may find that by waiting, adversarial situations—like all energy imbalances—may resolve themselves. Psychological advantage does not automatically result from a reluctance to fight, which may be viewed as intimidation or cowardice. What is meant here is that one should wait for the *right moment* to respond. Many initial attacks are merely an adversarial foray, to size up your reaction and perhaps learn something about your vulnerabilities or fight patterns. For instance, some fights may begin with a simple strong two-handed push, meant to startle, upset, and establish dominance. An adversary will give a hard shove, then stand ready, glaring and posturing. That is not really an attack. It is simply an aggressive gesture to see how the other person will respond.

Now, if this has just happened to you, even if you have been caught off guard and are shoved backward significantly, remember two things. One, this is not really an attack, and you are not really hurt. And two, right then is not a good time to respond physically, because the other person is completely ready for you to do so, and may actually want you to attack right then for a reason you have not discovered yet. If you can possibly muster the self-restraint, be patient and do nothing.

To ignore an adversary's initial attack is a strong martial insult, as though the adversary is incapable of significant effect. If you smile or laugh at him right then, it will likely enrage him to think he has not rattled you, has not even upset you. If he is going to escalate the confrontation, it will be at that moment. He will run out of patience and attack. He will most likely expect a repeat performance of his domination, and will probably attack in a forthright, non-deceptive manner, unaware that *you* are now waiting for *him* to attack. You have created a double advantage. You have injected uncertainty and frustration, and by exercising patience, have made his next move predictable—when you are ready for it.

Patience is necessary for preparedness. The patient warrior does not respond until he has considered all the information that might be valuable to him in a fight: the nature and strength of his adversary, the best place and time to respond, his own readiness for battle. Of course, sometimes there is no time to prepare, but the rash warrior is *never* fully prepared.

The enlightened ruler is prudent, and the good general is warned against rash action. – Sun Tsu, XII, (19)

Invulnerability

A predator will seek out any small niche in your spirit into which to inject doubt and uncertainty, the food of fear. You must learn to become impeccable, to have no openings physically, mentally, or spiritually for the adversary to find. Then the predatory mentality will begin to lose confidence, and question the probability of a successful attack.

Mitsugi Saotome wrote about a confrontation by his teacher, Morihei Ueshiba O-Sensei in his book, **_Aikido and the Harmony of Nature_**:

Once in Ayabe, when O-Sensei was perhaps fifty years of age, he was visited by a very accomplished kendo master. Anxious to test himself and to prove a point, the kendo master challenged O-Sensei. They walked into the garden together, the kendo master carrying his katana [long sword], O-Sensei empty handed. The sun flashed off the brightly polished steel at the kendo master moved into his kamae [fighting stance], O-Sensei standing quietly before him. And they stood. Sweat began to break on the kendo master's forehead, rolling down his cheeks like tears. It fell like a thousand prisms from the strained and glistening muscles of his powerfully developed forearms. And still they stood, O-Sensei calm and detached, aware but not waiting, his eyed only reflecting the image of the man and the sundrenched steel before him. Five, maybe ten minutes passed. Exhausted from the struggle of attempting to attack the universe, the kendo man surrendered. He had been unable to move. His acute sensitivity and perception had revealed no openings in O-Sensei's defense.

"It is a doctrine of war not to assume the enemy will not come, but rather to rely on one's readiness to meet him; not to presume that he will not attack, but rather to make oneself invincible." – Sun Tsu, VIII, (16)

"Always negotiate from a position of strength."
– Grandmaster Kim Sangcook

Tenacity

The most important ongoing psychological advantage is to develop personal tenacity—*kokorro,* or "indomitable spirit." You must practice holding onto your strategic goal with such persistence, such unwavering stubbornness, that nothing short of total unconsciousness will break your resolve. The best way to learn this is by practicing a martial art over a long period of time in a variety of settings. One particularly effective practice for developing tenacity is to compete in a full-contact martial tournament. It takes a fair amount of tenacity to step into the ring with someone who wants to hurt you.

I remember my tournament days, bowing to my opponent just before the referee signaled for the match to begin, and hearing my opponent's buddies shouting, "Knock his for a loop, so-and-so!" "Kill him!" "Kick his a--!" The only way to disregard those voices was to dig deep down within myself and find the inner strength and resolve to hurt the other guy first, and to keep on fighting no matter what happened. This is tenacity, and from my perspective, probably the most valuable lesson—maybe the only valuable lesson—to come out of my twenty years of competition.

However, tournaments and sparring practice cannot be depended upon to instill adequate tenacity. Tournaments and sparring are not real life situations. They are games with rules. Tenacity results from a life-long practice of not giving in to difficult situations, not allowing an outside influence to completely control your destiny. There is always something you can do to improve your situation. The trick is to discover it in time, and to follow through with it no matter what. Then, when you face someone who is totally antisocial and out of control, when you look into their eyes and see that indescribable predatory look, you will not be terror-stricken and freeze up. Instead of saying to yourself, *"This guy is going to hurt me,"* you'll find yourself saying, *"How can I turn this situation to my advantage?"* Practice not being dissuaded by adverse conditions and you will be much better prepared for that moment.

"Whenever you cross swords with an enemy, you must not think of cutting him either strongly or weakly; just think of cutting him and killing him."

-- Musashi

"The true Way of sword fencing is the craft of defeating the enemy in a fight, and nothing more than this."

-- Musashi

As a Confrontation Becomes Physical

At a certain point, an adversarial confrontation is no longer that—it becomes a fight. The psychological advantages we've discussed so far are meant to diffuse a situation, to avoid a fight, or stop it before it starts.

But once a fight is inevitable, it has already started, even if the first blow has not yet landed. At this point, an admonition is pointless.

An admonition is meant to dissuade an opponent from attacking, to appeal to his reasoning ability, to convey that his attack would be ill advised. But once a fight has begun, a reasonable mind in your opponent is too much to expect; other tactics become appropriate.

Goading

It is slightly easier to defend against a rash attack than it is to attack a defender who is both alert and prepared. Therefore, it is a slight advantage to be able to precipitate your opponent's attack. One way of doing this is to attack your opponent's calmness and motivate him to act rashly—and perhaps carelessly. That's the reason the two-handed pusher mentioned in the previous section acts the way he does. His intent is to upset his adversary and precipitate a response before that response is well thought out. However, such an act constitutes a physical attack, and legally justifies a physical defense. This would not be in the pusher's favor in a court of law; the pusher is guilty of assault. If the person he has pushed defends himself and is hurt, then the pusher is guilty of assault and battery, which is a felony.

There are an almost infinite number of ways to goad someone into rash action other than physically assaulting them. You can insult them, embarrass them, challenge them, or show disdain, such as spitting on them. It's easy to upset someone who is already riled. However, this should not be depended on to give you much of a psychological advantage. In fact, unless you have some other advantage, further enraging your enemy can easily work to your disadvantage, intensifying your opponent's tenacity and resolve. Goading an adversary into rash action is usually employed in conjunction with a deception—a hidden advantage that an opponent, acting rashly, might not notice, or an obvious advantage that a rational opponent would not attempt to overcome.

Tu Mu's comments on offensive strategy

In the later Wei [period], the Emporor T'ai Wu led one hundred thousand troops to attack the Sung General Tsang Chih at Yu T'ai. The emperor first asked Tsang Chih for some wine. (An exchange of gifts and compliments was a normal preliminary to battle.) Tsang Chih sealed up a pot full of urine and sent it to him. T'ai Wu was transported with rage and immediately attacked the city, ordering his troops to scale the high walls and engage in close combat. Corpses piled up to the top of the walls, and after thirty days of this, the dead exceeded half his force.

–Sun Tsu, III (9).

Baiting

Baiting is a tactic that is used to encourage an opponent to act in a certain manner, thus becoming rash or overextended, and predictable. You simply suggest a way of thinking about the situation that offers an irresistible conclusion on the part of your adversary. You may appeal to the adversary's vanity, or his pride, or strength, or greed. For the moment, the adversary must feel that he is about to gain the upper hand by saying or doing something that you have all but invited him to do. In his eagerness, he may overexpose himself, becoming vulnerable or distracted, not quite noticing in time that by being able to predict his next move, you have already begun to react before he was even aware of your manipulation of the situation. There are many examples in *The Art of War* of Chinese generals who baited their enemies, goading them to anger and rash acts, causing them to attack either before their soldiers were prepared, or before their leaders became aware of some hidden disadvantage.

First, attack the enemy's plans.
Second, attack the enemy's strategy.
Next, attack the enemy's calmness.
Last, attack the enemy's weapons.
Sun Tsu, on energies, (ch. V)

"Those skilled at making the enemy move do so by creating a situation to which he must conform; they entice him with something he is certain to take, and lured of ostensible profit, they await him in strength." -- Sun Tsu, V, (20)

An Incident of Baiting

I was dressing down after teaching my Hapkido class at the YMCA, my martial arts bag sitting beside me on the bench. A young man sauntered up and asked me, "Hey, man, do you box?" He pointed at my sparring gloves which stuck out of one end of my bag. "Only a little, as a part of my martial arts training," I answered. He said, "Hey, why don't you show me some moves?" I looked at him. He appeared to be about 17 or 18 years old, very muscular, not a bit of fat on him. I wouldn't want to fight him. He would be strong and fast. He was also standing where he could see himself in the full length mirror on the wall. I saw him turn this way and that, admiring and considering his own physique. Maybe I could use that.

He repeated his demand. "Show me some moves, man!"

I smiled and shrugged. "Not much point in that," I said.

He looked at me, trying to decide whether to be angry. "Wha'choo mean, man?" he said.

"Well," I answered, "You look pretty muscular. I'll bet you have a few moves of your own."

He grinned immediately, and said, "Yeah, I got some moves. I like to box. I got some combinations. I like to do this." He started to punch the wall in a strong 1-2-3-4 combination, two high punches, two low. He repeated the combination, stronger, shaking the wall. He stood back, bounced in place one hand in front of his face, the other downward in front, like Ali used to box. Then he turned and looked in the mirror again. After a moment of self admiration, he again turned to me, this time looking me square in the face, his chin up, like an unspoken challenge. "Show me some moves, man," he said.

"I already did," I answered.

"Wha'choo mean?" he said, his mouth open in an unfinished question.

I looked at him as close to without emotion as I could. I was afraid that if an emotion expressed itself, it would be laughter. "Well, I know a little bit about how you fight now, and you don't know anything at all about me. I'd say that gives me a slight advantage. That was my move," I answered. I turned sideways to him, but kept my hands down at my sides. I could raise them fast enough if I needed to.

The kid's eyes narrowed for a moment. I thought he was going to decide to be angry, but he grinned instead. A slight knowledge of how he was likely to move wasn't much of an advantage, but I had made him think that it was. He nodded, laughed, and walked away.

Deception

Deception is part of the natural order. The thrush fakes a broken wing to lure a predator away from its nest. The chameleon changes color to match branches in its background. Insects shaped like sticks hide among branches, insects shaped like leaves hide among leaves. Examples of deception in the animal world are endless.

Deceptive behavior of all kinds have manifested themselves into battles throughout man's recorded history. Deception is as much a part of warfare as swordplay or firepower. If, through deception, you can cause as opponent to overextend or exhaust his weapons, reveal or expose a vulnerability, overlook your position, or regard you as larger than life or unassailable, you have gained a significant advantage. Whatever you can do to make your opponent less effective in battle is a good tactic.

One of my favorite deception stories is from the Bible. Gideon was an ancient Israelite general who led a mere three hundred men to overcome the Midionite army of thousands. He gave each of his men a lantern, a pitcher, and a trumpet. He led his men to surround the valley where the Midionites were encamped in the middle of the night. He instructed them that when he gave the word, they were all to blow their trumpets, break their pitchers, light their lanterns, and shout, "The sword of the Lord!" at the top of their lungs. When they did this, the enemy army was scared out of their wits, and not knowing where or how many their attackers were, set to fighting among themselves, and many were killed before they fled the valley in complete disarray (Judges 6:15-22).

"All warfare is based on deception." -- *Sun Tsu.*

In sparring matches, feinting moves are common. A fighter will fake a high punch to cause his opponent to use a high block, raising his arm slightly, enough for the midline kick that follows a split second later. Feinting with a kick followed by a punch works just as well. The fake-front roundhouse combination is a standard kick sequence taught to martial arts beginners. There are an infinite number of ways to feint and counter. All of them work the same way; you lead the opponent's mind in a direction that results in an advantage for you.

On the street, deception is equally important, and equally prevalent. Muggers and other kinds of predators will feign affability, starting a conversation, asking the time, or asking assistance. They want to get close enough to you for their plan of attack to be effective. Then, when your guard is down, suddenly you are surrounded, or facing a short range weapon.

Deception is such an integral part of fighting that not only must you become adept at leading your opponent's mind, but you must constantly be on guard for deception to be present in any social encounter with adversarial potential. For this reason, most long-term martial artists don't like to talk about their martial experience with anyone outside their martial arts acquaintance, especially if they don't know that person. Sharing your martial knowledge, or even your style, is giving away a piece of information that could be valuable to someone who knows how to use it against you. It is a common rule among fighters to never reveal one's weapons until the moment one uses them.

When capable, feign incapacity. When active, feign inactivity. When near, make it appear that you are far away; when far away, that you are near. Offer the enemy a bait to lure him; feign disorder and strike him.
Anger his general and confuse him. Pretend inferiority and encourage his arrogance. Keep him under a strain and wear him down. When he is united, divide him. Attack when he is unprepared. –Sun Tsu

I make the enemy see my strengths as weaknesses, and my weaknesses as strengths. – Musashi

It is bad to repeat the same thing several times when fighting the enemy. If the enemy thinks of mountains, attack like the sea. If he thinks of the sea, attack like mountains. – Musashi

---

Surprise

Attack without warning, where the enemy is not expecting it... -- Musashi

The element of surprise holds the most significant immediate psychological advantage one can achieve in an adversarial confrontation. If your adversary does not expect you to attack, the fight will most likely be over before he realizes it has started. But to attack without warning or provocation is a legally indefensible act. This paradox must be fully examined and understood before one can truly embrace warrior mind.

You must understand that there is really no such thing as self-defense. There is only provoked attack. You must be very clear about this point. If you wait for you opponent to attack so that you can say to yourself, "I have only used my martial prowess in self-defense," then you have maximized your adversary's chances of success—maximized your own chances of being hurt. A fight does not have to be initiated physically for a strong response to be appropriate. It just has to appear to you to be imminent and unavoidable. The instant it does, you should attack your adversary with full strength and absolute determination to put him down. Remember, an attack is not neutralized until the attacker is immobilized, broken, or unconscious—until you can search him for hidden weapons at your leisure. If you adversary is surprised by this response to his actions—well, that is already a moot point.

A new student, a young man in his early twenties, told me about an incident that he experienced at a light-rail stop near a highway. A man approached him and asked for money for gas, explaining that his car was on the side of the road nearby. The man was black, dressed nicely, and was polite in his request, until a younger man nearby interjected, "He was here yesterday with the same story." The new student told the man to get lost. The black man approached within an arm's length of him, saying, "That guy is lying, you need to give me some gas money for my car." The black man wasn't much bigger than the student, but was aggressively posturing and pointing a finger at the student's face. The student was intimidated, but he mustered the courage to tell the man he didn't believe his story, and to please back off, that the man was scaring him. "You calling me a liar?" the black man said through clenched teeth, and his right hand disappeared behind his back. At that instant, the student kicked the man in the groin, doubling him over, and then kicked him in the face. The man fell onto his side, dazed and almost unconscious. His coat had ridden up his back in the fall, and there was a large folding knife in a pouch on his belt. The student ran away, missing his train. When he returned later, the man was gone, and no sign remained that anything had happened there.

After the new student told me the story, he asked me if I thought he had acted appropriately. I asked him if he had been hurt, and he answered, "No." Then I asked him if he would have done anything differently, and he said, "I wish I had disarmed him. I should have taken the knife and thrown it into the bushes. Other than that, I feel okay about what I did." I told him that approaching an armed man—even a temporarily dazed one—was extremely dangerous, should the man regain his senses while you are near him. I told him it sounded to me as though he had acted appropriately and prudently. He had been under imminent attack, and had taken the initiative away from his assailant and secured a means of escape.

I asked the student what he had been thinking the moment he began his first kick. He replied, "I saw his hand go behind his back, and I knew that when I saw it again, it would be holding something even scarier that the guy already was. I was thinking, *now or never*." I told the student that was his warrior mind speaking to him.

"At first, be shy as a maiden. When the enemy gives you an opening, be swift as a hare, and he will not be able to withstand you."

-- *Sun Tsu, XI, (60)*

Exploiting the Environment to your Advantage

The opportunity to establish a psychological advantage may not present itself. Suddenly, you may be facing an enraged attacker whose intentions are focused and unshakable. Now is *not* the time to consider looking around your environment for possible advantages to exploit. You should have such advantages already reviewed and prioritized in your mind.

Awareness must be practiced the same as technique must be practiced.

A warrior should constantly consider his surroundings and evaluate how to use the immediate environment to his best advantage, should the need arise. Think right this moment: Where is the nearest exit? Where is the nearest object that might be used as a weapon? Is there sufficient open space for kicking range fighting? There are an infinite variety of environmental variables worthy of the warrior's attention. I am only going to list a few in the hopes of stimulating a way of strategic thinking which the warrior must cultivate into an ongoing part of his awareness all of the time, not just in the heat of conflict.

There are five main environmental factors to always be aware of. They are: terrain, cover, escape routes, movable objects, and knowledge of the enemy.

Those skilled at war bring the enemy to the field of battle, and are not brought there by him. -- Sun Tsu
Chase the enemy onto uneven ground, into bad footholds, strike him when he stumbles, and do not let him recover. -- Musashi

---

The **ground surface** over which you pass along your way is just so much scenery to most people, but you must learn to pay closer attention to it. Is the surface upon which you are walking concrete, unforgiving if you had to take a fall on it? Is the surface loose gravel or sand which would shift beneath your feet if you were to take a widened stance? Is it mud, which will significantly show your foot movement?

Are there **obstructions** to your vision or your hearing nearby? A hill, the corner of a building, or a large boulder may hide a predator waiting to surprise you.

A work partner of mine told me about a large tree alongside a steep section of Cornell Road in Northwest Portland. About a hundred years ago, his great grandfather was robbed as he led his horse up the narrow stage road that at that point was too steep to ride. At its steepest point, when travelers would almost always be slowly walking their animals, a masked robber stepped out from behind a large tree with a shotgun. Ever since that time, that huge fir tree alongside of Cornell Road has been a public landmark known as Robber's Tree.

Are there **obstructions** nearby that will limit your movement? A wall, a fence, a river, a cliff, even a busy highway can present a direction that you may not travel safely. The warrior trains his senses to always be aware of areas that present inherent or potential danger, and directions that he may or may not travel. He will always be aware of his best ***escape route***. He will also train himself to take note of obstructions which can be used as ***cover***, to hide or protect himself if need be. It should be noted that there are two main types of cover: ***visual cover***, such as a bush or a curtain behind which you cannot be seen, and ***protective cover***, such as a large tree trunk, a boulder, or a cement wall which will stop a bullet.

If someone is shooting at you, don't hide behind a bush.

If you become aware of an impending fight situation soon enough, you may have time to choose the area of battle to your advantage. Generally, if you have few opponents, open ground which allows free movement is best, so that you may avoid being cornered. If you are facing many attackers, it may be impossible to keep from being surrounded in an open area. It may be to your advantage to seek an area of limited access, such as a narrow doorway, a footbridge, a stairwell—something that will limit your adversary's access to a few at a time, neutralizing their advantage of numbers.

"You must drive the enemy together, as in tying a line of fishes, and when they are seen to be piling up, cut them down strongly without giving them room to move." -- Musashi

In addition to immovable obstructions, there may be **movable objects** nearby. Outdoors, you may see rocks or sticks, both of which can be picked up and used as weapons in a pinch. Indoors, you may find furniture, electric appliances, and miscellaneous objects such as vases, tools, bottles, kitchen utensils—anything that can dent a head, cut skin, or cause a stumble is a potential weapon. It should be noted that anything you can use as a weapon can also be picked up and used against you. The trick is to be aware of this and use it before your opponent does.

---

*One of my early marital art acquaintances told me a story about a fight that took place in a tavern years before, when he was much younger, and much less temperate. He was sitting on a stool at the bar when two men started swinging fists at one another only a few yards away. He thought that since he was not involved, he would just ignore them. But, the two men both had friends with them, and soon, most of the tavern space was a mass of movement, swinging fists, and even a few kicks. Still, my friend sat on his stool at the far end of the bar, trying to keep out of the way. Eventually though, involvement became unavoidable when a young man backed into him forcefully. He was prepared to ignore it as an accident until the young man turned around, yelled "**Karate!**" and then struck him on the back of his neck with the edge of his hand. My friend was momentarily stunned, but fortunately, the young man had missed his mark by a few inches, and was preparing to strike again.*

*My friend hopped off his stool, picked it off the floor, and struck the young man in the head with it, yelling at the top of his lungs, "**Chair!**" He finished the story by saying, "If I had the opportunity to do that moment over, I'd have left the bar the moment the fight broke out. Even though I beat him, I still got hit."*

Another movable object that should not be overlooked as a weapon occurs in a multiple attacker situation—the attackers themselves. Almost all throwing arts teach that a good direction to throw your opponent is toward other opponents, who then have to momentarily stumble around a flying obstruction. Always remember to turn your opponents' energy back into them.

One source of information from your environment you should not overlook is **knowledge of your adversary.** Much information can be gathered by a trained eye, and a quick mind may discover subtle pieces of information about an enemy a warrior trains himself to observe. They are **appearance, consciousness, posturing, motivation,** and **allies.**

An adversary's **appearance** will reveal a great deal of information about his lifestyle. Is he nicely dressed, indicating that physical movement and fighting are probably not high on his agenda? Is he wearing dress shoes, indicating that style is more important to him than traction, or is he wearing athletic shoes, indicating quickness on his feet?

Perhaps he's wearing motorcycle boots—a formidable weapon on the feet of someone who kicks. Or is your opponent dressed in jeans and a sweatshirt, indicating he is not averse to working up a sweat? Does he have scars from previous fights? Does he have tattoos, especially those amateurish looking, blue-only tattoos that convicts give one another in prison? This might indicate a person who is quite at home in a hostile, adversarial situation. Are his hands clean and smooth, or rough and dirty? Is he wearing rings which may cut you if he punches, or wide leather wristbands to absorb the shock of hitting?

Your opponent's **level of consciousness** is a strong indication of his motivation. Generally speaking, there are four states of consciousness you may observe, and each one presents a different category of threat and a different response. The first level of consciousness is a sane, rational mind unaffected by drugs or alcohol. This is the most dangerous level of consciousness in an opponent, as he is able to plan at attack, deceive you, manipulate you, or surprise you. You must gather as much information you can about such an adversary to indicate any hidden motives or agendas.

The second state of consciousness to be aware of, all too common in our society, is drunkenness. Alcohol will impair an adversary's ability to plan an attack, but it will also decrease his social inhibitions to contain his emotions. A drunk may attack without warning or provocation, simply because he perceives the situation differently than you do. On the other hand, while a drunk may attack rashly, most likely his movements will be slowed and less coordinated. A drunk's balance can be taken from him more easily than a sober adversary's might be.

The third level of consciousness to take note of is an altered state because of a chemical imbalance—either metabolically caused, such as a diabetic crisis or post-seizure state, or a drug-induced state. There are two categories of altered consciousness; they are quite different, but both dangerous. The first is an agitated, maniacal state, usually caused by drugs which are stimulants, such as methamphetamine, cocaine, or angel dust. This is a state of adrenal overload, which includes stiff and spasming muscles, high body temperature, shouting and screaming, and often, hallucinations. This is a lousy choice for an opponent in a grappling situation. Such a person will be angry and fast moving, totally uncontrollable by techniques which work by inflicting pain or joint immobility. A "speeder" will be impervious to pain. He may even break his own bones in an attempt to grapple you and be unaware of it until later, after he has seriously hurt you. Your best defense against a speeder is to keep away from him.

The other category of altered state is any metabolical imbalance which causes a split from reality. These include the metabolic states mentioned above, as well as hallucinogenic drugs such as marijuana and LSD, euphorics such as opiates, or strong pain killers such as codeine and Demerol. This level of consciousness is usually a sluggish state accompanied by significantly slowed movement, but the user is also very likely to misunderstand his surroundings and social encounters. Normally, an altered state caused by metabolic imbalance or hallucinogenic drugs will be quite lethargic and confused; but you should not underestimate such a person's potential to be dangerous. They may suddenly misunderstand the situation they perceive themselves to be in, panic, and react to an imaginary threat suddenly, violently, and without personal regard. You may just represent a stumbling block on their way to self-destruction. Again, your best defense against such a person is to stay away from them, but since this kind of altered state is motivated to action by imagined fear, talking quietly and calmly (from a safe distance) may have a calming effect.

If you cannot get away from an adversary with an altered state of consciousness and they attack you, it won't matter if they are maniacal or panicked. You will not be able to control them. Your only defense is to make their body not physically work; you are either going to have to blind them, or break as many of their bones and joints as necessary to incapacitate them.

The fifth level of consciousness is simply one of incapacitation and does not matter how the person reached that stage. If they cannot stand up, cannot physically move fast enough to attack you, then they are not a threat to you—only to themselves. Your response to this situation is to relax your defensive posture, to have some compassion, and see to it they don't hurt themselves further than they already have.

The next observance to pay close attention to is **_posturing_** by your adversary. The type of posturing may be an indication of his motivation. Is he being defensive—that is, reacting to some perceived slight or threat to his manhood, his social standing, or his property? Is he acting protectively toward a friend or date?

Is your opponent acting aggressively? Generally, an adversary will only have the confidence to act aggressively for one of four reasons: they are physically bigger than you; they are in a mentally altered state; they have friends which outnumber you and your friends; or they are armed (or a trained fighter). They have probably already scoped you out and decided that their advantage is sufficient. Before you react to their posturing, you should try to figure out which of these advantages your opponent is depending on.

If your opponent does not come right out and tell you what is making him angry and aggressive, then most likely there is a **_hidden motivation_**. Usually a hidden motivation indicates a predatory mind and a hidden action agenda. Remember, predators see themselves in a constant state of war with the world, and all is fair in love and war. If you don't understand an adversarial situation, don't trust the other person's view of it. Deception is a common tool of war.

"Disrupt your enemy's alliances; do not allow your enemies to get together…" *--Sun Tsu, III, (5)*

If your opponent has friends with him, one tactic which may prove effective is to try and disrupt his alliances. If your adversary is not acting calmly or rationally, it may be worthwhile to appeal to his friends' sense of propriety, to try to motivate them to calm and control their own friend. Even if this tactic is not effective, it temporarily gives you and your adversary's friends a similar point of view: i.e. it puts you on the same side. Such a temporary alliance, though fragile, subtly causes your adversary's friends to view you as a reasonable guy, and thus instills a reluctance to adopt an adversarial role alongside their buddy.

If your adversary's friends appear to be equally unreasonable and solidly allied with your adversary, then you are obviously in a much more dangerous situation than facing a single opponent. If you cannot escape, then you best tactic may be to drop the first aggressor in his tracks with a quick, strong technique. His friends may be motivated to think twice about attacking you after seeing their most aggressive ally drop in a heap. At the very least, no one is going to want to be second. This may give you the time to escape.

No matter what situation you find yourself in, your primary advantage is going to be your early awareness of it. You must train yourself to be observant, strategic, and tenacious. This is not an opportunistic choice. This is an ongoing lifestyle. Developing warrior mind is an ongoing process with no discernable point at which you can consider yourself "done."

Zen Koan: Father and Son

A martial arts master had a son with the ambition to learn to fight. But rather than studying with his own father, the son preferred to study with first one teacher, then another. After ten years of practice, the son came to the father and said, "I, too, am a martial arts master." The father said, "Is that so? Let's see." The father picked up a staff and beat the son unmercifully, until the son yielded in embarrassment. The son studied ten more years, learning many forms, many styles. Again he came to the father and, taking a fighting stance, said, "I am as good as you now. Maybe better." The father said, "Is that so?" He picked up his staff and beat the son unmercifully, until the son yielded in disgrace.

Ten more years passed without the son approaching the father. Another year passed, then another, still the son did not approach the father. Finally, the father approached the son, and said, "Are you a master yet?" The son just shrugged silently. The father, wanting more of an answer, said, "Well, let's see," and picked up his staff. The son, seeing this, also picked up a large stick and waited calmly for his father to attack. The father bowed, and said, "Finally!"

- - from <u>Zen Flesh, Zen Bones</u>
edited by Paul Reps.

Angular Advantage

We have discussed seeking a psychological advantage, and also becoming aware of and exploiting the environment to your advantage. But there may be a time in your life in which these advantages do not prevent you from being attacked by a formidable adversary. However, the moment an attack becomes physical, one more advantage presents itself that most good fighters eventually learn to exploit—the proper use of fighting angles in relationship to one's opponent.

One of my most frustrating moments in martial arts was my introduction to the art of Judo in 1982. I was in my mid-thirties, in peak physical condition, and fairly confident that I could take on just about anybody (with the exception of my instructors). Then Mr. Garrison introduced me to an old Judo training partner of his by the name of Peggy Lee, a woman only half my size. Ms. Lee told me to grab her and throw her down. I took hold or her gi gingerly and attempted to unbalance her. The next thing I knew, I was face up on the mat with her hands around my throat. She told me not to be so gentle, to do my best. I was a little embarrassed to have been thrown by such a small woman, and was determined to not let it happen again. The next time I grabbed her, I tried hard to push her off balance, but I only made light contact with her. Again, before I knew what had happened, I was looking up at her from the mat, her fist in my face. I remember the feeling of having a solid hold of her gi, but it was always at a wrong angle for me to apply any pressure. The instant I grabbed onto her, I would find myself needing to hold onto her to keep my balance; and of course, she would just shift slightly to make sure that was impossible. The more firmly I grabbed her, the more off balance I became. It was a little bit like being dizzy, and was quite frustrating. Everyone in the room was having fun watching her—except me, of course. Finally, we stopped our randori (free practice grappling) at her request. I think she was afraid for my safety. Thoroughly frustrated, I asked how she managed to avoid my must stronger grip. She laughed and said, "I didn't avoid your strong grip, I avoided your strong angle. You're much too big to face straight on. I wanted to face you at my best angle, on my terms."

Later, Mr. Garrison informed me that Peggy Lee was a women's Judo national champion. I had an immediate appreciation for Ms. Lee's angles of advantage and disadvantage, but it has taken me many years since that first randori practice to learn how to apply them. After many years of practice, though, a marital artist learns to assume the angle of best advantage almost automatically, as a part of his fighting strategy. Finding and exploiting the angle of best advantage is the single most important aspect of a warrior's entry into an adversarial situation.

Understanding the Attack Angle

When an adversary approaches you, whether or not he is attacking, his attention becomes very focused on you—sizing you up, probably testing you for weakness. We may say that he has assumed a linear projection of his energy. The more aggressive he becomes—the more directly he attacks—the more focused and linear his energy becomes. That is to say, in most cases, he comes right at you, and his intentions are clear. This presents us with two facts that we can exploit to our advantage. The first is that his angle of attack is fairly narrow. The second is that his intent is, for a split second, somewhat predictable. The greatest advantage a warrior can gain by a single movement is to neutralize an adversary's angle of attack.

In order to understand how to take advantage of the attack angle, we need to take a look at balance in general for a moment. While standing and/or moving, everyone has strong and weak angles of balance, depending on how their feet are placed beneath them. The farther the feet are apart, the stronger the balance is along a line that connects the feet. Energy extended toward a person along this line, such as a push, will meet with considerable resistance. Energy that is at a sharp angle to that line will meet with varying degrees of less resistance, depending on the angle. A diagram of this energy might look like this:

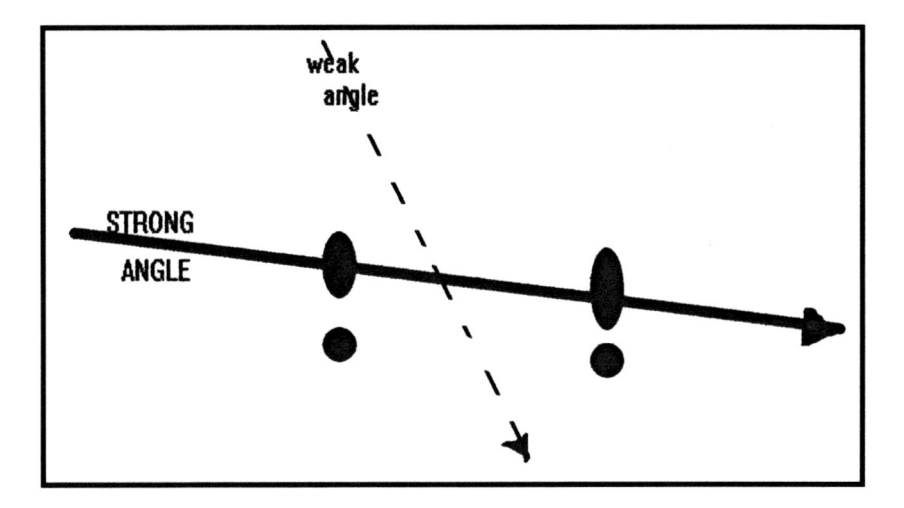

In grappling/throwing arts such as Judo, Jujistu, Hapkido, and Aikido, there are generally considered to be eight angles of balance. This is because angles are part of a full circle of 360 degrees, and in order for a line of force to significantly impact another line of force, it must be at least half of a perpendicular angle toward it. This is, of course, an approximate, but it makes the math easier. Half of 90 degrees is 45 degrees, and 45 goes into 360 exactly 8 times. (Coincidently, there is a short walking form in the art of Aikido called "The Eight Points of Balance".) A diagram of these eight lines of balance looks like this:

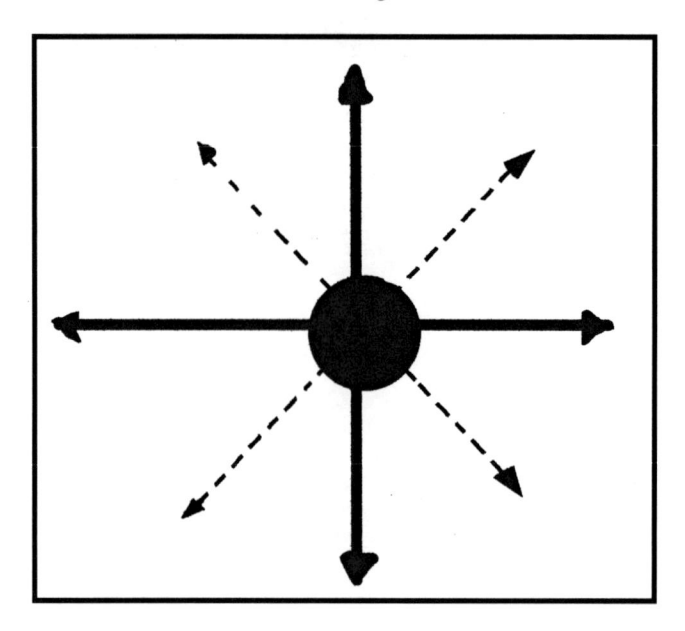

In the above diagram, if a person is standing on the horizontal line, then the strong lines will be his strong angles of balance. The broken lines will be his weak angles of balance. It must be noted that a force applied sideways, say, to the shoulder of a man standing with his feet apart, will meet with the strongest resistance. But a force applied directly to the front will also meet with considerable resistance. This is because a force meeting the body head-on encounters *bilateral resistance.* That is, weight and musculature is evenly distributed on both sides of the body. When we face a force straight on, we are coordinating our entire musculature and weight on resisting that force, or dealing with that problem. Meeting a force "head-on" is a universally understood term for meeting force with maximum resistance, and most likely, maximum damage as well.

Weak angles to our balance are at approximately 45 degrees from our strong angles because a force acting upon us a these angles can only be resisted *unilaterally*. That is, when we resist a force acting upon us from a weak angle, we are in such a position relative to that force that we can only use muscle groups on one side of the body. This isolated muscle use—especially if the force upon us causes us to resist with one-sided back muscles—results in weakness.

This should generate two thoughts in the competitive person. The first is that meeting a force head-on isn't necessarily the most effective way to deal with it. The second is, that if we have both strong angles and weak angles inherent in our balance all of the time, it makes much better strategic sense if we can somehow relate to our opponent from our own *strong angle,* and even better if we can relate to him through his *weak angle.* This sounds very complicated, but it's really not at all. Let's look at a diagram of two people and their strong angles.

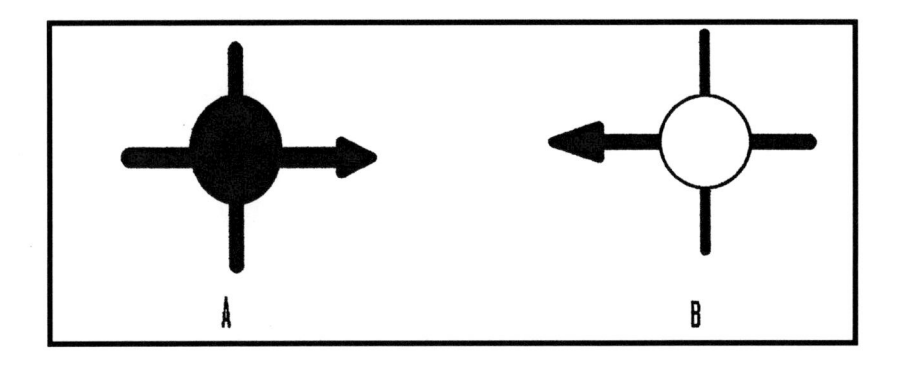

Let's assume "A" is the aggressor and "B" is the defender. In this configuration, both people are facing each other head-on. Neither has any angular advantage. Each faces the other's strongest force. Now, let's assume that person "A" has some other type of advantage; let's make "A" much bigger than "B":

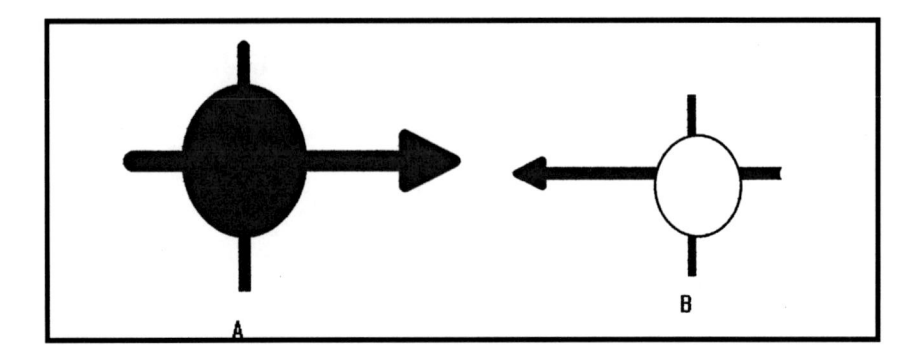

Now, if the situation becomes adversarial, person "B" would not be smart to remain directly in front of person "A"'s strongest angle; in a force-against-force confrontation, he will likely be overwhelmed. But here's the beauty of understanding the concept of an attack angle. When an opponent aggressively shows you his forceful side, he inadvertently shows you his weak side (angle) at the same time. An aggressor will instinctively align himself so that he is advancing along his strongest angle of balance, whether or not he is a trained fighter. It's just human nature. So the direction of the aggressor's attack is always his strong angle, *no matter what position his feet happen to take.* And once you know the strong angle—***the attack angle***—you know that the aggressor's weak angle is just 45 degrees to either side of it. Let's look at the figures above and add "A"'s weak angles:

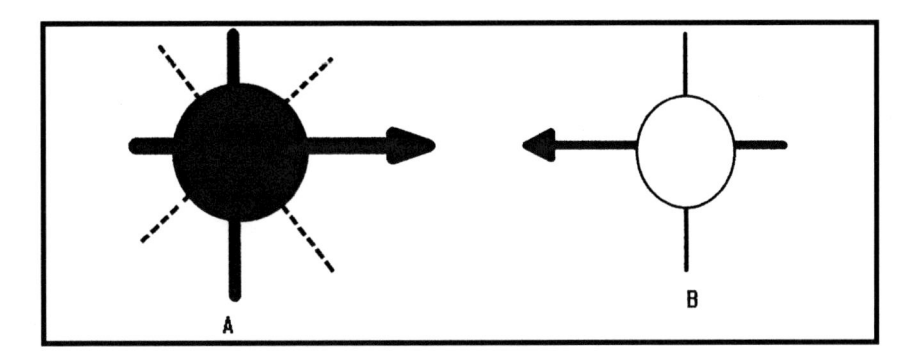

The need for "B" to reposition himself is obvious, and the direction he must move is clear as well. Let's assume that "A" has initiated some kind of aggressive move—an attack with forward momentum toward "B". If "B" moves away from "A"'s attack angle and positions himself along "A"'s weak angle, he may find an advantage to exploit. Let's look at the picture again:

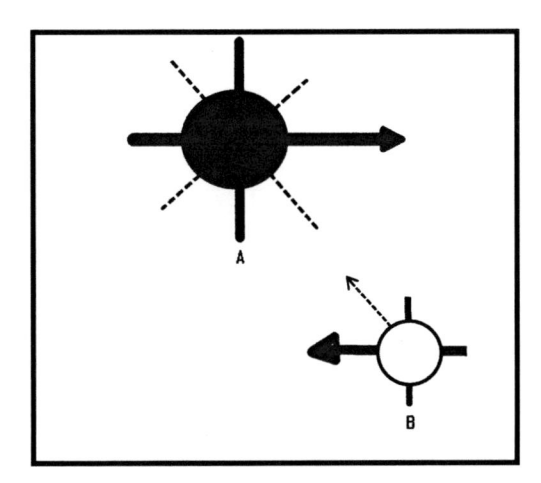

In the diagram above, "B" has successfully gotten out of "A"'s strong angle of attack and is safe, temporarily. But "B" is relating to person "A" through a weak angle, and must adjust his position (i.e. change direction) in order to apply any meaningful force or technique to "A" to discourage further attack. And while "B" is adjusting his position, "A" probably will be adjusting to "B"'s new angle as well. The result is that there is no angular advantage to "B"'s position. However, if "B" were to move so as to position his strong angle into "A"'s weak angle, the diagram above would look like this:

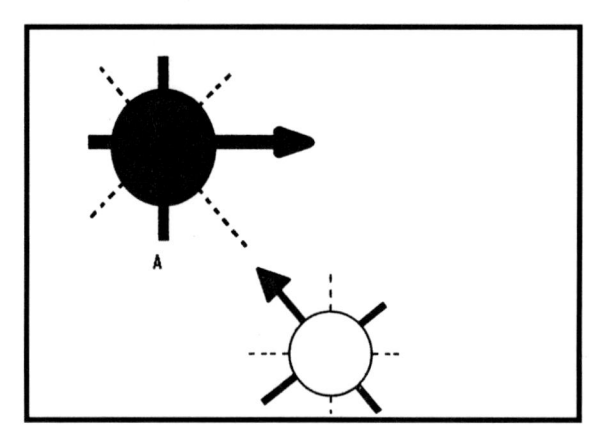

In this diagram, "B" is aligned with "A"'s centerline, and is now in position to apply maximum force toward "A" without changing position. "A" has applied force in a direction that is no longer a threat to "B", and in order to continue his attack, "A" will have to change direction, resulting in a slight delay. This is clearly a *temporary angular advantage* to "B". **As a general rule of strategy, it is best if you seek access to your opponent's centerline, and deny his access to your own.**

The Diamond Principle

So far, so good. We mentioned in the previous chapter the first rule of non-resistance, which is to get out of the way. Person "B" above, the smaller person, has wisely done just that. But nothing has changed except his position. If "A" has begun some type of aggression, chances are good that his aggression will continue until he is discouraged in some way. "B" can run away, and maybe "A" will get tired. But it could be that "A" is a better runner than "B", or maybe "B" is somehow cornered. Then "B" is going to have to deal with "A" directly. Physically. And quickly as well.

The key word in the above phrase *temporary angular advantage* is *temporary*. Person "A" has reached out with some kind of aggression, say a push or a punch. "B" has gotten out of the way, and aligned himself with "A"'s centerline. "B" has a split-second choice to make. "B"'s first choice is to access "A"'s centerline with a counterattack, such as a retaliatory punch or kick. The energy diagram of that move would look like this:

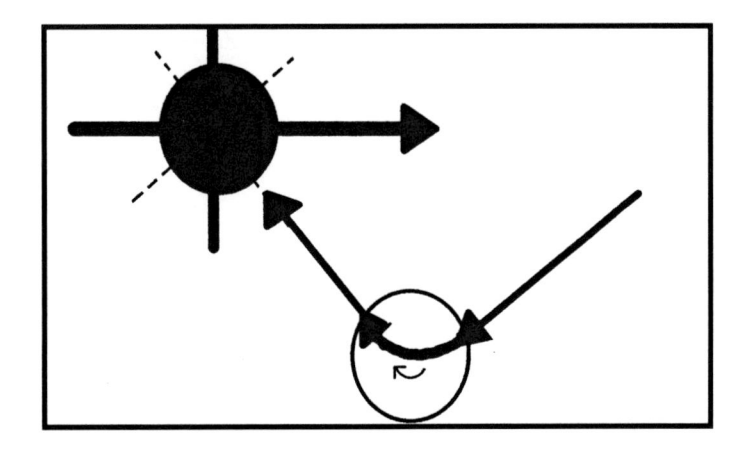

Here, "B" has moved to the side, pivoted at his center, and moved into "A"'s weak angle in a single two-part move. His path of movement roughly takes the shape of a wide angle, or one half of a diamond shape. The other half of the diamond would have been delineated had "B" moved to the other side of "A". "B"'s two choices together would look like this:

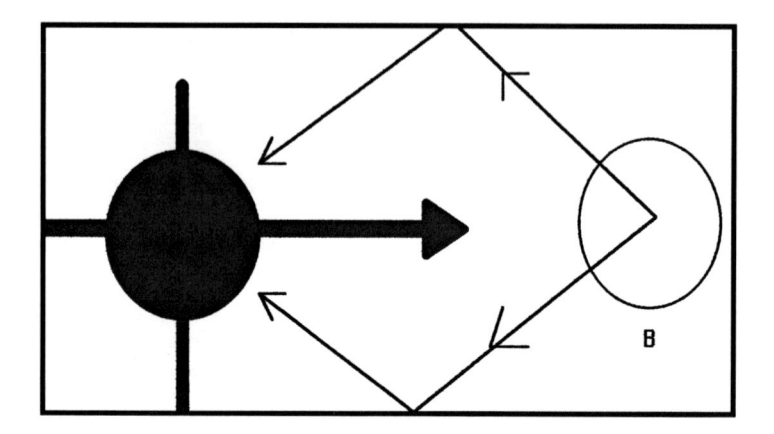

These lines constitute direct retaliations of force with force, while exploiting the weak angle of an opponent. The object here is to inflict enough pain or injury to dissuade the attacker from any further aggression. This strong angular defense, ***the diamond principle***, is used only when injurious force may be justified. *(See Chapter 5, Escalating Strategies.)* ***The diamond principle*** can be found in most of the basic defenses of all hard-style martial systems.

The Circle Principle

Person "B"'s second defensive choice is more complicated, and involves further understanding of strong and weak angles. Put simply, if we extend our energy into one of our strong angles, such as "A" has done above, considerable power can be projected in that direction. However, if we extend out energy into one of our own weak angles, not only will we be unable to extend very much power, but our own balance begins to weaken. The further we extend our energy into one of our own weak angles, the more unbalanced we become. If "B" doesn't want to hit "A", then his second choice is to lead "A" into one of "A"'s own weak angles and upset his balance. The first objective in such a strategy is to align oneself with the aggressor's attack angle. An energy diagram of such a move would look like this:

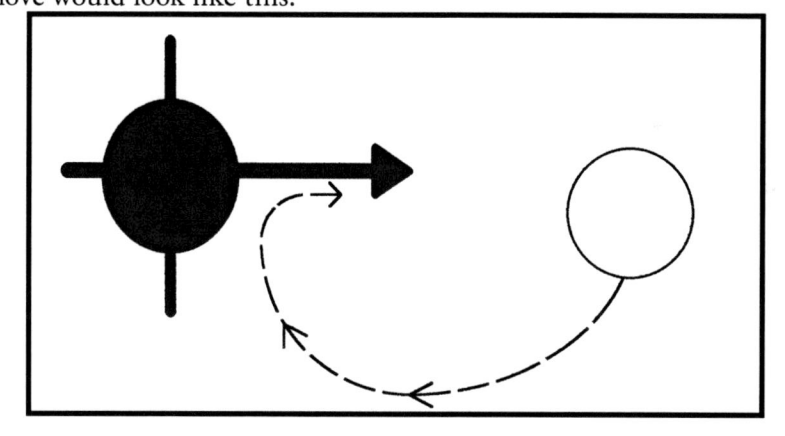

Here, "B" has moved to one side of the attack angle, and aligned himself so that "A"'s strong angle and his own are the same. "B" can even add some of his own energy to "A"'s energy, perhaps even causing "A" to extend his energy a little farther than he intended. Now, "B"

is in the perfect position to easily influence person "A"'s attack angle by applying ***secondary pressure.*** This is done by simply guiding "A"'s force off of his attack angle, and into a weak angle with gentle pressure against "A"'s main force in that direction. Since "B" is already aligned with "A"'s main force, he can easily do this with light lateral pressure in the direction he wants "A" to move. If this secondary pressure is applied before "A" has extended all of his attack energy, he will be unaware of it in time to resist. A diagram of this tactic, blending with an attacker's force and leading him into his own weak angle, might look like this:

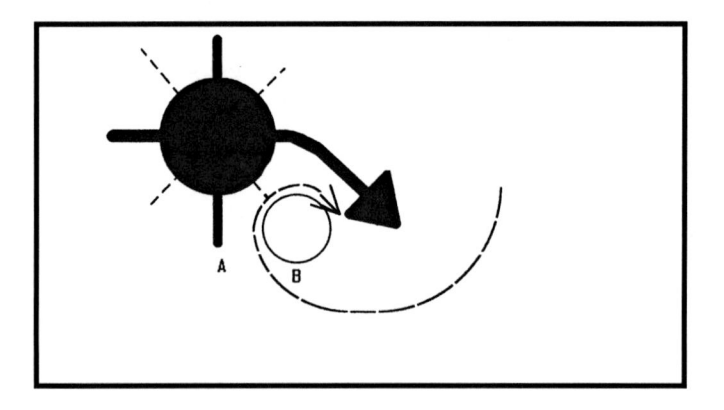

In the diagram above, defender "B" has aligned himself so that his strong angle is aligned with aggressor "A"'s attack angle, and by applying secondary pressure, "B" has guided "A"'s momentum away from his attack angle and into one of "A"'s own weak angles. The flow of "B"'s movement clearly circumscribes the better part of a circle, with himself at the center, and aggressor "A" as a tangential force. This is this heart of **the circle principle;** get out of the way, blend with the movement, become the center, and lead into imbalance. Almost all unbalancing techniques involve some application of the circle principle along with a thorough understanding of strong and weak angles. The circle principle can be found in almost all throwing techniques of the soft-style martial arts.

Review

In this chapter, we have learned that there are three main categories of advantage that a warrior must train himself to exploit. The first is a *psychological advantage,* consisting of the ongoing virtues of **correct behavior, patience, invulnerability,** and **tenacity,** and the opportunistic tactics of **baiting, goading, deception,** and **surprise.** The object of all psychological tactics is to create **doubt** and **hesitation** in the mind of one's opponent.

Failing to dissuade an opponent from his aggression, the warrior should seek some type of environmental advantage. A warrior should train himself to always be mindful of these environmental factors: *terrain, cover, escape routes, movable objects,* and *knowledge of the enemy.*

If an opponent physically attacks, the warrior still has an edge if he understands and exploits his **angular advantage.** All attacks become focused into a narrow angle of movement, called the **attack angle.** From this **strong angle,** a warrior learns to seek out one of his opponent's **weak angles**, and to coordinate his counterattack along that axis. He can either strike his opponent employing the **diamond principle,** or unbalance his opponent using the **circle principle.**

The proper time for ethics is before trouble starts, when good behavior and early awareness may help avoid it, and after the danger is eliminated, when mercy and forgiveness may be appropriate. *But the warrior must remember that when his survival is at risk, his imperative evolves. All his energy becomes focused on winning. Once the outcome objective is clear, any tactic that provides an advantage should be exploited. There is no such thing as fair play in fighting or in war.*

*****

Taking balance for osotogari leg sweep.

Chapter 8

Step into the Void

Precise timing creates and exploits gaps in an opponent's defenses.

"When the thunderclap comes,
There is no time to cover your ears."

-- Musashi

Regular practice in the original Sangcook Kim Hapkido School in downtown Portland was fairly rough in the 1970's. It was expected that a student learn how to fall impeccably, because he would get thrown down hard and often. It was expected that a student know how to block hard techniques to defend himself, but he was encouraged to be light on his feet, to move out of harm's way, because the punches and kicks were thrown with maximum power. Those of us who practiced regularly tried to learn to project such power, but we also tried to pull our punches and kicks just short of bone-jarring penetration out of respect for one another, tried to see that no one got hurt. Most of us, anyway.

But there was one black belt who didn't practice that way.

Mark was in his late teens, tall and lanky, and very fit. He was an excellent kicker; his specialty was a lightening-fast sliding side kick, which he used full force whenever students would spar. Even though his opponents knew he would probably use that kick, he was so good and so fast, it didn't matter. A match against him usually ended with his opponent holding his ribs in pain. It seemed that Mark enjoyed hurting people, and most of us who were not yet black belts were afraid of him.

One day during sparring practice, Mark side-kicked a smaller opponent across the room. When the other student got to his feet, he had some trouble breathing. Mark had clearly cracked one of his ribs. Mr. Kim turned to Mark and said, "Now, you will spar me."

They had only sparred a few seconds when Mark used his infamous sliding side kick straight for Mr. Kim's head. Mr. Kim leaned to one side of the kick so that it barely missed him. Then, at the same time as Mark retracted his kick, Mr. Kim simply corrected his lean without stepping, and hit Mark in the chest with an open palm strike. The force of the blow took Mark completely off his feet, but Mr. Kim was not done with his counterattack quite yet. As Mark arched backward into a fall, Mr. Kim stepped beside him and lashed out his palm a second time. The exact instant Mark's back hit the floor, Mr. Kim's hand struck, leaving five distinct fingernail cuts on Mark's forehead.

Dazed and confused, Mark asked Mr. Kim, "Why?'

Mr. Kim said, "If I had not ducked, you would have hit me. You were not sparring with respect. Don't come back for a month." Then Mr. Kim went into the dressing room and closed the door.

Mr. Garrison asked Mr. Kim about the incident later that day. Mr. Kim explained that to train without respect for your fellow students is totally unacceptable. Everyone else had gotten the message and had learned to take care not to hurt fellow students, so why didn't Mark get it? Mark needed an extra lesson, one carried to the next level. Mr. Kim had showed Mark that it would have been easy to seriously hurt him, but it hadn't been necessary. No one is infallible. Everyone has voids in his defenses. It's an easy matter for a trained fighter to step inside them and wreak havoc. It's all a matter of intention—and of ***timing***.

Timing is the most critical factor of an actual physical encounter. At some point in your life, you may have to react to a sudden situation instantly in order to save yourself from harm, and unless you are both physically and mentally prepared, your reaction will probably be too late. A person loses time if he doesn't perceive early enough, evaluate soon enough, or react quickly enough. For the warrior, time enough is the ultimate necessity. ***The whole point of developing your warrior mind is to minimize your reaction time so that your response will be*** *early enough to be effective.* This chapter will examine the dynamics of reaction time and how to minimize it.

There are three aspects of the warrior nature that affect reaction time to an attack. The first is **mental alertness**, which is critical to minimizing perception time. The second is **cognitive preparation**, which is critical to minimizing the time spent in the evaluation and decision process. The third is **physical training,** which determines how fast and effectively the physical response is executed. We'll take a more detailed look at each of these aspects.

Mental Alertness

Mental alertness must be practiced incessantly. It can never be raised in time. It must become the second nature of the warrior to never compromise his guard. There are three patterns of conduct which help to maximize one's level of alertness. They are: **staying calm, staying sober,** and **staying observant.**

Staying Calm

You are alone, walking back to your car from a late night gathering of friends. You remembered to park under a street light, but right now you are in between street lights. The sidewalk is dark, and tree shadows envelop everything. A figure steps out from behind a dumpster. You hear a rough voice say, "Hey, buddy!" Then there is a faint metallic double click. A knife blade glints in the dim light. You know that you are in imminent danger—that in the next few seconds you could lose your life. You feel your heartbeat in your throat. Your muscles stiffen, your mind struggles to step beyond its own disbelief...

No matter how fit you are, no matter how well-trained you are, you will not escape the physiological reality of such a moment. During any crisis that threatens your survival, adrenalin will flood into your bloodstream. Your heart will race, your muscles will tense up tight, and your senses will become distorted. Your thoughts will be jumbled and confused. Anyone who has experienced a massive adrenalin surge knows how the astonishment of that moment can completely overwhelm a person and cause him to freeze up.

The most serious deterioration to a warrior's timing is caused by a loss of calmness. Police officers, elite military personnel, and even some criminal types face threats to their survival quite often. Eventually they learn—if they survive—the best way to handle this stress, how to best operate under extreme survival stress conditions. If you are not immersed in one of these lifestyles, then you need to understand how profoundly survival stress will affect your reaction time, and what you can do to compensate for it.

There is an excellent book about this phenomenon. <u>Sharpening the Warrior's Edge</u>, written by Bruce K. Siddle, is a thorough examination of the effects of survival stress on combat performance. While the book is written primarily for law enforcement officers and focuses on the physical task of using a firearm, the principles discussed apply equally well to the unarmed martial artist.

In this book, Mr. Siddle, an internationally recognized expert on use of force training and the effects of combat stress, explains the direct relationship between the level of survival stress, and the deterioration of motor performance, visual processing, and cognitive reaction time. At the heart of his discussion is the ***combat paradox***, which is that the higher the perceived threat, the more the sympathetic nervous system is stimulated. This results in a rapidly rising heart rate, which precipitates a progression of loss of motor skills, perceptual narrowing, and cognitive impairment. If the threat continues to loom ever larger, the heart rate will rise to a level which precipitates complete dysfunction—irrational thinking and hyper-vigilance, or completely freezing up.

Mr. Siddle's point is that a person who trains in a combat art should consider what happens in a training session under moderate or minimal stress and what happens in an actual high-stress combat situation are very different. One may not be able to remember complex technique sequences, nor be able to actually perform them. This may result in confusion and hesitation—ultimately, a delay in reaction time, and can be deadly. It would be wise for students of combat or martial arts to keep the profound effects of the **combat paradox** in mind, and review the entire pattern of what they learn, and how they learn it.

"The key to successful survival training is finding methods to decrease the student's reaction time to a threat stimulus and provide training which will condition the students to an automatic response without hesitation."

-- Bruce K. Siddle, <u>Sharpening the Warrior's Edge</u>

You will not be able to prevent the release of adrenalin into your bloodstream during a life threatening situation, but there are a few key things you can do to minimize its effect on your reaction time. ***The most important key is to remember to control your breathing.*** There is a direct relationship between the heart rate and breathing. The faster the heart rate, the more rapid and irregular breathing becomes. And remember, a significant rise in heart rate will precipitate the perceptual narrowing, sensory distortion, and cognitive impairment discussed earlier.

But to a certain extent, we can control our breathing. If we slow down our breathing, we can slow the release of adrenalin into our blood stream. Tan-Jun breathing, or abdominal breathing—the slow, deep breaths many martial systems practice at the beginning and end of practice, can actually slow the heart rate. *(See chapter 3.)* And the slower the heart rate, the less profound the physiological and psychological deterioration of one's awareness, as well as one's fighting ability.

Another important key to remaining calm is to remember that in most cases, the focus of contention is probably not about you personally. Most people are just working through their own issues and you happen to be a stumbling block in their path. It's usually not personal. Even if your attacker is a professional predator, he is not likely to have picked you out because of who you are. It's just his business to look for potential victims who are in a position of vulnerability, or who have let their guard down.

Sometimes your adversary will be having such a bad day that he is already out of emotional control before you even cross his path. Remember, intense emotions such as anger are extremely contagious. An angry person can make you equally angry in short order even if you don't have a clear idea why. Don't be caught up in emotional turmoils that have nothing to do with you. Instead, try to disengage your ego from all your interactions, and try to get a sense of what else besides you could possibly be motivating your adversary. A wealth of hidden motivations may then appear. If not, at least your calmness may help diffuse the situation. If the situation is not diffused, then your defense can be dispassionately planned and executed so that you can get on with the more important aspects of your day. Keep strife impersonal. It's just business.

A third aspect that will aid calmness is to train so consistently that you will have a few favorite techniques that comprise an automatic response to such a situation. These are techniques you have practiced so long and so often that you don't have to think about them. Then you will be able to trust that they will happen when they need to happen. We'll discuss the automatic response pattern in more detail later in this chapter under **Physical Timing.**

Staying Sober

The second pattern of conduct is an obvious one. The warrior does not allow his level of alertness to deteriorate if there is the slightest chance that he will be exposed to a dangerous situation. Drugs and alcohol quickly erode mental alertness. But the term *sobriety* must be taken beyond the effects of drugs and alcohol. Any condition that affects alertness must be considered. A warrior who faces the potential of battle dare not overeat. A rich, full meal will make him drowsy and careless. He must also find the time for adequate rest and stress release. An exhausted brain is as untrustworthy as an inebriated one. The warrior's path is one of self discipline—an ongoing effort to create and maintain the sharpness of mind which will maximize his safety and his success in battle.

One of movie star Arnold Swartzeneggar's first movies was entitled Stay Hungry, which he explained in an interview was his own personal motto during his early years as a body builder. A hungry man will work much harder for success than a man who is dulled by regular satiation.

Staying Observant

The third pattern of conduct is to practice the art of continuous observation. Alertness is not simply becoming aware of what comes your way. You must reach out to the farthest level of your senses and probe your surroundings. Observe everything; process every detail, no matter how trifling, no matter how distant. The earlier you have information of an impending threat, the more time you have to react to it. Also, the earlier you have information, the less rapid your adrenalin release will be, and breath control will have a much greater influence on your system.

Cognitive Perception

Martial arts practice is as much mental as it is physical. A good practice accomplishes more than just learning a few techniques. It trains the mind for early recognition of, and automatic response to, the various dynamics of an attack. This is the only way to provide an opportunity for timely response. It is called being **mentally grounded.** Being mentally grounded involves connecting the body and mind into one experience, and being able to react instantly to a perception of threat.

The warrior, through his ongoing practice of **correct repetition,** combined with **visualization of successful action**, learns to alter his behavior and awareness automatically to take the best advantage of his circumstances without having to think about it. His practice is a form of creating a situation in which he can practice various reactions ahead of time. Then, when the real situation happens, it is more a form of recognition than a situation which needs analysis. This strategic analysis and visualization of response is an ongoing process, not confined to the classroom or *dojang* (practice hall). It is a continuous practice that helps to define the warrior's relationship with the rest of the world. The more he visualizes situations and their resolutions, the less surprised he will be to find himself in a similar situation, and thus the more spontaneous his response becomes (*See chapter 4*).

Another aspect of cognitive preparation is much more subtle and difficult to describe, as it will be different in every situation. ***You must learn to think independently.*** There are many constraints on modern life that we don't regularly examine. We just say, that's the way life is in this neighborhood, or this country, or this day and age. There are styles we don't question, there are manners, there are traffic lights, and checkout lanes, and telephone rings, and police sirens—all requiring certain well-known responses, and almost always getting our compliance without a second thought. You must develop those second thoughts, learn to do things by choice, not by habit. Each action becomes a practice and a product of consideration, evaluation and decision, even if your action is the same as every other person's action. The warrior practices ongoing ***mindfulness***, so that if a situation arises that may require a unique response, a road not often taken, he will be adept at making quick decisions that may or may not fit the generally accepted pattern.

A violent response is just another tool of social interaction in a large toolbox of social possibilities. A balanced individual will prefer to use other social methods: avoidance, compromise, diplomacy, persuasion, acquiescence. But a warrior knows that as a last resort, he can choose a violent response if the situation warrants it, and he will be practiced in its application and comfortable in its use if need be. The capability to instantly step outside social boundaries radiates a distinct force-of-being around a warrior which sets him apart from other people, and warns others that he is a person not to be trifled with.

An essential part of cognitive preparation is emotional training. You must challenge yourself to practice beyond your comfort zone. You must throw yourself into what you are practicing beyond your ability to control or predict what will happen. If you have a good instructor, he will establish and maintain this level of intensity as much as he can, short of compromising the safety of his students. He will insist that you face your practice partner, no matter who he may be, and do your utmost best. The teacher will interrupt or stop the practice if he thinks it's gotten too dangerous. Grandmaster Garrison calls this *"courage training."*

Fear is not the enemy. It's just nature's way of saying *"pay attention."* Get used to feeling a little bit afraid, and doing what you need to do in spite of it. Courage is not an emotional state. It is a conditioned response to adversity. It is developing the self-discipline of tenacity—of never giving up.

Cognitive preparation is learning to quiet the inner dialogue and focus one's mental energy into awareness, calm the emotions, practice independent thinking, develop unyielding tenacity, and trust the automaticity of the body to respond appropriately. Without this preparation, a timely physical response is not possible.

"Courage…is a man doing what he must—in spite of personal consequences, in spite of obstacles and dangers and pressures—and that is the basis of all morality." – John F. Kennedy, <u>Profiles in Courage</u>

Cognitive Preparation Accidentally Saves the Day

Recently, I had an opportunity to meet with several other writers during a literary convention I was attending out of state. As a close friend and I approached the host's home, we glanced in the front picture window and saw a young man in an animated conversation with an attractive young woman. The instant the young man saw us outside the window, he crouched in an exaggerated horse stance with his hands in a sparring posture, left fist high and forward, right fist held close into his chest. He was facing the window, as though we had startled him into his defensive reaction, even though we were on the other side of the window.

When we entered, I was introduced to half a dozen people by my friend, and I found myself shaking hands with the horse-stance man, whose name was Nathan. My friend, a teacher who is not a martial artist, asked about the posturing he had seen as we arrived. Nathan answered that he was a student of Kajukenbo, which he described as a very quick and devastating martial art. He explained that he was so well trained that his response to being startled was an automatic fighting stance. He had reached the level of brown belt, and his whole body was a weapon, he said. My friend, must to my discomfort, introduced me as a fellow martial artist. Nathan asked what rank I was, and I answered that I was a black belt. He said, "Really?" he looked me up and down with obvious distain. "You look out of shape, not much of a challenge." I replied that I didn't represent any challenge at all, since I was not looking for a fight. "Good thing," he said in a louder than necessary voice. "I might hurt you."

That was clearly meant for other ears, since we were seated less than two feet apart—probably meant for the attractive woman seated on the other side of him. And while part of me understood that the statement was not personal, another part of me doesn't much like being insulted. So I said to him, "Let's look at this from another perspective. I've been training thirty years for this exact moment. What makes you think I'm not ready for you?"

The young man's eyebrows went up, and his lips tightened. I took this as a sign of emotional overload and instability. I didn't have the faintest idea how he would take my question, but I reasoned that whatever happened, I was probably sitting too close to someone who had shown himself to be young, athletic, macho, and emotionally unstable. I probably ought to move back. This conclusion had happened almost instantly, and within just a second or two, I began sliding backwards to the chair next to mine, placing an empty chair between the young man and I. At the exact moment I started to move, Nathan threw a backfist at my face and shouted a loud *"Kiai!"* But I had already moved out of range, and Nathan's fist slid through the air where my face had been. By the time his brain registered that he had missed, I was seated comfortably two chairs away.

"How did you do that?" he stammered, open-mouthed. I just smiled and said nothing. He didn't need to know it was only a coincidence.

Physical Timing

"Attack [the enemy] when he does not expect it; avoid his strength and attack his emptiness." – Sun Tsu, IV (20)

I remember training with Kali Master Dan Inosanto at a seminar at Camp Danzan Ryu, in California several years ago. He was demonstrating the art of double-stick fighting with one of his senior students. They were swinging their two sticks at each other so fast that their motions were difficult to follow, yet I could hear the staccato cracking of the rattan sticks as they hit. Master Inosanto kept increasing the pace until it appeared that his student was at his maximum speed. Suddenly, Master Inosanto's two sticks blurred out of sight, and there was a dull thump in between each of the sharp cracks of the sticks. Master Inosanto had doubled his speed, smacking the student's chest in between each meeting of the sticks.

A person with Dan Inosanto's speed doesn't have to worry much about reaction-time lag. But for the rest of us with ordinary speed, we need an extra edge. It is crucial to our defense that we be able to perceive the right instant to initiate our response, and to move in a way that makes the best use of the brief moment we have to respond. **Good timing is about creating and exploiting gaps in an opponent's defenses. Good timing is more important than superior speed.**

Let's assume you have followed the precepts of Warrior Mind so far; you are in good shape and in touch with your body, well trained, calm, grounded, sober and alert. You find yourself in an adversarial confrontation despite your best efforts to diffuse the situation, and a physical attack is imminent. Your adversary has ignored your admonition and has assumed a threatening posture. There is no time to retreat to a better position, or to appeal to others for help. There is only you and your opponent, and he is starting to move toward you, his intentions obvious. What do you do?

You must escalate your own intentions in both speed and intensity. Remember, there is no such thing as *self-defense*. There is only *counterattack*. Once you understand that an attack in underway, you must instantly evolve your outcome objective. Whereas before the fight began, your objective was to diffuse the situation and avoid a physical encounter, now your objective becomes to win the fight. You must take the initiative away from your adversary by attacking him.

You can never be completely prepared for the unexpected; that is a contradictory concept. But you can be prepared to ask yourself some initial questions, such as, Is this situation dangerous to me? And when is the best time for me to respond? If the answer to the last question is <u>now</u>, then you'd best be moving already.

If a warrior is well trained, it doesn't really matter what techniques his adversary uses in his attack. The warrior learns to continuously apply the martial principles of advantage to gain the upper hand no matter what his opponent does. But because the methods of attack are endless, the application of martial advantage constantly changes. The principles themselves do not.

That's why ongoing physical training is so important. You can never learn all the techniques there are to know, never complete a list of appropriate responses to every situation. Even if you could, the adrenalin released into your brain at such a moment would prevent you from sifting out precisely the right one. It is far more practical to understand the martial principles of advantage, and to have a few favorite techniques that you have honed to consistent dependability—a good left hook, a strong front kick, a flawless hip throw. These few techniques must be practiced so regularly and consistently that you can do them perfectly without having to think about their execution. They just happen instantly when they need to happen.

"If you enter with intent, make use of the proper angles, move from the center so that your hips project your power, your opponent will always be playing 'catchup' to your counterattack." – James R. Garrison

---

There is a recent book about Hapkido that I shall not name which claims to present illustrations of all of Hapkido's 3,600 techniques. When I think of such a book, I also think of my good friend Mike, who has been a police officer for twenty years, and presently is a S.W.A.T. team instructor. Recently, I asked him how many techniques he knew. "Four," he replied. "Maybe five, in a pinch." But here is a man who has used those few techniques hundreds of times against bad guys who didn't want to be subdued. "What I do has to work," Mike says. "Otherwise, I have to shoot them."

The whole point of understanding and applying the martial principles of advantage is to gain time enough to apply a technique which will decide the fight in your favor. You may have less than a second for your response. You cannot waste even a fraction of a second deciding what to do, or wondering whether you can do it. Therefore, the principles of timing are of prime importance and precede all other martial principles. The principles of timing are:

1. Draw the opponent in
2. Initiate the entry
3. Employ simultaneous attack and defense
4. Step into the void
5. Use your best weapon

1. Draw the Opponent in

Encourage your opponent to believe he is in control and has an advantage up until the last possible instant. This can be as much mental as it is physical. Do not appear resolved or formidable, unless this has a chance to dissuade an attack. Assuming your opponent is *already* attacking, you do not want to appear to be able to understand or respond to his attack until the instant it is necessary to move. (This is why many martial arts teachers discourage "*Karate face*", the grimacing, scowling and posturing that sometimes precedes the execution of technique in some schools. It makes your opponent wary.) You want your opponent to be so overconfident of his success that he commits himself to completing his movement.

Timing is just as much about not moving too soon as it is about not moving too late. If you react too soon, your opponent will become aware that his target has changed, and he will compensate—adjust his aim or change his technique. You want him to think that he is about to succeed in whatever attempt he is making until it's too late for him to change his momentum. As your opponent follows through with his motion, you can take advantage of this short moment of predictability, move off the line of his target acquisition, and initiate your response while he is busy recovering from his unsuccessful attack.

2. Initiate the Entry

> *"We must defeat [the enemy] at the start of his attack, in the spirit of treading him down with the feet, so that he cannot rise again to the attack."* -- Musashi

The countdown to the resolution of a fight begins the moment it becomes inevitable. The longer that countdown lasts, the greater the chances you'll be hurt. You must remember that your intention has now evolved. Your goal is to end the fight decidedly in your favor. The earlier you take the initiative to achieve this end, the better off you'll be.

The first move that you make in an adversarial confrontation is called *your entry,* and it establishes all your potential for defense or attack. There are two principles of entry which significantly alter the timing of an adversarial interaction in your favor. They are: ***stepping into an advantageous angle and closing with the opponent.***

Stepping into an advantageous angle frees up the defender from the obligation of blocking, of the obligation of reacting solely to the force of attack. If the defender steps out of the intended target area, then he is free to counterattack his opponent as an initial move. His opponent will have to adjust to the new angle before he can resume his attack, but the defender does not. This creates a slight timing advantage.

If the defender closes with his opponent—that is, moves toward his attacker, he cuts down the time to impact which the attacker has subconsciously calculated in his head. If the defender moves toward an attack, the initial impact almost always happens before the attacker is ready for it to happen. This interrupts his timing. Now he has to alter his plan of attack, which causes even more of a delay. These two tactics comprise the basis of the timing advantage during entry.

As a general rule, you should seek to enter your opponent's personal space; do not let him penetrate your personal space.

3. Employ Simultaneous Attack and Defense

If you have utilized the two principles of entry above, you will control the initial impact of the confrontation. This enables you to apply this impact toward achieving your entry objectives. **Remember, your angular movement is your defense. Your entry is an attack.**

During my early years in Hapkido, occasionally, Mr. Kim would put on gloves and a chest pad and join us in our sparring. When we sparred, he would hit me at his leisure no matter what I did. Mr. Kim never seemed to block any technique I attempted, yet my arms would be sore after practice. I would watch him spar the others, and I could see that he was hitting instead of blocking, but I still had to ask Mr. Garrison to explain what Mr. Kim was doing.

"He is cutting off his opponent's power," Mr. Garrison explained. "If you step off the angle of your opponent's attack and then punch back into your opponent's centerline, your punch will cross his attack at an angle that is stronger for you than it is for your attacker. For example, if you step to the outside and punch over the top of your opponent's arm, his punching arm is blocked automatically, while yours hits a target behind it. Mr. Kim uses this movement as his defense. He stopped actual blocking years ago. He calls it a wasted motion, a missed opportunity."

"If you are going to hit an opponent, hit his vital spots, not his weapons."

-- Grandmaster Kim Sangcook

Unbalancing an attacker with your entry works exactly the same way. You step out of your opponent's attack angle and apply your force into an angle which is stronger for you than for your opponent. If you lead him far enough into his own weak angle, he will fall down. (The decision to strike an opponent or unbalance him involves many factors. That decision is discussed more fully in chapter 5.)

4. Step into the Void

"You defeat the enemy by remaining in the void. There is timing in the void; by knowing your enemy's timing, you can use a timing which he does not expect." – Musashi

I've discussed how to draw an attacker in, invite him to commit his energy to a predictable movement, how to step out of his target acquisition, establish a more advantageous angle of entry, and step in with one's own counterattack. The two remaining questions about entry are *when* and *where*? The *when* of entry is the moment you perceive you are under attack. The *where* of entry is fairly simple as well: you enter your opponent's openings—his *voids*. **A void is simply a weakness in your opponent's defenses that can be exploited to your advantage.**

No matter how many times I face my teacher on the mat, when he says, *"Throw a punch at me,"* I am always startled by his response. Before my punch reaches its culmination point, I will have already been hit at least once. It's really just the result of my teacher's mental groundedness. He knows that the instant I begin my punch, I will be programmed to complete it. That gives him a split second of time during which he knows what I will do, how I will move. He reacts within that short span of time, and I am not able to perceive it quickly enough to change my motion.

Sometimes, an instructor will step away from the first punch, become critical, and correct some minor irregularity in the puncher's form. This accomplishes two things; first, it instructs the *uke* in the fine art of punching correctly. But second, it also gets the *uke* to concentrate so intently on his punch that he will strongly program himself to complete it no matter what. That lengthens the moment of predictability for the teacher. I had to learn this the hard way.

Musashi's Void

In the early 1990's, Master Garrison guided his senior black belts toward becoming dan rank in Aikido in order to broaden our martial training. To supplement our training, he sponsored several seminars with an Aikido master, Walter Todd. Todd Shihan was a first generation Aikidoka, a student of O-Sensei Ueshiba himself. He was an irascible old man with a sharp sense of humor that was just short of mean; but he was a genius in the art of movement, balance, and timing.

Todd Shihan had an artificial hip and two bad knees, yet his defensive timing was so refined that no one could get the better of him even at the age of 70. When asked about the concept of timing, he answered, "It's simple. Just step into the void."

The hardest fall I ever took in my life happened right after my next question. I asked him, "Todd Shihan, what do you mean by *void*?"

He smiled and said, "I mean the same thing as Musashi meant in the last chapter of *The Book of Five Rings*. Musashi's void."

I said I still didn't understand, perhaps that was a mistake on my part. I could have asked Mr. Garrison to explain it later, but I spoke up instead.

"What is Musashi's void?" I said.

Todd Shihan grinned, and said, "Let me show you. Throw a punch at me."

I threw a fairly good punch, but Todd Shihan just stepped back away from it.

"That was nothing!" he said with obvious disdain. "I don't have to defend myself against that. Aren't you one of Garrison's black belts? Don't you know how to punch?"

I was a bit embarrassed and angry then, so I threw a really strong punch straight at his face. But as I did so, Todd Shihan moved to the outside of it, slid his right arm up mine, and hit my face with a knifehand block just as my punch was reaching its culmination. My whole body was still moving forward, except that now, my head stopped. My feet left the mat, swept up into the air, and I fell flat on my back from about four feet in the air. I slapped, but still had the wind knocked out of me.

"That's Musashi's void, boy. It's inside your guard, behind your weapons, any place you're weak. It's always where you least expect it," Todd Shihan said, grinning.

"The spirit of timing is to check the enemy's attack at the syllable 'at'…when he jumps, to check his jump at the syllable 'ju'…to check his cut at 'cu'…" -- Musashi, <u>The Book of Five Rings</u>

After that seminar, Mr. Garrison also explained a few things about Walter Todd Shihan. Todd Shihan trained in Japan just after World War II, when the Japanese people held much quiet resentment about the military occupation of their homeland by U.S. troops. Walter Todd was a U.S. serviceman, and the only non-oriental in the Hombu Dojo at that time. Consequestly, he was thrown down as often and as roughly as the other students could manage. Mr. Todd learned not to ask questions, and not to volunteer to be *uke* for anyone. Years of this kind of rough training imbued in him a kind of "old school Japanese" consciousness about volunteering to be *uke*. He had seen my asking questions and volunteering to be *uke* for him as a challenge, a questioning of his ability. He would have felt it his duty to throw me down as roughly as possible, which he succeeded in doing very well. It was not the last time I acted as an *uke* for Todd Shihan, but it was the last time I volunteered to do so.

Todd Shihan explained that a void is created by an imbalance of energy in a fighter's defense. A summary of his view begins with this idea: a fighter at rest represents energy at rest, or in balance. As soon as a fighter moves, such as when initiating an attack, he must direct his energy in the direction of the target. His energy is no longer in balance. Just as there is a positive thrust of energy forward, such as a moving fist, there is a negative vacuum of energy left behind, such as an exposed ribcage. These negative areas of energy are areas of imbalance. They are like holes in a warrior's armor. These energy imbalances, or "voids," as Todd Shihan calls them, come and go as fleeting as waves upon water, but awareness of them can mean victory or defeat. *The secret of good timing is to seek out and step into your opponent's void with your initial movement,"* says Todd Shihan.

The most common void is **target oriented**, such as a vulnerable exposure behind a punch or kick. A warrior knows, for instance, that if his opponent throws a right cross, his left shoulder will be weak; if he flows in that direction, a target may open up there. He knows that if his opponent throws a left roundhouse kick, his right hip will momentarily dip, and the right knee will temporarily be exposed. He will automatically flow away from the strong kick and toward the weak base leg, in hopes that a target will present itself there.

Such voids are like windows of opportunity which open and close more rapidly than the conscious mind is capable of processing. But "seeing" these opportunities for counterattack is less a matter of using the eyes than it is of applying an understanding of body kinetics that gradually develops after years of practice. The long-term practitioner eventually acquires an intuitive awareness of an opponent's motion, a recognition of similar movements encountered hundreds of times in practice. He has reacted to these movements and sought out the voids behind them countless times, and he can react to them without having to think about it. The longer a person stays in practice, the more spontaneous his reactions become. ***The ultimate goal is to move simultaneously with one's opponent.*** Realistically, this is impossible, but the long-term practitioner continuously strives to achieve it anyway. Seeking out your opponent's voids is how you refine your timing.

Another kind of void that is always present during an attack is **balance oriented**. A person at rest can remain well grounded, strong in multiple directions. But a person moving into an attack usually focuses his energy into a single direction, called the attack angle *(see chapter 7)*. During his attack, secondary force applied at a sharp angle to an opponent's movement can easily unbalance him. These weak angles are also referred to as voids.

Mr. Garrison has elaborated on this theme countless times. *"Do not contend with an opponent's strengths,"* he says. *"Simply avoid them. Instead, attack his weaknesses. Exploit your opponent's imbalances, and he will throw himself. Constant awareness and exploitation of these voids are ways that traditional Hapkido and Aikido are convergent."*

Voids can also be **mental** or **emotional**, such as exhibiting overconfidence or emotional overload. Any chance a warrior has of encouraging his opponent to drop his guard or of goading him into a rash and predictable action will increase that opponent's vulnerability—his voids. (For more information about establishing a mental advantage, see *chapter 7*.)

Thus remaining within the void, as espoused by both Todd Shihan and Mr. Garrison, means simply to keep an opponent continuously off balance—that is, to apply constant pressure in the form of an ongoing counterattack, so that the opponent had no time or opportunity to recover.

"Fix your eye on the enemy's collapse, and chase him, attacking so that you do not let him recover his position." – Musashi

5. Use Your Best Weapon

Once you have stepped into your opponent's void, you must take advantage of the opportunity to gain the upper hand, and you will have only a fraction of a second to do something. There is not enough time to concoct a plan of attack; by the time you think of something, that short window of opportunity will have closed up tight. What do you do? You do what you are best at, what you have practiced so diligently that it happens automatically.

You must learn to trust your training. This is accomplished by practicing a few basic moves until they become as natural as breathing. Most martial systems teach students a rich variety of techniques in order to keep their interest level high. Consequently, most martial artists who have been practicing more than a year or two have so many techniques stacked up in their heads that they have a hard time remembering which one to execute. A combat situation in which your life is threatened will most likely cause such an adrenalin flood into your brain that you will not be able to remember your own name, let alone one of five hundred techniques. While it's a good idea to learn as much about your martial art as you can, a good personal combat plan is to **practice a few—perhaps half a dozen—favorite basic techniques until they become so ingrained into your being that their application becomes automatic, and you don't have to think about them.** You must know these moves so well that you not only know how they work on various body types, but how they can be countered and how to counter those counters. If a single technique is practice the same way many times, the body's muscles themselves begin to retain the memory of how to move automatically. Thus the recall of that particular movement bypasses the brain, or at least the conscious memory part.

Also you should remember that fine muscle control will deteriorate under the influence of massive amounts of adrenalin. You should keep your emergency moves simple—easy to remember, easy to perform. It's best if these moves involve whole-body movement and depend on the use of large muscle groups. Minute, subtle techniques such as nerve pinches and wrist or finger locks may work in the movies, but you won't be able to effectively employ them in a real, threatening situation. Moreover, your adversary will also have such a load of adrenalin in his system that he may not feel such subtle techniques anyway.

You must be able to incorporate your emergency techniques into a continuous flow of movement. Ask yourself, what follows your best move? Does it set you up for another favorite move? Can you retain your balance, continue your entry, and guard your vital spots if your favorite move doesn't work?

The energy of a fight is like trying to catch an ocean wave on a surfboard. If you remain stationary, the wave will roll under you, and you'll find yourself on the back side of it, trying to catch up. If you want to be on the front side of that wave of action, you must initiate the effort. You must learn to flow into the voids as they appear (or are created) in your opponent's defenses, attacking repeatedly, continuously, until he is clearly defeated. You must stay half a step ahead of your opponent. Movement never stops. The whole point of attacking is to take his balance (and his confidence) away from him. Any pause in the application of your counterattack gives him a chance to recover his balance and composure, and minimize the voids in his defenses. Remember, you are safe only as long as you remain in your opponent's void.

In all techniques, you must understand it is never step one, step two, step three. There is always only one move. – Cory Underhill, 7th Dan, Hapkido

Review

There are three factors which affect reaction time. The first is **mental alertness**, which is critical to minimizing perception time. The second is **cognitive preparation**, which is critical to minimizing the time spent in the evaluation and decision process. The third is **physical reaction time**, which determines how fast and effectively the physical response to the threat is executed. The whole point of understanding and applying the martial principles of advantage is to gain enough time to apply a technique which will decide the fight in your favor. The physical principles of timing are:

1. Draw the opponent in
2. Initiate the entry
3. Employ simultaneous attack and defense
4. Step into the void
5. Use your best weapon

Practice accomplishes more than just learning the technique. It trains the mind for early recognition of, and automatic response to, the various dynamics of an attack. This is the only way to provide an opportunity for timely response.

"The ideal survival skill should be kept as simple as possible in technique complexity, technique response time, and theory of application…Preventing mental stalls is a matter of developing pre-planned strategies."
-- Bruce K. Siddle, <u>Sharpening the Warrior's Edge</u>

Good timing begins with a prepared mind.

*****

Mr. Garrison and Mr. Morgan at the WOMAF Fall 2008 Seminar.

Chapter 9

Flow with Change

During a recent seminar, Grandmaster Garrison shared with students from around the country some of his early history training with Grandmaster Kim Sangcook.

"I had recently graduated from my master's program in clinical psychology, and I had just been hired at a new job," began Mr. Garrison. "Circumstances were looking up for me, but I didn't have enough money to pay all my bills, secure a decent place to live, and still practice martial arts. Of course, the martial arts came first. So basically, I was living out of my truck, cleaning up at work, and practicing with Mr. Kim every chance I got. During this time, Mr. Kim said to me at practice one day, 'I'm going to Korea next week. You are coming with me. You need to practice Hapkido in Korea.'

"I told him I didn't have any money. He said, 'Well, what do you have?' I told him all I had was my truck, and he said, 'Sell it.'

"So, I sold my truck, got my Visa papers in order, and went in to talk to my new boss. 'I have to go to Korea,' I said. My boss said, 'When will you be back?' and I had to say that I didn't know. So a few days later, I was on my way to Korea alone. Mr. Kim had left a few days before. I had no money, I didn't know what was going to happen when I arrived, or whether I'd have a job when I got back to the U.S. I didn't even know where to go once I arrived at the airport in Seoul, but Mr. Kim had said, 'Don't worry. Everything will be taken care of.'

"When I arrived at the airport in Seoul, I was somewhat bewildered. My Korean was terrible, the line through customs was a block long, and I didn't know a soul. But very soon, a Korean man in a suit came walking down alongside the customs line holding my picture, and when he saw me, he said, 'Mister Jim! Come with me!' And we walked right by customs without checking through, got into a limousine, and drove off.

"That was when I met Mr. Kim's teacher for the first time—Chungdo Kwan Grandmaster Woon Kyu Uhm, who is now president of the World TaeKwanDo Federation, and likely the most senior TKD man in the world today. I met Mr. Kim's practice partners—Mr. Chung, Mr. Park, and Mr. Lee. Mr. Park was the main influence in the creation and development of the Tae Geuk Forms, which are now the official WTF forms. Mr. Kim had me practice with Mr. Park and Mr. Lee several hours a day for weeks, until I learned all of the Tae Geuk forms. Mr.

Lee is now the official coach for the French National Olympic TKD team, and has a large following in France. And Mr.Chung has a large martial arts organization on the East Coast, in Boston.

"Working out with and studying under these men was awe-inspiring. The dedication to the martial arts they exhibited, their precision of movement, their unwillingness to accept any technique short of its perfect manifestation—well, it completely revitalized my study of the martial arts.

"Had I been the least bit hesitant to go to Korea, Mr. Kim would have gone without me. He would have stayed two or three months, and I would have stayed in the U.S., comfortable and secure, teaching in the Sangcook Kim Dojoang. Nothing would have changed, and my training would likely have become stale. But Mr. Kim saw something in me that he knew would benefit from training in Korea, and so he insisted I go. Saying 'No' to Mr. Kim was not an option, if I were to remain his student. And because I was dedicated to remaining his student and disciplined to that end, and because I trusted him implicitly, I followed his directions. It turned out to be a great learning experience-- a turning point in my career."

Grandmaster Garrison finished by saying, "A good teacher will guide you in such a way that your training will continually be exciting and intimidating, and will definitely never be the same. But you must do your part as well. You must develop the self-discipline to train regularly without fail, and you must be open to whatever experience your teacher demands of you. You must develop implicit trust in both your teacher and his art. If the art is approached this way, both the art and the student will evolve gracefully."

Tradition is honoring our teachers
by opening ourselves to their hard-won lessons;
Tradition and respect are the same.

This chapter is about mastering the flow of constant change in your martial art. Being able to adapt both physically and mentally to a rapidly changing scenario is of paramount importance to a warrior—the main purpose and culmination of all of his training, the heart of his martial quest.

There are three general aspects of continuous change which we can explore to help us in our readiness:

1. How both the art and the artist can evolve gracefully.

2. How to maximize adaptability in an unpredictable situation.

3. How to anticipate change in your opponent and take advantage of it.

Graceful Evolution of the Student

A Cup of Tea

Nan-in, a Japanese master during the Meiji era (1868-1912), received a university professor who came to inquire about Zen.

Nan-in served tea as the professor spoke at length about his thoughts on Zen. He poured his visitor's cup full, and then kept pouring. The professor watched the overflow until he could no longer restrain himself. "It is overfull. No more can go in!"

"Like this cup," Nan-in said, "you are full of your own opinions and speculations. How can I show you Zen unless you first empty your cup?"

-- from <u>Zen Flesh, Zen Bones</u>

This is perhaps the best known of the cryptic Zen stories called *Koans* or Zen puzzles. The point of the *Koans* is to provide the reader with some understanding that will help guide his path toward enlightenment. Enlightenment is a difficult concept to explain or even define; I won't presume to accomplish that here. It is presented in many of the *Koans* as a spiritual understanding that happens suddenly and fully. In others, though, such understanding appears to take years, even decades.

I suspect that enlightenment happens in small increments, like placing the pieces of a puzzle together until a picture takes form. The picture may appear significantly different as each piece is set in its place, but if one is patient, the intended picture will eventually become clear.

I have struggled with this picture of the martial arts for over forty years—the past thirty of them in Hapkido. The first five of those years, I practiced under Grandmaster Sangcook Kim, and for more than twenty-five years, I have studied under the always intense and sometimes harsh guidance of his senior student, Grandmaster James R. Garrison. Grandmaster Garrison has continued to open up new doors to my perception, continued to guide me in directions that have stimulated my personal growth and awareness. Often I don't understand a lesson at the time of its presentation, but I trust that my teachers have had more experience in the learning/teaching process. And I trust they are providing me with an experience which will ultimately prove invaluable. In fact, statements and lessons that Mr. Kim taught me decades ago in the original Sangcook Kim School come back to me still, and fill out the pattern, form connections and perspectives on the art that entirely escaped me at the time. Ultimately, studying a traditional art in a traditional way becomes a leap of faith.

Recently, this was re-substantiated as I practiced Judo with the black belts at Pacific Rim Martial Arts Academy. We were doing a *randori* practice combining a foot sweep, followed by an opposite side tai-otoshi throw. I was working with Michael Martyn, who has excellent Judo skills. I was having a difficult time understanding the ease with which he loaded me up. Even though I outweighed him by at least fifty pounds, his movement and my consequent unbalancing were effortless. But each time he loaded me up, he seemed to move differently. I watched as his right foot shot past my foot, and said, "Oh, you just put it there!"

He said, "Yes, *that time*. Next time it'll be different. It's different every time."

"But how can anyone learn a move that way?" I asked.

"You have to practice over and over, a hundred times to just get a feel for it," he answered. "Then you have to do it a hundred more times before you can begin to have confidence that your body can do it without your having to think so hard about it. Then, after a hundred more times, you begin to understand how it works. After about five hundred times, the movement becomes automatic. Then you begin to feel what your opponent is doing, how big he is, where his energy is flowing. That's really the beginning of learning a technique. *Learning Judo really isn't about perfecting a technique. A perfect technique never changes. Judo is learning about how to connect with your opponent, where his balance is, and how to take it from him. That constantly changes.*"

"You need not fear the warrior who has done ten thousand techniques once. Fear the warrior who has done one technique ten thousand times."

-- Ancient Chinese maxim

I immediately experienced a memory flashback to an Aikido class Mr. Garrison had taught years before. Mr. Garrison had talked at length about the essence of Aikido, and its purity as a martial art. "The techniques either work and are effortless, or they don't work at all," he had said. "Completing techniques when they are not working is brutish, ego in motion. Blending with one's opponent is the key, the real art. Seeking out the opponent's imbalance and exploiting it is the goal, not the completion of the technique. *One needs to let go of the art in order to truly embrace it. Practice relating to the opponent in terms of correct angle, superior positioning, and superior posture, and prevailing becomes inevitable.*"

Look for a teacher who is knowledgeable, strict, articulate, and intolerant of mediocrity.

I believe the best teachers remain students of their own art, both in receiving new instruction from those with more experience, and also in rediscovering nuances within the art as they struggle to awaken its potential in others.

But this approach to martial arts is not universal.

For a variety of reasons, some martial artists stop being students. They declare themselves to be finished, complete, totally enlightened. Theirs is the best way, the only way to approach martial arts. Any comments or suggestions are met with, "Yes, but…" or, "Well, my way works for me," or even, "Our way is so advanced, you just don't understand." They have concluded prematurely what all the pieces in the big picture mean. But after they conclude their personal truth, their picture never changes, never evolves further; enlightenment remains incomplete. In the martial arts, these impatient practitioners are often referred to as "overfilled cups."

I can only guess at their reasons for this way of thinking. Perhaps they have never had a teacher who could guide them past their own limitations, or they had a teacher who also stopped being a student before addressing all of his own flaws. Or perhaps they just stopped listening. Consequently, there are many martial arts teachers who consider the whole purpose of martial arts to be to receive rank and accolades. They only want external reward for their brilliance and perceived expertise. It is not important to them that they learn and grow. They are not bothered that what they are passing on to their students may be subtly flawed.

When a technique is flawed, such a practitioner probably will not realize it until the end of its execution, when it doesn't work. So the next time they execute the technique with more intensity rather than examine each of its phases. This is how many students get hurt. Mr. Kim used to use the analogy of buttoning a shirt. If you don't get the buttons aligned with the proper holes, you may not realize this until the whole front of the shirt is buttoned up wrong, and you end up with a left-over button at the top. The only way to correct this mistake is to start over and pay better attention.

Good students continually start over and allow themselves to change. They acknowledge their humility, muster their courage, exercise their patience, and guard their behavior against lapses in respect. They embrace their beginnings, their basic moves, the roots of their training, and closely examine them for flaws. Good students welcome continuous challenge and re-evaluation of the inner self. By inner self, I'm talking about internal values such as personal integrity, honesty, self discipline, ethics and manners—all qualities necessary for improving one's art—and one's life. The Japanese have a wonderful word for this mindset; the word is **Shoshin**, which translates as, *"beginner's mind."* I believe that maintaining a beginner's mind is absolutely essential to making any sort of progress in the martial arts—or any art for that matter.

Consider two different approaches to training I have encountered recently. The first was related to me by Mr. Martyn, a fifth dan at Pacific Rim, who attended a Judo seminar in Canada last year. At this seminar there were several members of the Judo team from Tokei University in

Tokyo. These Japanese students were accomplished Judoka, but spoke no English, and Mr. Martyn spoke no Japanese.

Mr. Martyn noticed that the seminar had separated into two distinct groups—the Japanese students were pairing up with each other, and the Americans were also pairing up only with each other. Mr. Martyn, being both adventurous and determined, walked over to one of the senior Japanese students and stood in front of him, saying one of the few phrases common among all Judoka. "Onigashimatsu," meaning, *Thank you for what you are about to teach me.* The Japanese student seemed less than thrilled to be paired up with an American, and Mr. Martyn paid for that by taking several hard falls. Fortunately, Mr. Martyn is an excellent faller. Each time, he would get up off the mat, show his enjoyment at the experience, stand in front of the Japanese judoka and, smiling politely, say, *"Onigashimatsu!"*

After awhile the Japanese judoka realized that Mr. Martyn was a sincere student with good manners, and his attitude started to change. Eventually, the Japanese student started to slow down his movements so Mr. Martyn could copy them. For more than two hours, they worked on one technique, Osotogari (leg sweep), and the Japanese student started taking falls for Mr. Martyn. Mr. Martyn related that this seminar was one of the most fun experiences he's ever had at a seminar. He came home with a positive experience, new friends, and new insights into Osotogari.

[The warrior] is confident in the face of opposition. Respectful behavior will bring good fortune. -- <u>I Ching</u>, Hexagram 6: Conflict

Compare that training experience with the following:

Recently, a special WOMAF seminar was held at Pacific Rim Martial Arts Academy to honor guests who had come all the way from the East Coast to train. Fairly early on, though, it appeared that these martial artists were not so much interested in learning as they were in impressing upon all who watched how wonderful they were at martial arts. They began throwing students of lower rank without regard for their safety, adding on extra techniques to the ones Mr. Garrison was teaching. Their senior ranking member was not subtle in his assumption that he should be promoted to a high rank which he thought suitable.

After the morning training ended, the students were asked to leave the mat area so the people from the east coast could put on a prearranged demonstration. Chairs were placed so that President Kim and Mr. Garrison could watch from the best vantage point.

The head teacher from the east coast began the demonstration by speaking about how well trained he was, and how his system was so much more "progressive" than "regular Hapkido." The demonstration quickly became a lecture on how he had eliminated several aspects of traditional Hapkido such as forms training, horse stance, and Tan-Jun breathing, and how he had changed some of the basics to his own predilection. When he demonstrated his modification of a basic fighting stance, President Kim walked onto the mat to give him some advice on how to improve his technique. But the East Coast headmaster would not listen. "Our system works for us the way it is," he said.

President Kim shrugged his shoulders, shook his head, and walked off the mat. The East Coast headmaster didn't even realize that there in front of him for a few brief moments stood the most accomplished martial artist he would probably ever meet in his lifetime, and he didn't even have enough good sense or manners to listen. The opportunity to learn and grow was lost.

Think of the two men in these stories.

The first has consistently sought a sense of personal growth and evolution toward becoming a better martial artist; a man who, by exhibiting common courtesies and unwavering respect, gained invaluable insights from someone who didn't even speak his language.

The second has cut himself off from his own teachers and pared down his traditions without understanding them fully, exhibiting an arrogant conceit—that he understands his art better than his own seniors in that art.

Who do you think is the more accomplished student? Which of these two men will be better at their martial art in ten years? Which of these two would you want to be paired up with in a training session? Which of these two approaches to learning would you embrace as your tradition?

"Those who follow Karate-do must never forsake a humble mind and gentle manner. It is the small minded individual who likes to brag upon acquiring some small skill, and those with little knowledge who carry on as if they were experts are childish."

-- Gichin Funakoshi, 10th dan, founder on Shodokan Karate

A good student will continuously strive to learn ever more about his art all his life. The term *art* actually refers to any study which helps us to understand ourselves and our place in the universe around us. There is never going to be an end to new things to learn—unless you close your mind to the possibility. A person needs to develop a sufficiently strong center so he can allow himself to change and grow. Evolution of the body, mind and spirit can only occur in a well balanced and confident person. Insecure people resist change.

> *"In the case of the martial arts, the issue is not how we change the techniques as much as it is in how we change ourselves by understanding these techniques."*
>
> -- Kensho Furuya, <u>Kodo: Ancient Ways</u>

Maximizing Your Adaptability

A few days ago, I was drawn into a conversation with a teenaged boy who had just found out I practiced martial arts, a brief exchange that went something like this:

"Are you any good?" the boy asked.

"I've learned a few things in the last forty years," I answered.

"Are you as good as Keanu Reeves?"

"Keanu Reeves is an actor."

"Yeah, but he can dodge bullets!"

"Well, I can't dodge bullets, or fly, or shrug off fifty people," I said. "But you know what? Neither can he." This was said into thin air, as the boy had already dismissed me as a fraud and relocated his attention deficit onto other friends.

It was an unimportant conversation, as I have no particular need to explain myself to adolescent boys. But it never ceases to surprise me how the general public's conception of the martial arts is so completely distorted by the media. The list of movie stars who have performed spectacular martial arts scenes is huge—Keanu Reeves, Uma Thurman, Drew Barrymore, Cameron Diaz, Ben Affleck, Matt Damon—and on and on. And after every popular movie with a martial arts scene in it, there is a surge of starry-eyed kids into the front door of the nearest dojang.

The hard work of daily practice quickly thins their ranks. The rest linger on for a few months, thinking that if they can just master the spinning turn-back kick, they have what it takes to be the next Jet Li.

Even many people who practice the martial arts hold onto unrealistic and distorted conceptions of what constitutes martial expertise. If a person can throw a decent side kick, punch through a pine board, execute a graceful shoulder throw, and spar without getting sucker-punched in the first ten seconds, then he's mastered the martial arts, right? There is a line in *Enter the Dragon* when Jim Kelly says to the villain Han, "I'll be too busy looking good!" That seems to be what counts today.

The truth is, martial expertise has nothing in common with those larger than life superheroes in the movies who fly through the air, dodge bullets and walk on water. Such feats are popular fictions portrayed by actors with the help of guywires, trick photography, and a well-practiced script. Anything is possible in the movies, and anyone can be a Kung

Fu master when that person knows what's going to happen and gets to rehearse his response over and over again.

But in real life, anything can happen—and there are no guywires.

Martial arts training is more about being ready for the unknown and the unpredictable turn of events than it is about practicing the perfect response to a certain kind of attack. No one can master techniques appropriate for all possible situations. We must understand that we practice specific techniques over and over again, not just to perfect the movement, but to incorporate them deep into our subconscious so that when the technique becomes appropriate, its execution will be automatic. Our minds have more important duties to protect us in dangerous and unpredictable situations: paying attention to our surroundings, becoming aware of subtle changes in the energies around us, remaining strong, resolute, indomitable. **Our mental preparedness is far more important in the face of perpetual change than is our physical expertise.**

"Mind and techniques are to become one in true karate."
-- Gichin Kunakoshi, 10th dan, founder on Shodokan Karate

All martial training is aimed at increasing physical and mental preparedness for the unknown. The following is a list of eight martial principles previously discussed in *Warrior Mind* which are revisited in light of the concept of flowing with change:

1. True Strength Comes from Within

The first rule of flowing with change is to totally believe in yourself and in your choices. Knowing who you are and what values you stand for will prepare you to quickly recognize situations which require immediate or forceful action, and provide the confidence to act without hesitation.

You must continually assess what constitutes appropriate conduct in order to quickly recognize inappropriate conduct, and ascertain the moment when it may become necessary to act. This is best accomplished by strictly adhering to a code of conduct which is universal among martial arts of all types. Shodokan Karate founder Gichin Funikoshi stated it this way more than seventy years ago:

> *"Karate is no different from other martial arts in fostering the traits of courage, courtesy, integrity, humility, and self-control in those who have found its essence."*

The ethical man is more practiced at disciplined behavior, at resolute dedication to a chosen path, and at having confidence that he is acting correctly. This inner strength results in less doubt and less hesitation when a quick decision must be made.

If the mind is in a quandary, the body will hesitate to act.

---

2. Mind and Body are One Flow

You must turn off the inner voice that maintains an ongoing description of your day, your actions, your feelings. If you have to analyze what's happening to you and arrive at a logical conclusion about what to do, you will be too late to counter a real attack. But with the mind's voice silenced, the body can flow as soon as it perceives the need. The body, through regular and consistent training, acquires its own movement intelligence. Learn to let your body react automatically, as it knows best; this is *mushin*.

"If there is a single moment of reflection when you are attacked, it's too late. The thought cannot exist in your mind before performing

the movement. It must be instinctual, without thought. With constant training, the movements become automatic, like a reflex. If you don't do Judo like that, it's not Judo."

-- Shozo Awazu, 9th dan, Judo

---

3. Control your Breath, Expand Awareness

Calmness is crucial to our preparedness for change. An agitated state is really just an out-of-control ego. When our anger or fear gets out of control, we become wrapped up in our own feelings; everything becomes about *us*. We may be so busy commiserating with ourselves that we fail to notice an escalating threat. Or we may be so startled by a central event that we fail to notice a peripheral event that may be even more dangerous to us.

Breath control is the key to remaining in control of our emotions; emotional control is the key to expanding our awareness. Nearly all martial arts teach some form of abdominal (or *ki*) breathing to help the warrior remain calm, enabling him to make rapid and rational decisions. But the real benefit of calmness is that our minds are not so wrapped up in ourselves.

A warrior's mind has a far more vital task—to pay attention to everything around him, no matter how subtle the stimulus might be. The warrior most likely to survive is the one who develops a 360 degree circle of awareness. What happens in front of him may be only a distraction for someone about to blind-side him from behind.

In times of danger, take a deep breath, get control of your emotions, and surround yourself with awareness—this is the beginning of zanshin.

A student of mine named Mary works as a hospice nurse, visiting the homes of terminally ill patients. At the home of a schizophrenic man with cancer, she was attacked by the man's equally schizophrenic mother. Mary was standing to one side as the patient and his mother got into a terrible argument. Mary was looking at the patient and assessing how he was doing when she suddenly felt a change of energy in the room. The mother had gotten behind her and puffing herself up from her normal meek and bent-over demeanor, she was lunging at Mary with her clawed fingers outstretched. Mary dodged aside just in time to avoid any contact, and quickly left the house. What had alerted her in time? She says it's what she had learned in class the Friday before, about extending her awareness out into her environment, and being aware of subtle changes in the energies around her. She had become aware of a change of energy in the room, and she had raised her guard just in time.

---

4. Guard your Balance.

It is a natural instinct to want to root yourself to the ground in a crisis. Almost all beginning fighters are guilty of this. But the instant you do, you become rigid—easy prey for a throw. You want *your opponent* to become rooted. When you settle into a rooted position, for that instant, your feet are probably in the right spot. But an instant later, the situation has changed; your opponent has moved, shifted his weight, readjusted his attack angle, or charged into you. If you aren't already in motion, it's too late. The whole point of learning to be grounded, of learning to move from the center, is so that you can maintain your balance during movement, and be rooted *less*.

Develop what Mr. Kim calls a ready-for-anything stance. Keep your knees slightly bent, your weight on the balls of your feet, and your back as straight as possible. Hold your hands loosely at shoulder level with your elbows in close to your body. Learn to move in any direction while maintaining this posture. Learn to initiate all movement from your *Tan-Jun* center, just below your navel. This is called, **One-Point Movement.**

The better prepared you are to move your whole body in any direction, the quicker you'll be able to respond. Remember that all effective attacks and defenses are executed by whole-body movement, not by isolated hand or arm motions. Keeping your balance during this flow is essential.

5. Surge Forward Like Water

Water flows easily when unobstructed, and eddies around obstacles in its path. If totally blocked, it pools, patiently awaiting the first chance for release. Water only flows forward—downhill. It does not change its nature, nor reassess its path.

Like water, the warrior only surges forward into the choice of his resolution. To back up is to let go of his resolve. But also like water, he is constantly aware of and adapting to the ebb and flow of energies around himself. Like water, he is ready to change his course instantly, while his goal remains clear in his mind.

Keeping in mind the personal values you hold, you continuously work on developing acceptable patterns of behavior. (If such-and-such happened, I would act in this manner.) Remember, while your central ethical standards may not change, your strategies for adhering to them *will change*, according to the situation.

You must develop and have in place a thoroughly examined set of **escalating action strategies**—how you believe you should react to emergency conditions and threats in a variety of circumstances. Formulating these response patterns is an ongoing practice, both in and out of the dojang. Then, hopefully, when the real thing happens, your mind will be prepared for early recognition and instant response. You will not need to stop and analyze the situation or define your ethical path; that work is already done. To maintain your ethical identity, you simply have to remain within your predetermined action boundaries.

Your permission to react instantly and automatically to a threat must be preconditioned. It must be a natural expression of your inner self.

6. Practice Non-attachment

The more you practice an isolated technique, the more you tend to view it as the best response to a particular form of attack. The more times you execute that technique, the more you become mentally and emotionally invested in its completion, even if you have to force it. This approach to learning almost always works in class, where the *uke* cooperates with his own defeat.

But the flow of energy during a real attack is never predictable. Your opponent's balance, momentum, speed, and reactions to your movement are all changing constantly. You begin a technique only to find that the dynamics of balance and impetus have evolved, and that technique is no longer appropriate. How can you continue?

You must let go of the idea of technique completion and concentrate on remaining in touch with your opponent's balance and momentum. Learn to blend with your opponent's movement without any agenda for it. In fact, be eager to help him along his path; add a little of your own energy to his, so that he may extend his movement farther than intended. Then he may temporarily unbalance himself, and the possibility of a technique may reappear.

But even so, it's best to have no investment in finishing a certain way. It's better to learn how techniques flow into one another. As one technique encounters insurmountable resistance, the potential for others will arise. As you seek to remain in contact with your opponent's energy, reversal of momentum may occur several times. Remain unattached to any outcome until either a target is exposed, or your opponent is so overextended and unbalanced that a technique which occurs to you is already halfway completed, effortless.

Remember, it is the ego which demands a certain path, a certain outcome, and closes the mind to other possibilities. The assertion of one's ego all but guarantees contention and struggle. Learn to approach life in a selfless, receptive manner, and you will better flow with the ever-changing energies around you, thus avoiding much adversarial resistance.

> *Judo (Jujitsu) master Henry Seishiro Okazaki wrote, "Only by cultivating a receptive state of mind, without preconceived thoughts, can one master the secret art of reacting spontaneously and naturally without hesitation and without purposeless resistance."*
> *-- from "The Esoteric Principles of Judo" (unpublished paper)*

7. Exploit All Advantages

You must develop a critical eye for your environment, which you exercise at all times. Wherever you find yourself, you will automatically assess advantageous and detrimental conditions. Which direction is the safest exit? Where is the greatest danger? How far from me is the best cover? Is there anything nearby that anyone could use as a weapon? How close is this person to me? What kind of fighter is he likely to be? Can I see both of his hands? Where are this person's strong and weak angles of balance?

Ask yourself often, *How can I turn this situation to my advantage?*

This ongoing practice of strategic thinking is essential for quick response to the unexpected. Continually assessing your surroundings helps to keep your circle of awareness large, your will to prevail strong, and your mind sharp and ready to respond. In addition, critical assessment of your environment helps to separate the known from and the unknown, reducing the possibility of surprise. An ongoing awareness of an adversary's angular relationship allows a fighter to quickly establish an angular advantage the instant a confrontation turns physical.

8. Understand Good Timing: Step into the Void

The whole point of understanding and applying the martial principles of advantage is to gain time enough to apply a technique which will decide the fight in your favor. All thoughts and actions must be focused on creating this timing advantage.

Your timing is determined by your entry. There are four principles of entry which significantly alter the timing of an adversarial interaction in your favor. They are: ***stepping into an advantageous angle, closing with the opponent, using simultaneous attack and defense,*** and ***entering the void.***

Remember, your angular movement is your defense; your entry is an attack. Ideally, your initial move is both. You avoid your opponent's strength by getting out of his path, and you attack his weaknesses—his exposed areas or his imbalance—at the same time.

These weaknesses are called *voids*; they are like holes in a warrior's armor, windows of opportunity which open and close more rapidly than the conscious mind is capable of processing. But "seeing" these opportunities for counterattack is less a matter of using the eyes than it is of applying an understanding of body kinetics that gradually develops through years of practice. Eventually, you acquire an intuitive awareness of your opponent's motions, and you can react to them without having to think about it. The longer you stay in practice, the more spontaneous your reactions become. The ultimate goal is to move simultaneously with your opponent, continuously attacking his weaknesses before he has a chance to recover. In his *Book of Five Rings*, the great swordsman Musashi called this **"entering the void"**. You are safe as long as you can remain in your opponent's void.

"The secret of good timing is to seek out and step into your opponent's void with your initial movement." – Walter Todd Shihan

---

Martial arts practice must evolve beyond just learning technique. It must prepare the mind for instant recognition of, and automatic response to, the various dynamics of an attack. Over time, proper practice evolves this mindset into a continuous flow, which is often referred to as *warrior mind*. Warrior mind is learning to quiet the inner dialogue and focus one's mental energy into awareness, calm the emotions, develop unyielding tenacity, practice strategic thinking, and trust in the automaticity of the body to respond instantly and appropriately. Without this preparation, you cannot flow with change; you cannot face the unknown without fear.

"The essence of martial arts is that the mind should not be detained by anything nor stopped anywhere. Mind must be empty, allowing attention to flow naturally wherever it needs to go. Then many things are possible. Whatever you have trained yourself to do will be performed automatically, like a flash of lightning. The ultimate focus is no focus, beyond distinguishing between self and other. The kick or punch becomes an extension of you, and correct technique happens instinctively, in a natural response to the situation. This is made possible by responding to each moment of challenge as it comes, without thought. The ultimate strategy is no strategy."

-- Takuan Soho, Zen Priest, <u>The Unfettered Mind</u>

Anticipating the Flow of Change

At the original Sangcook Kim Hapkido Dojang in the early 1970's, sparring was a bit rougher than what is practiced today. We always wore body pads, mouthpieces, and heavy gloves, but that was not enough to protect us completely. We sparred almost every class, and often, someone would get knocked down by a well-executed punch or kick.

When Mr. Kim put on the pads and gloves, the rest of us swallowed hard; someone was likely to go flying. When it was my turn to spar with Mr. Kim, I did my best: but just about the time I'd think, *Aha, an opening!* he would throw a sliding front or side kick, and then withdraw, crouching into a low back stance. I would move backwards to avoid the kick, and then, as he faded back, it looked like a large space opening up between us. I would step into that space to reach him for a counterattack, but before my front foot would touch the ground, Mr. Kim would execute a turnback-side kick from his crouched position which would hit me square in the chest and knock the wind out of me. Mr. Kim would use this combination fairly often, and although all of us knew about it, none of us could manage to avoid getting hit.

Out of sheer frustration, I asked Mr. Garrison how this was possible. He explained, "Mr. Kim isn't just sparring with you physically, he's sparring with you mentally. He sets up your mind to perceive a certain way. Then your reaction becomes predictable. In that particular move, he makes you believe there's an opening. So when you step into it, he already knows what you're going to do before you do it. He can start his kick the instant you start your movement, and because you're programmed to take that step before attacking, his kick lands while you are unguarded every time." Mr. Garrison smiled uneasily. "You know, he hits me with that one too. No matter how many times I see it happening, I still get caught by it. I believe it's because Mr. Kim watches the way his opponent *thinks*."

Sparring represents the ultimate flow of rapid and constant change in a martial setting. Consequently, an examination of the strategies and tactics of sparring will reveal a good deal of information about this flow which will be valuable in all adversarial situations.

If you spar reactively—if you wait and see what your opponent does before reacting to it—you will never catch up to the present moment because of reaction-time lag. The very best you can do is to manage to block your opponent's moves and come out even. But, your opponent is still free to attack you again. Your goal is to stop his attack. In order to do so, you have to be able to move beyond mere reactive thinking.

The traditional understanding is that there are two approaches to sparring: offensive and defensive. However, while there are some physical techniques which are more offensive or defensive in nature, there is only one effective mental approach. ***A good fighter is always on the attack.*** Even when forced to move defensively, his intention is still clear—to take control of the action and guide it toward an advantage over his opponent.

The ultimate goal of sparring is to be able to cause an opponent to expose a weakness, or void, and to be able to attack that void before it disappears. To accomplish this, a fighter needs to learn how to anticipate his opponent's intentions. If his opponent's movement can be predicted, then the fighter can start his response ahead of time. A good fighter quickly learns to think of his opponent's posture, demeanor, and movement as a gateway to his mind. He learns to read his opponent's patterns, assess his predilections, and offer opportunities for his opponent to move predictably. A good fighter plants the seed that causes his opponent to think a certain way. In effect, *he leads his opponent's mind.*

Successful sparring requires mental dominance, yet constant transitional flow as well. A popular paradox used in Judo to describe randori (grappling practice) is, "Practice total commitment, yet infinite variation."

The goal of an effective fighter is to lead his opponent into making a strategic mistake—one that results in a momentary advantage. There are basically three types of situational advantage sought in an opponent: ***a position of imbalance or overextension, a target exposure (void), or a predictability of movement.*** All sparring tactics intend to take advantage of one or more of these. The following are a few examples of each.

Causing Imbalance or Overextension

When a fighter is able to cause an imbalance in his opponent, he creates a double advantage. The first is that he may be able to throw his opponent to the ground. The second advantage is that an unbalanced opponent will temporarily have to deal with his own balance before he can continue any further attack.

In a real fight, bouncing your adversary's head on the ground—which may stun him or knock the wind out of him—is a fine advantage. But in sparring, grabbing your opponent in any way is usually against the rules. However, there are a few ways to cause imbalance in your opponent without applying a completely obvious Judo throw.

One tactic which invites a slight imbalance is to turn toward every attack and apply a circular block. If your opponent throws a punch, you can step around it and block in such a way as to add some of your own force to the momentum of that punch, and your opponent may overextend himself for a moment. Many martial arts styles teach blocking with cupped hands. This makes it easier to grab an attacker's arm and lead him off-balance. In competition sparring, cupped-hand blocking and grabbing is illegal, but this is still an effective tactic in a real fight.

Your opponent will have to recover from whatever imbalance you can create. He will have to retract his overextension and turn toward your new angle in relation to him in order to continue his attack. That gives you a split second of freedom to attack him first.

Another tactic that invites an opponent to overextend himself is to control the angle of relationship and the distance between the two of you. Usually, your opponent will instinctively focus on your centerline; that is, he will automatically arrange his stance so that all his weapons can be unleashed straight at you. This is his attack angle. It is advantageous to *him* if you remain in line with his attack angle. It is advantageous to *you* if you move off of this line. If your opponent initiates an attack from an awkward angle, he will likely overextend himself, or become slightly off balance.

The distance between fighters is a dynamic, ever-changing focus of contention. Every fighting style favors an optimum distance to an opponent. Kickers prefer a greater distance than punchers; punchers prefer a greater distance than grapplers. Establishing a preferred distance between a fighter and his opponent is so critical that this struggle has its own word in the Japanese martial arts. The distance between fighters is called *ma*.

By controlling *ma*, you can apply two tactics to unbalance and frustrate your opponent. The first is to stay just beyond his reach, so that he may attempt to stretch out his techniques in an attempt to strike you. This will result in slowed techniques and possibly a slight overextension you can exploit.

If the *ma* is beyond an opponent's reach, he may be lured into taking a step before executing an attack. A common attack sequence in most martial arts is the stepping or sliding kick, meant to cover an extended distance quickly and efficiently. An experienced fighter may position himself just beyond the reach of his opponent's kicking distance, but well within reach of a one-step sliding kick. Consequently, the second fighter's initial move becomes predictable. He will have to take at least one step before he attacks. At the moment the second fighter moves, the first fighter can safely initiate a counterattack because he knows what step the second fighter is taking, and where he will be at its completion. This is a common exploitation of *ma*.

The second tactic to exploit *ma* is to close the distance suddenly, jamming up your opponent's attack before it has unfolded. This is dangerous, in that it always results in significant impact, but it usually results in upsetting your opponent's balance as well. One trick to successful jamming is to move off your opponent's attack angle slightly just before you step into him. Then your opponent's energy into you is minimized, and your energy into him is at an awkward angle for him. This is a common exploitation of *ma* preferred by fighters who are comfortable with grappling. Their intent is to stay so close to their opponents that punching and kicking becomes awkward. They seek to unbalance their opponents, throw them down and apply a pin, a lock or a choke. Overextension doesn't have to be a long-reaching move. It can happen without any movement at all. It is simply any momentary physical or mental lapse which results in the loss of *ma*.

Another strategy which may result in your opponent overextending himself is to invite your opponent to become overconfident. There are many ways to do this. The most frequently used are feigning weakness or imbalance, and offering an irresistible target.

There is a beautiful fight scene in the movie *The 13th Warrior*, starring Antonio Bandares, which illustrates feigning a weakness. A fight breaks out between two men, one of whom is considerably bigger and obviously stronger. The stronger fighter pounds the smaller fighter mercilessly, hacking apart several wooden shields, until the smaller fighter is kneeling, breathless, apparently beaten, on the verge of despair. Antonio Bandares comments, "You don't appear to be doing so well." The smaller fighter replies between gasps, "On the contrary, I've got him right where I want him." This seems humorously ironic, until the much bigger fighter grins triumphantly and steps in for the killing blow. As the giant man's axe falls straight down, the smaller fighter dodges aside and circles his own axe onto his adversary's neck, killing him. The big man's overconfidence had resulted in a predictable move.

There are many fighting styles which employ the constant feigning of imbalance. Two of the most popular are a form of Chinese Kung Fu known as *Drunken Monkey Style* and a Brazilian fighting style called *Capoera*. Both styles employ a series of apparent stumbles, falls, rolls and handsprings which appear awkward and accidental, but which are intended to close the distance between opponents before an attack is recognized. It appears this kind of stylilst is just having bad luck with his balance, and suddenly, his opponent is hit.

Once, many years ago, I witnessed a fight in a tavern in which a method of feigning vulnerability was used. One man threatened another man, pointing and shaking his finger, and saying something I didn't hear across the room. But the second man held up a hand, palm outward, feigning a slight limp, and grasped the back of a chair for balance. As soon as the second man had a hold on the chair-back, he laughed and said something that was probably insulting to the first man, who immediately stepped in to throw a punch. At that moment, the second man simply swung the chair between them and forced it into his attacker's legs, tripping him. The attacker hit his head against a nearby table on the way down, and the fight was over before it really started. I never forgot that lesson—deception prevailed. There's no such thing as foul play in a real fight.

There is another method of inviting overconfidence which is very dangerous. This is to offer a target, inviting your opponent to focus on it and move in a way that may be predictable. But there are many variables inherent in this tactic which may result in an undesirable outcome. First, your opponent may not react predictably. He may feign an attack, knowing that you will probably react predictably to his attack. And second, he may simply hit the target you present.

Many years ago, Mr. Garrison took a few of his black belts to a sparring session with a character he had met in his travels. The man was a disabled Green Beret who had returned from Vietnam ten years earlier with an eye patch and a steel hook for a right hand. The man, whose name was Ron, was as classic a case of post-traumatic stress disorder as I've ever met, bordering on maniacal paranoia. But he was a fairly good fighter.

When it was my turn to spar him, I moved about, circling, looking for an opening which I couldn't find. I was young and fairly fast. I thought I'd try to bait him into moving in a way I could predict. So I threw a front kick which he avoided easily, and then I turned my back toward him for a moment, to spin into a turn-back kick. Ron stopped the fight and said, "Don't turn your back to me. Never do that." Well, I thought I'd just moved too slow, so the next time, I threw two kicks, and spun confidently into a fast turn-back side kick. I never made it all the way around. Ron sank his steel hook into the center of my back, and I went down like a sack of potatoes, in searing pain. "It could have been worse," he said. Now, twenty years later, I still have a small white scar perfectly located between my left shoulder blade and left kidney, two inches from my spine. Don't offer what you can't protect.

Causing Your Opponent to Expose a Void

Actually, voids are present in every fighter's defense almost all of the time. Every time a fighter attacks, his energy shifts from his center to his projecting weapon, leaving some other part of his body exposed. However, this information is not as useful as it sounds. Most fighters learn how to minimize their exposure as a normal part of their movement. For example, seasoned fighters learn to hold their hands high, at face level, to block incoming blows. And when they punch, their opposite hand may even raise up a little, rather like a sword striking out beneath a shield. This minimizes the voids in their attack, and is often referred to as *sword and shield* technique. Voids that occur during a fighter's attack are also hard to access for another very good reason; their opponent is usually too busy defending himself at the time to take advantage of it. By the time the opponent has defended himself, recovered and counterattacked, the void is long gone.

Overextensions, momentary imbalances, and exposed vulnerabilities are all incredibly transient events. It's all but impossible to take advantage of any of them as they occur—unless you can learn to cause them. But there is one fight dynamic that is usually constant: your opponent dislikes you and wants to thwart your efforts. This is an exploitable energy.

Whatever you attempt, your opponent will do his best to counter, and in that split second, he becomes predictable. For example, suppose you are sparring an opponent who holds his forward hand fairly high and far away from his body, in an exaggerated "karate" stance. If you just sweep his hand downward and immediately follow that with a kick from *underneath* it, he will likely be so focused on moving his hand upward back into its original position, he will not perceive the kick until it's too late. This is called, ***exploiting adversarial energy.***

Most seasoned fighters use **combination moves** to exploit adversarial energy. That is to say, a fighter can depend on his opponent reacting defensively to any attack. That makes the opponent somewhat predictable for a split second. For instance, if a fighter throws a high punch, his opponent will probably raise his forward hand—his shield—in automatic response. That leaves the area behind and underneath that hand momentarily exposed. If the fighter throws that high punch and follows it immediately with a low kick, that kick has a better chance of landing in an exposed area. In fact, experienced fighters rarely throw single, isolated techniques. They expect the first technique to be blocked, but the second or third has an increasingly better chance of getting through. The best fighters employ techniques which rapidly change directions, left and right, high and low, seeking to exploit the adversarial response. This is called ***three-dimensional fighting.***

Another tactic often used to exploit adversarial energy and expose a target is ***broken-rhythm timing.*** An experienced fighter may consciously establish a pattern of attack. If he can lure his opponent into anticipating his attack by responding predictably, then he can simply break either the pattern or the rhythm to take advantage of his opponent's known defense.

An example of this tactic is the fighter who throws two or three straight front kicks in a row followed by a fake-front roundhouse kick. As his opponent is driven backwards by the successive front kicks (which are thrown all at the same low target with the same speed) the opponent will likely be lulled into using the same defensive down-blocks. The fake-front roundhouse kick is meant to cause the perception that another front kick is on its way. But just as the opponent begins another down-block, the first fighter's foot swings up over the top of the downward moving arm and connects into the exposed upper body or head. Establishing a pattern and then breaking it—or establishing a rhythm and then breaking it—are almost always effective tactics to expose a target because they lead an opponent's mind.

An experienced fighter may recognize the broken rhythm tactic and choose to thwart it before its completion. He does this by counterattacking instead of defending. When he perceives an attack, an experienced fighter will step into an advantageous angle and launch his response back into the opponent, deflecting his opponent's forward energy and hitting a target at the same time. This is called ***cutting off your opponent's energy.*** An example of this is an angular punch that slides over the top of an opponent's punch.

Another example of cutting off your opponent's energy is ***placing a barrier*** between yourself and your opponent's strength. For instance, many large men are used to using their strength and size to best advantage. They prefer to grab their opponent and either bear-hug them, or lift them up and throw them as far as they can. If such a large man grabs you, you're at a distinct disadvantage, but you may be able to interrupt his intent by turning into him and shoving an arm into his face or neck. Now he has to apply his power around a barrier. And while he is distracted by your arm, you may have an opportunity to punch with your other arm, or attack his legs with a kick. A strong man can only apply his strength if he has his balance. Your best strategy is to not let him get a hold of you, but if he does, don't fight his strength. Try to establish a barrier he has to work around, and then attack his balance.

Causing Predictability

Being able to predict your opponent's next move is the most definitive advantage a fighter can gain. Instead of waiting to see what an opponent will do and then reacting to it, you can start your counterattack at the exact instant your opponent initiates an attack. The trick is to be accurate in your assumptions. The best way to increase your accuracy is to convince your opponent that he needs to move in a way that you have suggested. There are two main methods of accomplishing this: ***transitional countering*** and ***limiting options.***

Countering and transition between techniques is a vital skill that most martial artists never master. Many never even understand the concept. The majority of martial arts styles are technique oriented. That is to say, a student practices a certain technique over and over again until he feels a certain automatic flow from beginning to end. This is a fine way to learn an isolated technique, but it's only a starting point. What happens when the *uke* [training partner] resists? What happens when your technique reaches a point that it cannot possibly be completed?

Let's assume you are trying to apply a throwing technique on an attacker. He has thrown a punch. You have moved off to one side, cup-blocked his arm, and are leading him into an imbalance, intending to apply a wrist throw (*kotogaeshi*). But now you feel tremendous resistance in the direction of your lead—your opponent is drawing his arm back toward himself, pulling his elbow closer to his side. The wrist throw is no longer likely to succeed. But there is still a lead; your opponent has just changed its direction. Initially, you wanted to cause his arm to be over-extended forward, but he has countered that by applying reverse energy. Your opponent wants to draw his arm into himself, so you simply let go of your original intent and flow with this new direction. There are several new techniques now possible—an arm bar, chicken-wing lock, leg-sweep or choke hold. If your opponent resists by moving his arm out away from his body again, then the possibility of the wrist throw reappears.

The idea behind countering and transition is to learn to tune into your opponent's balance and energy and flow with it. If your lead is successful, you can complete your technique. If your lead is unsuccessful, your opponent is still acting in a predictable manner by applying an opposing force. Either way, his energy is predictable and exploitable. The art of *Ho Shin Sul* (Hapkido grappling techniques) is taught in groups of two or three techniques, to teach their energy relationship.

Mr. Garrison used to teach us by applying a technique loosely and then saying, "How would you defend yourself? How are you going to move now?" However his *uke* would move, he would say, *"Oh, good!"* and throw us down with some other technique we had unwittingly stepped into. *"Oh, good!"* became a catch phrase indicating a continuous blending with an opponent's energy, changing techniques as his energy changed. *"Oh, good!"* always drew a chuckle from the class because we all knew the *uke* would soon hit the mat—he just didn't know how it would happen.

Limiting Options

There are two strategies to limit an opponent's options, thus making his next move slightly more predictable. The first is to create an opportunity for him which appears advantageous. You may temporarily expose a target, or appear to be off balance or appear to be distracted. Your opponent will size you up and decide there is an opening, and initiate a predictable move toward it. But you had better really be on balance, paying attention, and able to protect your exposed area. You had better have a move ready to initiate the instant your opponent begins his attack, or your response may be too late, and your feigned disadvantage may become a real disadvantage.

The second strategy is to limit your opponent's options, so that he must move in a certain way to regain position. An example of this is a common tactic in sparring called **herding**. This is when one fighter moves in such a way as to apply attack pressure in one direction, forcing his opponent back in that direction. For instance, if a fighter applies pressure by dominating *ma* so that his opponent is forced backward into a barrier such as a wall, then steps slightly to one side so that an opening appears for the opponent to get away from his trapped position, he will invariably step toward that opening. At that moment, both the opponent's timing and his direction become predictable. The fighter can attack the space where the opponent will step almost before he decides to step there.

This tactic can also be used in competition. Almost all sparring competition takes place in "rings" which are not rings, but squares. An opponent can be herded into a corner and then let out through a supposed opening along an opposite side—but when the opponent begins his first step in that direction, he becomes a predictable target.

If you are caught in just such a limited-option situation, attack straight forward instead. Your opponent will not expect that, and may fall back a step, creating a real opening—or at least creating more options for you to move, thus maintaining your unpredictability.

These sparring tactics are just a few examples of an infinite variety of ways to help a fighter predict the next move of his opponent. As a fighter gains more experience, his physical movement during sparring becomes more spontaneous and automatic. Sparring itself becomes more of a mental exercise. In order to maximize the possibility of success, an experienced fighter constantly pays attention to clues which reveal his opponent's mindset, his emotions, his patterns of movement. He looks for mental lapses in his opponent. Any defensive move or readjustment of position that is not a direct attack is a disengagement of the opponent's mind—and a time to attack *him*. The best fighters constantly seek ways to *cause* mental lapses in their opponent. They plant the seeds of perception which their opponent is likely to interpret a certain way, and react predictably. The moment a fighter becomes predictable, he is already beaten. The best fighters are unpredictable because they remain in a state of continuous physical and mental flow.

Become like water. If your mind flows continuously without fixation, your body will flow easily from movement to movement. If your mind holds onto one thought or goal, your body will tense up and stop its flow.

Review

The only constant in the universe is that all things change. We can choose to embrace new knowledge with humility and receptiveness and evolve gracefully. Or we can resist change with egotistical stubbornness and arrogance, and our world view will be increasingly outdated and inappropriate.

To maximize our preparedness for change, we must: **develop internal strength and confidence; quiet our mental chatter, control** *our breathing, expand our awareness, guard our balance, flow like water, practice non-attachment, recognize and exploit all possible advantages, and seek out and step into our opponent's void with our initial movement.*

The goal of an effective fighter is to lead his opponent into making a strategic mistake—one that results in a momentary advantage. There are basically three types of situational advantages sought in an opponent: *a position of imbalance or overextension, a target exposure (void), or a predictability of movement.*

Examples of ways to invite imbalance or overextension are *using circular movement and blocks, controlling the angle and distance between fighters, and feigning weakness or imbalance, perhaps even offering a target.*

Examples of ways to cause a void in your opponent are *using combination moves and three-dimensional fighting, exploiting your opponent's adversarial energy, and using broken-rhythm timing.*

Examples of ways to exploit predictability in your opponent are by *employing continuous transitional countering, and by limiting your opponent's options.*

A fight is less apt to be won by the fighter who is the more brutal than by the fighter who is the more cunning. The best fighters do not depend on favorite techniques; they favor the techniques suggested by the conflict itself.

The warrior's mind passes freely through the moment, aware of it, yet detached from it. He knows that all things ebb and flow, that which seems fixed is merely a reflection, like the moon upon water.

Those who resist change will be overwhelmed by it. Those who learn to flow with change will not be unbalanced by it. Those who can anticipate change will learn how to turn it to great advantage.

Chance favors the prepared mind.

*****

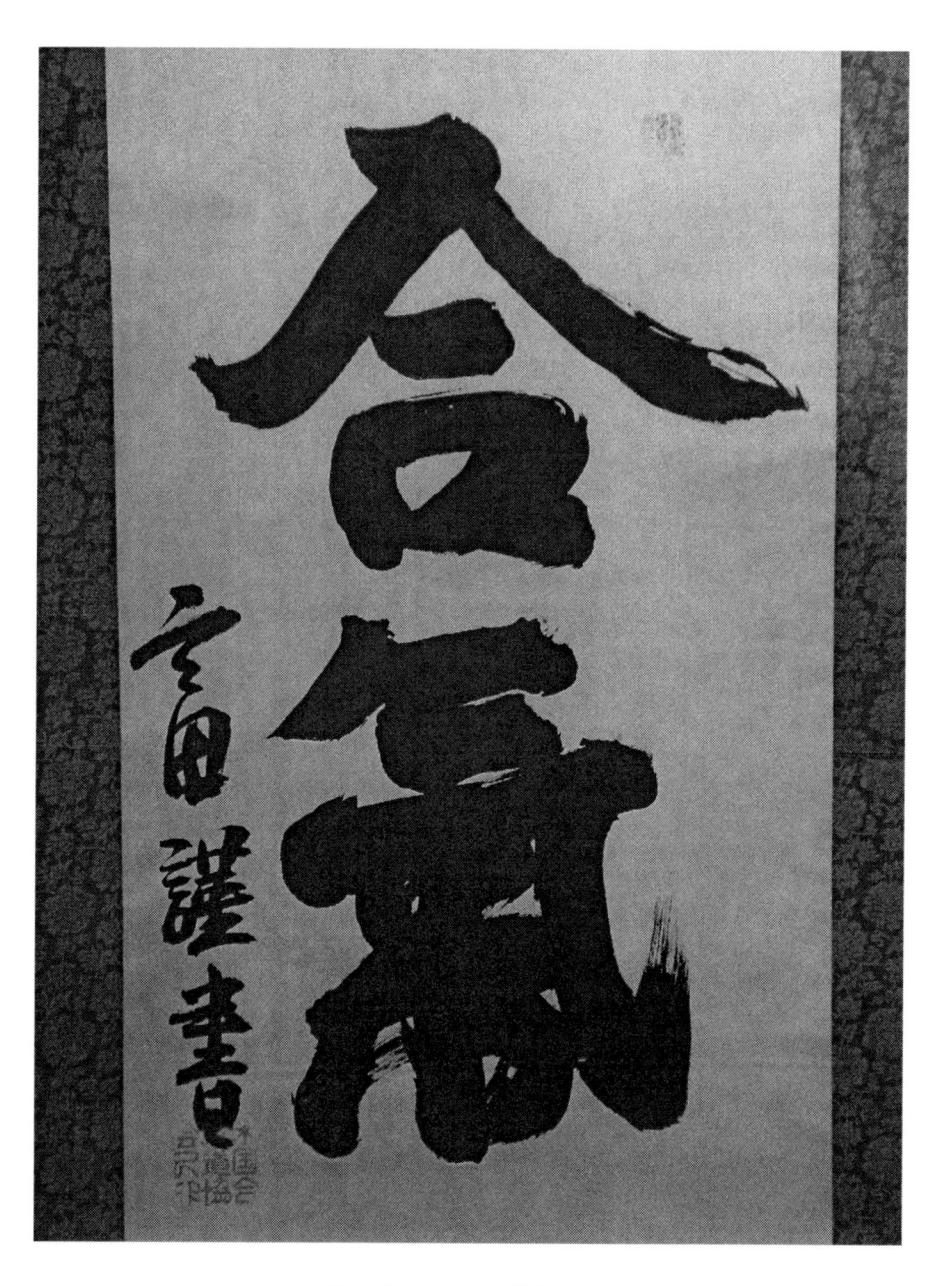

Aiki- the energy of Harmony

Chapter 10

Honor Your Spirit

The Meaning of *Budo*

Two recent experiences have caused my martial arts study to evolve in a new direction.

About a year ago, Grandmaster Kim visited the Pacific Rom Martial Arts Academy to visit with Mr. Garrison. I found myself momentarily alone with Grandmaster Kim in the office. He smiled and greeted me, as I have been in practice long enough that I am one of the faces he recognizes. Then he said, "You have been in practice a long time, haven't you?" I answered yes. "How long?" he said. I answered: "I've been practicing Hapkido for thirty years. Before that, I practiced Kenpo for almost ten years. I guess I've been practicing for about forty years now."

Grandmaster Kim nodded and sat silently for a moment, his brow furrowed slightly. "How many fights have you been in, in the last year?"

I thought it a strange question. "You mean, like in tournaments—like sparring?" I asked.

"No. Not tournaments, not sparring. How many real fights?"

"Well…none," I answered.

"How many fights in the last ten years?" he asked.

I though back over the last several years. When I was in my twenties, there were occasionally a few scuffles which rarely amounted to much. I'd been hit a few times in my youth, and I'd hit a few guys too. But now at 60, I reflected that I had mellowed a bit due to my diminishing speed and flexibility. I'd given up tournament competition several years before. I didn't go out on the town in the evenings any more except to go to practice. Whenever there seemed like a potential for a physical confrontation, I'd take steps to diffuse or avoid it. "I don't think I've been in any real fights in the past ten years," I answered.

Grandmaster Kim nodded. "Then you must be practicing for some other reason." He smiled and leaned closer. "Maybe just good energy," he said, and walked away.

It surprised me to realize that he was right. I was studying the martial arts for some other reason than using them. But what was that reason? My being ready to fight defined my existence—yet I had not been in a real fight in the past twenty years! This inconsistency puzzled me, now that it had been pointed out. Clearly there was a need to redefine my goals, my life definition, but I had no idea how to proceed.

The second experience happened about six months later. I was asked to assist Grandmaster Garrison as an *uke* during a half-day seminar. It was Mr. Garrison's task to introduce a class of future social workers from the University of Portland to the art of Aikido, which he called "compassionate self-defense." Those attending were all graduate students, but none had any martial arts experience or self defense knowledge at all.

Mr. Garrison lectured for more than two hours, with just a brief introduction to simple defensive movement, mainly a "turning out of the way" move called *tenkan*. A few seemed to drink in the information as though it were life-sustaining nectar; others seemed to let it wash over them and run off without moistening their mental skin.

Most of these graduate students had never experienced an adversarial confrontation that had become physical. Fighting was perceived as barbaric and uncultured. The thought of having to physically defend themselves against an angry or delusional patient had never occurred to them. The dominant thought was, "Surely, reasonable minds will prevail." Mr. Garrison patiently pointed out to them that if everyone were reasonable and cooperative, none of them would end up with a job. Sooner or later, if they continued their pursuit of professions which were meant to give aid or understanding to needy and/or dysfunctional members of society, they would at some point come face to face with someone who would try to hurt them. The question was, what would they do? How would they handle such a situation?

"Get help," someone said.

"Get a baseball bat," said another.

"Kick them in the groin!" shouted one woman.

Mr. Garrison nodded thoughtfully saying those were all reasonable responses, given the scenario. "But they all have one common conclusion," he said. "They assume that the other person is an adversary and must be overcome, controlled, or beaten down. This is a common mental construct in our society. Good guys and bad guys. Friend or foe. It's us against them. But it colors the way in which we perceive everything around us.

"Most people just want to get through the day with enough to eat, and with some shelter and safety. In your dealings with them, they may begin to see you as an obstruction to their needs. They don't hate you; they just want you to get out of their way. It's not personal. Most people aren't by nature adversarial. It is our defining them that way and treating them that way that leads them into becoming adversarial. We become defensive, and because of this, outcome options are limited. An adversarial confrontation becomes inevitable."

"How do you treat an adversary any other way but adversarial-ly?" The speaker stumbled on the word.

"By treating them with respect and with compassion," Mr. Garrison answered. "Simply ask yourself, what does this person really want? Follow that with, can I reconcile myself to helping them achieve their goal? Remember, victory does not belong just to you. It's belongs to them as much as it does to you."

"What if they just want to hurt you?" A stout man with a graying beard asked.

"That is a problem. But what if they just want to get past you to reach a family member they perceive to be in trouble? What if they begin to see you as an obstruction to their freedom, or their food? If there is a fight, your injuries will hurt just the same, no matter what the other person's motivations. In a real fight, trust me; everybody gets hurt. So the key to victory is to figure out how to avoid fighting. One way to do that is to change your mindset. You don't have control over the other guy and often not even over the situation," Mr. Garrison answered. "You only have control over how you respond to it, and what energy you inject into it. If you bring a mind full of fear and distrust, contention and resistance, the situation is much more likely to develop into a fight. But if you bring calmness, neutrality, and a willingness to listen, the situation is more likely to resolve itself without a struggle.

"A person with a strong center, a strong identity, does not need self-substantiation or ego-strokes. Such a person doesn't need a victory just to prove himself. This lack of contentiousness helps calm a potentially adversarial situation, and may help to avoid a fight altogether."

I was confused. "What do you mean when you say a strong person does not need victory?" I asked. "What if the person is beating on you?"

"*Why* are they beating on you?" Mr. Garrison turned his attention to me.

"Who cares? Maybe they're just mad," I answered.

"Well, in that case, you've already failed at a compassionate connection with this person, and you may have to hurt them in order to save yourself. And that's unfortunate. Wouldn't it be better if you could have avoided hurting that person?"

"Well, of course," I said.

"So, it would be better to ask yourself *how can I resolve this situation peacefully* beforehand, rather than after a fight has already begun," Mr. Garrison said.

I nodded, but also shrugged. "How do you resolve a fight before the fight?" I asked.

"It doesn't begin with the fight," Mr. Garrison continued. "It begins with your intent to fight."

"What do you mean?"

Mr. Garrison came up close, directly in front of me. "Let me ask you a different question," he said. "When you feel adversarial energy coming from another person, what do you want to happen? What do you need in order to consider the situation satisfactorily resolved?"

"I want the other person to see the error of their ways," I answered. "I want them to understand that they have an inferior position, that their logic has flaws, or that their position is indefensible strategically."

"Why?" Mr. Garrison asked.

"I want to feel that I've won," I answered.

"But why do you feel that you need to win?"

I had no answer.

"Intending to win, to 'put the other guy in his place' creates contention, separation. When you state your intent in this way, an adversarial confrontation has already begun. Contentiousness is not a sign of strength. True strength, inner strength, is self-sustained, not needy. Inner strength is learning self-acceptance, hardening resolve, developing confidence and optimism. People with inner strength don't need external symbols of victory because they are already victorious."

"But what if they just attack you?" the stout man asked.

"Then you have to neutralize that attack. But there are many ways to accomplish this without beating the other guy senseless. The first step is not to fear or hate the other person, not to want to hurt them. Your ethical standard must guide you toward resolving a situation as non-violently as possible. You must never lose sight of the other guy's humanity, or you lose sight of your own. Your humanity—your ongoing connection with others—is the source of your inner strength. This connection with everybody and everything around you, this joining into a universal harmony, infuses a person with great energy. In Japan, this energy is called *Ki*. One of the translations for this word is *spirit*."

"The ultimate goal of the martial arts is to neutralize an attack without diminishing one's Ki, or spirit," Mr. Garrison said. **"You do this by maintaining your respect and compassion for others, even as you exert control over the situation. This is the only justifiable victory."**

That statement has had an enormous impact on my thinking. I found myself struggling with the quintessential warrior dilemma. I had practiced the martial arts for more than 40 years. Martial strategy and logic had long become automatic. It was my training to seek out tactical advantages and exploit them to my opponent's detriment. I was pre-programmed to seek his defeat. If there was any trouble, I would be ready. I looked for it out of the corner of my eye with every step.

My brain was immersed in the concept of *me winning*. It was difficult to imagine living any other way. It was necessary for my emotional balance for my opponent to know that he'd been defeated. He didn't have to be hurt. In fact, it would be a cleaner win if he were unhurt, as long as he realized that he'd been put into a position of disadvantage and not hurting him was *my* choice. Tantamount to humiliating him, actually.

If the only tool you have is a hammer, everything starts to look like a nail. *–pioneer adage*

Why did I seek this essentially negative emotion from my opponent? Why did I even conceptualize the dichotomy of self interest and opposing interest? I began to explore the possibility of regarding the whole adversarial concept—me against the world—as an artificial construct; an adversary might not really be an adversary unless I made him one in my mind. *What if I simply didn't do that?* This idea was like a dam bursting and a river of thoughts flooding out over a desert.

I remembered Mr. Kim's casual statement, *"Oh, you must be practicing for some other reason."* It had never occurred to me that practicing a fighting art could be about something other than fighting. But here it was. It had to be, or else I was stuck in an unevolvable concept of the world. But if I were to give up that perspective, what lay on the other side of it? *"Maybe just good energy,"* Mr. Kim had said. What did that mean?

This chapter is about exploring this question, about clarifying the *some other reason* which sooner or later all long-time martial artists must discover if they intend to continue evolving—not just into better marital artists, but into better people as well.

Karate is no different from other martial arts in fostering the traits of courage, courtesy, integrity, humility, and self-control in those who have found its essence.
– Gichen Funikoshi, founder of Shodokan Karate

NEW DIRECTIONS, NEW DEFINITIONS

Sooner or later, a person will reach the limits of his (or her) physical development; his body will reach its peak performance level. Through regular exercise and disciplined diet, he can extend the duration of this peak, but eventually, he will not be able to improve his performance. Mentally, he may experience a similar peaking phenomenon, although continued mental stimulation helps to prevent stagnation. So to continue evolving into a better person, he must look outside of himself for fulfillment; he must learn to develop *socially* and *spiritually*. The following are a few basic concepts and redefinitions that must be explored if the warrior wants to continue his evolution into what Confucius referred to as "the Superior Man" *ie* a man of high moral character, a man worthy of the admiration of others. They are:

1. Letting go of adversarial presumption
2. Transcending the martial mindset
3. Expanding one's personal definition
4. Redefining personal strength and energy
5. Understanding the nature of Ki
6. Spiritual realization

Letting Go of Adversarial Presumption

The goal is not to bring the enemy to his knees, but to bring him to his senses.

-- Mahatma Gandhi

There is a tendency among the warrior class to view the world as perpetually at war, and to see violence as an appropriate solution to many of society's problems. But there are serious downsides to this world view. The first is that adversarial perception tends to recapitulate itself. We begin to expect opposition wherever we look. Half of everything we see is suspicious and threatening. This tendency is presumptuous and judgmental, as well as dangerous. We may choose to go to war before other, more peaceful options are explored. Fighting is actually a manifestation of social failure at some level: failed diplomacy, failed compromises, the loss of calmness and patience, or simply avaricious greed.

How can perpetuating an adversarial dichotomy help us to evolve socially? Viewing the self as good allows for far more than self respect; there is the danger of self righteousness—a disrespectful, disconnecting energy. Viewing the other guy as suspicious at best, and openly antagonistic at worst, devalues that person and denies the possibility of connection—also very disrespectful. So in a sense, this whole conceptualization is awash with unrecognized negative energy.

A second downside to a sustained martial consciousness is one of the warrior's greatest assets—the strategically trained mental process. If a warrior views the world as a continuous strife in which the entity with the greatest advantage is the most likely to prevail, then he has already significantly narrowed the possibilities of outcome. He has already ruled out the harmony of accord, mutual sustenance, shared pleasure.

Many of life's richest moments have no inherent strife in them at all. But the warrior, immersed in his combat training and strategic mindset, may overlook these moments completely. Mutual love and respect have prerequisites of trust and empathy and compromise as their beginning place, yet the traditional warrior has little training in these social skills. Is the warrior then doomed to a life without trustworthy companions? A life of conniving, backstabbing, and suspicion? This would be a tragic condemnation of all warrior professions.

Third, a continuous and unrelenting defensive posture against imagined enemies is exhausting. All one's energy is expended, but none is returned.

Clearly, maintaining an adversarial perspective leads to a social dead-end.

Here is the central dilemma of the warrior: he spends years developing the warrior persona: someone who does not give up, someone who does not tolerate disrespect, rudeness, or aggressive behavior. These are all adversarial behavior patterns the warrior instantly recognizes, and to which he automatically reacts. Warriors tend to view their social interactions in strategic terms; that is, they tend to expect adversarial energy and consequently find it all around themselves. The result of thinking this way tends to evolve a personality that is competitive, intolerant, judgmental, and quick to react with force—fighting traits.

Fortunately, a warrior's social stance usually mellows with maturity. As he learns the arts of compromise and diplomacy through dealing with friends and family, he begins to realize that an adversarial perspective isn't always appropriate. As he increasingly participates in the social structure—holds a job, supports a family, joins activist or interest organizations—he observes that most of the roles of the people around him are not adversarial. Oh, there will always be those fringe elements, the reckless, the selfish, the predatory; he knows how to deal with these types. But, days and weeks go by when he doesn't have to. And the strategies of adversarial interaction don't really serve him well in his primary relationships. He needs to figure out how to be strong without being armed to the teeth and quick to unsheathe the sword. He must find the strength within himself to explore all social options for resolution of conflict, for soothing and reconnecting dissonant energies without the use of deadly force. Consequently, the ultimate task of the warrior is to transcend his own warrior mindset.

The basic idea is to transcend confrontation. – Hirosho Tada

Transcending the Warrior Mindset

How does someone who has studied martial technique and strategy for years—even decades—renounce what has been so diligently constructed? How do we reconfigure our entire universe? What do we keep and what do we throw away?

A reconfiguration of our reality begins with revisiting our values and redefining our personal concepts. We may choose to keep some values and terms; for instance, we will not discard our training, nor our fitness and our vitality, nor our alert mindfulness. But other values and definitions may change or fade away altogether.

If we abandon the automatic assumption of adversarial energy, then we need not remain as obsessive about strengthening our defenses. In fact, the whole definition of **personal strength** will evolve in a new direction.

If we stop viewing ourselves as alone and separate, then our ego will have less dominance over our decisions, and our definition of the term *self* will evolve into being a part of a larger whole.

If we begin to view ourselves as a part of a group, then our life purpose—our *intent*—will evolve as well. The warrior's role, now connected to others, becomes that of protector, guardian or shepherd—a keeper of the peace, not a proponent of war. The concept of **victory** is no longer personal; it becomes the result with the most positive social outcome, even if he himself is defeated or killed in the process.

Ultimately, as we begin to share the common struggles and hopes of the world around us, we will begin to experience a social unity, and a propitious **collective energy**, the more we connect with others.

Redefining Personal Strength

Grandmaster Kim has said countless times to his students over the years:

"A warrior must always negotiate from a position of strength."

This is universally true. A warrior's lifelong *raison d'etre* will be to maximize his personal vitality and the safety of his position. Yet even truisms evolve. If we ourselves are to continue evolving socially and spiritually, then we must redefine the word *strength*.

Both of the above definitions of strength are relative values. Great physical strength is no help against a sniper with a rifle. A better position on the playing field or a more cunning defense occurs in temporary moments that pass away as conditions change. There is no such thing as an impregnable castle.

Once a month or so, I'll watch on the evening news as a squad of SWAT team members tear-gas a house, bash in a door, and drag someone out by his handcuffed wrists. The point is, strategic strength is tenuous and precarious. There are always going to be greater and lesser forces, and there are whole organizations funded with your own tax money whose job it is to see that you are the lesser force. No amount of weaponry, no certain minimum thickness of your cement bunker walls, no amount of pumping up on the steroid of your choice will ever make you impregnable to usurpation. So instead of seeking to evolve into one of those steroid-swollen hulks with gravelly voices spraying spittle when they rant like those WWE Wrestle-Mania Smack-Down guys on the sports channel, the warrior must seek some other definition for strength: one that does not rely on outside comparisons for its meaning.

The concept of personal strength must evolve beyond the need to compare, to compete with, to win. That approach encourages adversarial presumption. To continue his social and spiritual evolution, the warrior must learn to measure his personal strength in non-combative desirables; such as calmness, happiness, confidence, vitality, maximum awareness and inter-personal connection. And he must learn to eliminate negative mindsets that weaken him, such as doubt, hatred, malice or fear.

An often overlooked dimension of strength, one which can achieve all of these goals, is *inner strength.* Inner strength develops as a result of consistently directing one's life toward a chosen goal. ***Inner strength is developed by focused living.*** Disciplining one's life to adhere to a chosen path causes an intensification of being, resulting in robust vitality, clear intent, relentless determination, uncompromising integrity, and indefatigable optimism. A person with inner strength has the confidence and the tenacity to remain true to his ethics, his ideals, and his goals despite the onset of adversity. Such a unified focus of personal energy radiates from the warrior like a powerful and indomitable force-of-being. *(See chapter 1.)*

Inner strength is developed by four basic practices:

1. Clarify your goals

Intent is much stronger if the intended goal is clearly visualized, and the path to achieving it is arranged into manageable segments. The warrior asks himself, what am I doing to become closer to my goal right now? What can I accomplish today?

2. Eliminate interference

John Lennon said, *"Life is what happens when you're busy planning other things."* This is all too often true, but the warrior must try to eliminate interruptions of his plan of action. If his plan is to go to practice every day, then he should not allow interference with that goal. He will also maximize his health and vitality so that he will not undermine his own will to succeed.

We become what we do; we are the sum of our choices.

3. Establish a goal-oriented pattern of living

We can't control many of the outside influences on our lives; we can't control the weather, natural disasters, or various social frenzies that may spill over into our space. But we can control our diet, our health habits, our attire, our allotment of time and energy. The best way to succeed at any endeavor is to make it a regular part of our day. Success is rarely a lucky accident; it is more likely to occur to those who have planned for it, and who have habitualized their efforts to achieve it.

4. Redefine yourself as already successful

The warrior's path does not have an end, at which time a warrior can say, *"I am done now."* Many martial arts teachers have dangled the coveted black belt in front of their students as if that were the ultimate goal of all martial study. But the truth is that black belts just signify that a student has completed a course of training designed by a particular teacher. Black belts from different teachers and different schools signify vastly different levels of training. Consequently, the black belt doesn't really signify anything. The true warrior realizes that the path of learning has no end at all. He must be satisfied to know that he remains on the path each day. His concept of success becomes living his life in a conscious, chosen manner, rather than achieving an external reward.

Developing inner strength and personal integrity are the natural consequences of living a goal-directed life. Both are essential for the warrior to expand his consciousness beyond himself, and so begin his evolution toward spiritual awakening.

The Evolution of Intent

Much of the time during practice, Grandmaster Garrison would step onto the mat after warm-ups and instruct a new technique or a new way of looking at a familiar technique. He would often urge the advanced students to move with more fluidity, have more feeling behind their moves, clearer intent in their execution. After such a lecture, practice seemed to intensify a notch or two; punches were closer to the mark, and people got thrown down harder.

Recently, during one such session, I was paired with a brown belt, a young man with considerable skill, who knew how to fall very well. So as he punched, I moved straight into him, blocking his shoulder at an angle and forcing him off balance into a hard fall. Mr. Garrison came up and stood in front of me. "I've just told the others to move with more fluid balance and clearer intent," he said, "What was *your* intent?"

"To throw him down," I said.

"But why?" he said.

"Because that's the point of the exercise, isn't it?"

"Maybe for them. Not for you," Mr. Garrison said. "You should be at a point in your training where you transcend the need to force someone into anything. You should exemplify smoothness, not force. Hapkido is about blending, not brute dominance. Your intent should be to finesse the person into an imbalance, not force him. He should not even feel your touch. The less force you use, the better your Hapkido. The ultimate goal is to use no force at all."

"How is that possible?" I asked.

"You simply guide your opponent's energy into its own collapse."

My face must have registered a certain amount of confusion, so Mr. Garrison continued to speak.

"Let me tell you about a confrontation I experienced many years ago. I was working as a part of the security force at the Paramount Theater during a live music performance. The audience was made up of mostly young, drunk, and scary-looking people who wore leather and chains. One night, a big, muscular guy started a fight and the security team had to help break it up. After we took the fighters out of the theater, the big guy broke loose from the security man holding him. The big guy took a fighting stance, waving his arms in the air as though he knew kung-fu, but not in a way that indicated an actual trained person. But it was obvious that he meant to hit anyone who came close to him. I had stepped in front of another guard to block the big guy's attempt to punch him, and suddenly, it was just him and me face to face. I could hear sirens coming nearer, but quite a ways off yet. And the big guy was focusing on me.

"I wasn't afraid. The guy was huge, naked from the waist up, and cursing like a sailor, but he was staggering drunk. If we had a tussle, I would throw him down easily. But you never know about that lucky punch you don't see. I'd been sucker punched before—I'd lost the same tooth three times to sucker punches. So I didn't really want to fight. But it was also obvious that this guy was a social menace and had to be taken into custody. There was no backing away. So I told him, calmly, that he was going to jail. He answered with a string of foul language, saying he'd fix anyone who tried to take him.

"After his ranting and swearing wound down a bit, I asked him if he was done with that. I tried to speak even more calmly this time. I slowly put my hands into my pockets, to indicate self-assurance, and that I really didn't intend harm to come to him. I said, 'Well, we can make this easy, or we can make this hard. Either way, there a lot of us, and in just a moment, the police will be here to finish the job. You may be hit with nightsticks or maced or, if you actually manage to beat the odds for a little bit, they may just shoot you. But, one way or another, you're going to jail. What shape you're in when you get there is up to you. So, why don't you just bend yourself over that car hood and put your hands behind your back for the handcuffs? That's the way this is going to end anyway.'

"He looked at me in silence for the longest moment, said the 'f' word, then turned around and put his hands behind his back for handcuffs to be applied. To this day, I wonder what that fight might have been like. I'm glad it didn't take place, but in a way, it did. We had a clash of wills about how things were going to turn out. My intent was to control the situation with the minimum amount of struggle, but I had no doubt that I would be on the winning side. I believe that he felt the strength of my intent, saw the three other guys behind me, heard the sirens, and his will caved in on him. We didn't fight because it wasn't necessary. But I also believe there was no fight because I talked with him as though he were a regular person. I remained respectful and meant no harm to come to him unless it became unavoidable.

"That's what I'm talking about here," Mr. Garrison said. "You've been practicing Hapkido for over thirty years. We know you can kick and punch and be rough. But can you be compassionate? Can you be successful using a lighter touch? Practice the energy of connection. That will result in a more positive outcome—both for your *uke* and for you as well."

I was still a bit confused. I understood how a lighter touch would benefit my training partner, but I was not at all certain what I would get out of it. What was the energy of connection? At that moment, I recalled Mr. Kim's words. *"Maybe just good energy,"* he had said. Maybe he had simply meant, as Mr. Garrison had just said to me, energy that resulted in a positive outcome.

I knew that I always felt energized after an intense practice in which everyone learned something, but none of my training partners got hurt. The more intense the practice, the more conscientious we had to be of each other's safety. Respect never lapsed; we had learned to take care of one another. The senior members of our practice group felt like family.

This had to be the energy of connection, the good energy that Mr. Kim had mentioned. Could this be the most important reason for practice?

I now believe both Mr. Kim and Mr. Garrison were implying that the most important growth and development we can exercise happens within us, on a non-physical, energetic level. The most valuable learning experiences connect the individual to a more expanded, collective reality, within which he is only a part. His intent becomes less about himself, and more about the success and well being of the group. Attaining this expanded awareness is the warrior's greatest achievement.

The originally pragmatic idea of the art of combat—how to fight better, how to get better at dominating an opponent—takes on the additional, complimentary objective of how to become better as a human being. And, with age, this complimentary objective progressively becomes the practitioner's primary objective... That is the meaning of Budo.

-- Kenji Tokitsu, in <u>Ki and the Way of the Martial Arts</u>

REDEFINING PERSONAL ENERGY

A widespread belief within most Oriental cultures is that we exist on both a physical level and an energetic level. A corollary of this belief system is that our thoughts are a focus of that energy. Consequently, it is believed that our thoughts, if strong and consistent, are able to influence our physical selves. The way we view our reality becomes our reality.

Recent discoveries in quantum physics seem to support this Oriental belief system. Quantum physics suggest that all matter in the universe has energy which surrounds it and infuses it. The smallest particles in the known universe have been found to be infinitesimally small, rapidly vibrating, string-like entities that sometimes act like matter, and sometimes act like energy. So, at the quantum level, matter and energy can't readily be distinguished. Quantum theory proposes that matter and energy are just alternate forms of the same essence. In fact, matter and energy are actually thought to be *interactive*.

There was an experiment done in Japan by a photographer named Dr. Masaru Emoto; he taped pieces of paper with different words printed on them to glasses of water, and left them that way for a day or two. Then, he refracted light into the water and photographed it using an electron microscope. What he found was that the water molecules took on more brightness, more symmetrical shapes when they had benevolent thoughts connected with them. A water molecule that had been blessed was quite beautiful, like a snowflake. Water molecules which had been cursed were discolored, yellowish, disorganized. The point of this was, if thoughts can do this to water, just imagine what they can do to you.

-- from the film, "What the #@&% Do We Know?"

Although quantum physics are really more a series of mathematical calculations than they are certainties, they still present a variety of fascinating conclusions. We have heretofore thought of ourselves as just so much biological tissue, but what if our real selves include the energy fields that surround our bodies? What if our physical bodies were interactive with these changeable, indistinct energy auras—even dependent on them? This would present a profound change in the way we think of ourselves.

The idea of an *energetic body* is a profound concept, but it is a cumbersome phrase. The word *Ki* has been used in Oriental cultures for over 3,000 years to indicate the energy fields that surround and infuse every living thing. Our bodies co-exist with a dynamic, animated aura of *Ki* which changes as we move, changes even as we think. The physical body and the *Ki* surrounding it are intricately locked together in a dynamic symbiosis, each dependent on the other for vitality.

It is generally accepted in Eastern thought that robust physical health supports the presence of a strong and vital *Ki* flow around an individual. This apparently also works in reverse. Acupuncturists stimulate specific points on the body in order to restore and revitalize the *Ki* flow around it, thereby relieving physical symptoms and restoring physical health.

But essential questions for the average person are, what exactly is *Ki*, and, without the esoteric knowledge of an acupuncturist, how can we make our *Ki* stronger?

By seeking to develop sensitivity to Ki, we can improve our efficiency in combat and find in combat another meaning beyond the mere attempt to win. We spontaneously become open to an ethical dimension.

-- Kenji Tokitsu, <u>Ki and the Way of the Martial Arts</u>

THE NATURE OF KI

Your *Ki* is your non-physical Self. Your body is not your whole Self; it is only a tool of your real Self. Your *Ki* is your personal vitality, the life-force that you generate through the condition of being alive. *Ki* is sometimes referred to as bio-energy, or life-force, but *Ki* is not divided into separate bits of life. *Ki* circulates and pools around a living being, but is not confined by it. The *Ki* that you generate as a living being simply adds to and becomes a part of the *Ki* that surrounds us all.

The universe is the self, and the self is the universe. *– Ueshiba*

Ki is the creative vitality of the universe. It is everywhere, within everything, uncontainable by any one thing. *Ki*, as pure energy, is not bound be the laws of particle physics. The laws of gravity, mathematics, geometric confinement, even temporality may not apply. *Ki* is not visible, not detectable, and not discrete. Even as *Ki* within the individual is in constant flux, *Ki* itself, in the larger sense, ebbs and flows throughout the universe, passing into and out of our lives as naturally as a river passing over a stone.

Your *Ki* is like a cup of seawater. If you think to yourself, that's all the *Ki* I can contain, then the cup is all that you will see. But if you think of the same cup slowly sinking into the ocean, then the seawater in the cup is the same as the seawater outside and all around the cup. The more you think about the cup, the more your ego is in control of your thoughts, and the more isolated you become. But the more you think of *Ki* as like the seawater—the same within you and all around you too—the more aware you become of its infinite accessibility.

The universe itself is filled with creative energy; it is interactive, accommodating, evolving, sentient. *Ki*, the effusion of its spirit, is all around us, flowing into and out of us with each breath. The more in touch with our surroundings we are, the more *Ki* we can draw to ourselves.

Control of the mind and body, control of ki and, finally, control of your life begins by maintaining a strong consciousness. The activity of the mind determines the strength of one's life-force because a spiritual being's first function is to receive the universal energy that is the force sustaining life.

-- Kouzo Kaku, in The Mysterious Power of Ki

Ask, and ye shall receive. *– Matthew 7:7*

How to Strengthen your *Ki*

The more *Ki* an individual can access, the stronger his vitality, the more dominant his force-of-being. A strong *Ki* field around a person is a great asset, whether that person is at peace or in a struggle. The person who brings the most energy into a confrontation will be the one most likely to dominate the interchange and determine the outcome. It is to a warrior's distinct advantage to know how to maximize his *Ki*.

There are three ways to strengthen your personal *Ki*: **physical conditioning** (fitness), **mental imaging** (visualization), and **spiritual realization** (connection).

Ki and Physical Conditioning

Everyone has *Ki*. Every physical act involves some flow or change within the aura of *Ki* that surrounds the physical body. A strong and healthy body generates and sustains much more *Ki* energy than a weak or unhealthy one. Vibrant health is like fertile soil for the creative vitality of the universe to take root in. compromised and dissipated health is like desert sand in which precious little will grow. A person who takes his warrior nature seriously will exercise his body to peak performance level, consume only healthy foods, drink plenty of water, and get enough rest to regenerate maximum energy.

Yet the warrior knows that this is not enough by itself to give him much of an edge. Even bad guys can have strong physical *Ki*. Bullies almost always have more *Ki* than their victims, or they wouldn't be able to intimidate and demoralize them. Strong physical *Ki* does not mean a person is admirable or trustworthy, it only means a person has made good health choices, or that his poor choices haven't caught up with him yet.

The true warrior will establish a pattern of behavior that will maximize his physical health and vitality, but his efforts to increase his *Ki* will not stop there.

Ki and Mental Imaging

Another way to increase the power and intensity of our *Ki* is simply to imagine it becoming so. There is an ancient Japanese proverb which says, **"Where the mind goes, Ki follows."**

Our inner strength and vitality, bolstered by our supply of *Ki*, can be greatly enhanced by mental imaging and autosuggestion. We draw toward us what we imagine.

Most people don't give what they imagine much importance, and drift through life like derelict flotsam, experiencing come-what-may as powerless, wave-tossed victims of circumstance. But a warrior must take his imagination seriously. He must focus it onto what he wishes to happen, and learn to stop focusing on what he doesn't want to happen. The warrior must learn to visualize his own success, and allow no doubt to erode that mental picture. Mental *Ki* is only as strong as one's determination.

Even when I have not one iota of strength left in my body, I will always continue to fight.* — Charles Nungesser, WWI flying ace*

The principle characteristic that people with strong mental *Ki* have in common is that they all visualize themselves as capable of success. More than capable, they visualize themselves as unstoppable. They have in mind the goal they wish to accomplish, and they visualize themselves succeeding completely. They do not entertain any thoughts of failure.

People with strong mental *Ki* develop a kind of positive thinking process, or *victory mind*, which results in several distinct mannerisms. Mentally strong people are never pessimistic about anything; they develop an indefatigable optimism. They never think in terms of impossibility; they think in terms of infinite possibility. They do not complain about their circumstances, or blame other people for them. They are always open to new ideas and approaches, always willing to listen to others' opinions. They have great patience; they do not get angry at setbacks to their plans. They are quick to forgive, and do not begrudge others who may complicate their progress. They maintain a sense of thankfulness, a feeling of having been given what they need in abundance. And they are constantly aware of their inner dialogue; if they catch themselves thinking or saying a pessimistic or self defeating phrase, they will disavow it, and change it to a more self-affirming aphorism that reinforces their optimism and bolsters their hope.

Dr. Deepak Chopra wrote, **"Whatever you put your attention on grows stronger in your life."** If you place your attention on success, your determination will become stronger. If you are filled with determination and hope, you are supercharging your mental *Ki*.

You must be the change you wish to see in the world. – *Mahatma Gandhi*

Mental *Ki* is mental focus. *Ki* has little power if it is not focused, like a storm without an eye. But, when *Ki* is directed toward a goal by the mind, a marvelous dynamic results. Since *Ki* energy is the same within a person as it is around him, his personal *Ki* energy begins to resonate with and influence the *Ki* around him. If his intent is strong and clear, a person will create an aura of sympathetic energy around himself, and he will become aware of serendipitous events which support his efforts.

However, if a person should concentrate consistently on something he most fears, he may draw that toward himself as well. His *Ki* will not know the difference between desirable and undesirable goals. The universe only wants him to arrive; it is up to the individual to choose the path.

Human beings have only one important choice to make in their lives; they must decide whether they live in a benevolent universe, or a hostile one. That decision will make all the difference. – Albert Einstein

There is no doubt that directed mindfulness is a great generator of personal *Ki*. However, there are many destructive people in the world who generate tremendously strong intent but who focus on exploitative or hurtful goals. The warrior will not rely on physical prowess and mental focus alone, for these bad guys may visualize themselves as invincible warriors as well. Their physical and mental *Ki* may be just as strong as his own.

But there is another dimension of *Ki* that only a man of honor can access-- one which can give him the definitive advantage. A warrior must learn to transcend his own personal experience, expand his awareness, and connect with the universe, thereby receiving the bounty of unlimited *Ki* energy which surrounds him. This is the warrior's ultimate goal—the path of spiritual realization.

Place your mind where there is no evil. – Musashi's advice for new warriors

Ki and Spiritual Realization

Grandmaster Garrison has met many martial artists in his extensive travels and has heard many claims of martial expertise. Many years ago, when he had newly returned from a trip to a martial arts camp in California, he was having dinner with Grandmaster Kim and sharing his experiences. He told Mr. Kim about a journalist he had met, who insisted that she had witnessed a group of Chinese Kung Fu practitioners in San Francisco who could knock their opponents unconscious from several feet away just by extending their *Ki* power through the air.

"She said she was told there were masters of this art who could actually kill someone by directing their *Ki* at that person," Mr. Garrison said.

"Very handy," Mr. Kim said. "But how do they practice?"

Mr. Kim undoubtedly knew that *Ki* does not work this way. *Ki* can be gathered and focused into a powerful force behind one's intent, but it cannot be hoarded for personal aggrandizement. *Ki* belongs to everybody. It is the endless, invisible thread of energy which joins us together into the fabric of the universe. And *Ki* cannot be used to diminish itself.

Whether we realize it or not, we are one with our environment; the same energy flows through us all. But our egos sometimes convince us that we are separate and preeminent. Such a perspective will influence our conduct, and predetermine our positive or negative experience. If we conduct ourselves with empathy and compassion, in harmony with our surroundings, we will likely enjoy the experience and become energized by it. But if we try to control, exploit, or destroy that which surrounds us, our personal energy will detach from the universal energy and dissipate, leaving us isolated, frustrated, and exhausted by our efforts. *Ki*, the creative energy of an interactive universe, is never in conflict with itself; it is either honored and abundantly available, or it is ignored, isolated, and soon exhausted.

The intensity of the *Ki* within us is a reflection of our ability to let go of the limitations of our ego and embrace our surroundings with empathy and compassion, connecting us with the infinite source of *Ki* all around us. Therefore, the path of the warrior must take a new direction; he must learn the art of ***maintaining connection.***

***Life's most persistent and urgent question is, what are you doing for others?** – Martin Luther King Jr.*

Learning how to connect and to remain connected, how to associate the self as a part of something larger than the self, is the beginning of spiritual growth. One of the many translations of *Ki* is *Spirit*. In fact, *Ki* and *Spirit* are just words from different cultures which describe the same energy.

Spiritual energy is the energy of connection. – Deepak Chopra

---

Your spiritual self is larger than your physical self; it is not defined or limited by your body. It is the part of you which reaches out and connects with everyone and everything around you. And once you are connected, there is no separateness, no ego. There is only mutual empathy, benevolence, and support. When your spirit joins into the great flow of energy around yourself, you become stronger. You become embraced by a collective vitality.

Your spiritual awakening begins when you realize that we all share a single experience. Spiritual growth occurs when you begin to perceive others to be just as important as you are and wish them no harm. Your spirit is strengthened by honoring the connections you have with others.

Aikido Shihan Mitsugi Saotome has written a wonderful description of the energy of connectedness in his book, *The Principles of Aikido*. He wrote that the energy of connectedness was like a "seventh sense:"

The seventh sense is the sense that enables you to erase the boundaries between yourself and your fellow human beings, to know that to harm another is to harm yourself, to feel the pain of others as your own pain—to sense the world as a whole entity rather than a collection of individual parts at war. Think of how you hear music. You do not listen to it note by note. You hear a whole piece and understand its beauty. The seventh sense is the ability to hear the whole music of the universe in which you participate, to hear how the note that is yours to sound fits into the song of which it is a part... -- Mitsugi Saotome Shihan

People who connect with others in their lives—exchanging energy in the form of caring, respect, compassion, and kindness—receive a tremendous boost of inner strength from this behavior. They gain a sense of worth and belonging, a sense of purpose, and a boost to their determination and intent to succeed at this process. People who live with this sense of connection have discovered the ultimate wellspring of both vitality and happiness. By remaining connected with others, their spiritual *Ki* is constantly renewed. Thus, connectedness represents not only a philosophical choice, but a strategic one as well.

My religion is kindness. *– the Dalai Lama*

We go about in our lives, either consciously or unconsciously, creating energy surpluses or energy deficits, depending on our individual life choices. People who make poor choices, such as indolent behavior, bad diet, the use of drugs or physiologic toxins, deplete their own energy. Consequently, they have only enough energy to look out for themselves and have no concern at all for anyone else. These are the selfish, the careless, the negligent, and the predatory people we see around us.

Evil isn't a cosmological riddle, only just selfish human behavior.
-- Joyce Carol Oates

People who are self-centered and self-serving harm themselves slowly by not caring, not connecting. Their actions return no sympathetic energy; they have severed their connection with the infinite source of *Ki* all around themselves. They become greedy, suspicious, distrusting, exhausting all their energy in defensive posturing. Such people are so devoid of personal strength they often seek to replenish themselves by draining the energy, exploiting the emotions, and stealing the wealth of others.

Expending one's energy in such a disrespectful manner will always have a negative outcome. This disconnected energy state is sometimes referred to as "negative *Ki*," but *Ki* is never negative; this state simply represents an absence of *Ki*. Negative, disrespectful, selfish behavior can never lead to happiness; there is no *Ki* in it.

True, lasting happiness can only be achieved by a benevolent heart which welcomes *Ki* into itself.

Only positive energy emanates from an enlightened man.

This is the warrior's edge—spiritual realization. This awareness is cultivated by practicing the art of connectedness through the continuous emanation of respect, benevolence, and compassion. Energy which is expended attempting to connect people with one another in this manner is much more likely to have a positive outcome, more likely to result in a positive energy return. And with this infusion of energy, the warrior grows stronger.

Gaining mere literal knowledge and technical skill is not the goal of Aikido practice. You must work to improve your character and raise your consciousness to a higher level. The study of Aikido cannot be a selfish study. You must develop your sensitivity toward others and your concern for them in your daily interactions, both in practice and in your daily life.

-- Mitsugi Saotome

The Importance of Respect

The most important practice in maintaining a sense of connection is to develop continuous and unwavering respect and compassion for those around you. This is the basis for all ethics.

Many martial arts practice halls post written rules of behavior for all the students to contemplate. *These are the rules which must be obeyed at all times,* such wall plaques say. So students observe and obey only those rules. Some of the students may think, well, if these are the only rules, then areas the rules don't cover are fair game for any kind of behavior. Or worse, some may think, how can I get around these rules but not technically disobey them? So if there are twenty rules posted, eventually, there will be a twenty-first situation, and these students will not know how to behave.

Behavioral discipline must be more deeply ingrained than just being able to read and follow rules; it must be internalized as a part of a warrior's self-definition, so that correct behavior can be figured out and applied in all situations, even unknown ones. For this reason, Grandmaster Garrison had been adamant about no lists of rules being posted in his dojang. *"There is only one rule,"* he has said many times. *"Show unwavering respect at all times. All other rules are just applications of this."*

New students are sometimes uncomfortable with this apparent lack of guidance. But they learn from being corrected, and by observing the behavior of higher ranked students. Black belts wouldn't be black belts if they had poor manners. By paying close attention, and by desiring to be perceived as a good student, students gradually learn how to act courteously and have genuine consideration for others. Eventually, good behavior will emanate from within, and a student will be able to figure our how to behave even in unusual situations. He will be practiced at choosing the correct mental and emotional stance and will guess correctly how to act. Eventually, he becomes confident in his correctness and is able to act spontaneously, without doubt or hesitation.

A warrior is known by his courtesy. *– Japanese proverb*

Effective training in the martial arts is impossible without connection with and unwavering respect for one's group of training partners. Martial arts cannot be learned in a vacuum, from studying pictures in magazines, or shadow boxing alone in an empty field.

Every once in a while one hears about or reads about someone who has gone deep into the forest and meditated for months or years, after which they emerge, claiming to have had some sort of supreme revelation of martial expertise. Of course, they all become tenth degree masters because they claim to have been completely enlightened. But the truth is there are no "forest conversions"; the warrior as a loner is a sad delusion.

There are no instant masters. Martial art mastery is only achieved by hard work with other like-minded, dedicated practitioners who come to practice several times a week, and keep doing so month after month, year after year, with no thoughts of advancing in rank or receiving extraneous honors.

This kind of ongoing practice fine-tunes one's interaction to other people's movement and balance, and sharpens one's focus of power towards moving targets. It deepens one's intuition for another's intent and patterns of thinking. It alternately exhilarates and humbles the practitioners but always keeps their ego under control because the most important goal of training is to not hurt one another. One has to respect one's partner enough to never lose sight of his well-being and trust that he is doing the same for you. The more complete the trust, the more deadly the techniques that can be practiced. This mental connection sharpens an adversarial acuity, a fluidity under fire that is not learned any other way except combat itself. Both mental and physical training must be undertaken together in order for either of them to be effective.

Anticipating Your Opponent's Mind

There is another distinct advantage to expanding one's awareness through the energy of connectedness. By viewing himself as a nexus within a vast field of energy, the warrior can become connected with the *Ki* flowing through his immediate environment on a subconscious, visceral level. Eventually, his awareness is able to include his surroundings without sensual input or conscious thought.

The average person is aware of his surroundings only when it is demanded of him. The warrior is aware of his surroundings all of the time.

-- Carlos Castenada

By striving to achieve a high degree of harmony with his surroundings, the warrior will become more aware of dissonant energy, emanations from someone who intends him harm. The true warrior honors his enemy, regards the enemy's choices with respect, learns to empathize with him. Within this connection, the warrior will find how to read his enemy's motivation and predict his next move. Respecting his enemy will give the warrior the earliest awareness that such a person may be preparing to attack him.

It is said that if the mind is pure, you will be able to know what the other person is thinking. "The purer you become, the more clearly you will feel another's intention to kill you." – Morihei Ueshiba

---

There are many stories of warriors who develop a kind of sixth sense for becoming aware of dangerous situations around themselves even before those situations fully develop. They are simply assessing the degree of harmony that is returned on their investment. A warrior with a high degree of connectedness will sublimate his ego and empty his mind of personal concerns. His mind becomes like a tranquil pool, in which the reflection of the moon is without distortion. His mind will become so connected, his opponent's thoughts will be reflected in his own mind simultaneously, and he will be able to react instantly to whatever act his opponent initiates. The warrior emanates harmonious intent; if a dissimilar energy is returned to him, he will sense the other person's intent even before any commitment to action is made. The warrior who spends much time in a field of battle will not live long without this sixth sense.

The sixth sense allows you to see intent, to see the action forming in the body before any move is made. It allows you to read the feelings of others.

-- Mitsugi Saotome

Musashi wrote in *The Book of Five Rings* to "pay attention to trifles." This means to reach out with the mind, test the air around you, feel the ground, see into the shadows, read the eyes of the approaching stranger. Do not relax your awareness simply because a beguiling voice asks you to. Do not relax your courtesy or respect, for these help you to keep your awareness expanded. Do not allow your emotions to cloud your decisions, or you will lose sight of your goal.

The warrior walks a razor's edge. On one side, diplomacy, capitulation, civility. On the other, he must still have at the ready the martial skill, courage, and resoluteness to meet that purely sociopathic energy, resist it, dominate it, and, if necessary, destroy it—*but not be affected by it.* Perhaps that is too much to expect; perhaps the best the warrior may aspire to is not to be traumatized by it. That takes clearly defined ethical values and formidable inner strength. It takes all the *Ki* one can access.

We must, as warriors, seek the position of superior strength. This is not only a physical and strategic imperative, but also a mental imperative. We must develop clear ideas of how to behave, clear intent to succeed, acute attentiveness and receptivity, and accurate perception. Ultimately, we will seek inner, spiritual strength as well. We do this by joining with the world around us and becoming a part of it. Spirituality is not so much a personal experience as it is a collective experience.

One practices a martial art for the same reason one practices any other art: to improve the person as a whole, to have a stronger center, and ultimately, to improve society by improving oneself.

The soul that beholds beauty, becomes beautiful. – *Plotinus*

I believe this: place two people in adversarial roles on equal ground and with equal resources; one who opens himself to the *Ki* energy around him, who has learned to participate in a beneficent universe, and the other, a totally self-centered, self-absorbed person whose ethical base is "What's good is what's best for me"—and the person who has the spirit with an ongoing *Ki* exchange in the universe will prevail.

Why?

Because he is adept at tapping into sources of energy which continuously bolster his inner strength. He can muster the intent to seek the best outcome and instantly dedicate himself to that cause without hesitation. And he will be able to reach out with his mind and read his opponent like an open book.

The selfish person will have a capricious character, depending on his own personal needs, and consequently, he will have little integrity or inner strength. He will prefer not to have a direct confrontation with someone who does. He will not be able to employ his favorite tactics on a person with such strong mental focus, who is not easily manipulated, emotionally exploited, intimidated, or deceived. With no tactical advantage and little inner strength to draw upon, the self-absorbed person will be confused about his best course of action and plagued by doubt. Because of his inner nature, he will defeat himself before the conflict even begins.

This is an old Martial Arts idea—the one who wins the fight is of the lowest class. The one who wins without fighting is best. The one that fights maybe wins maybe loses. But without fighting, you never lose, you train and work hard and finally there is self-development. Then when you face your opponent, they become scared of your strength and you stop their actions. This is best.

-- Hidetaka Nishiyama, 9th dan, Karate-Do

Warrior Mind, Warrior Spirit

Warrior mind is a mind focused on achieving a goal and practiced in the strategies of successful effort. It is a mind with a central doctrine and no doubt of its appropriateness. It is a mind rooted in action, in instantaneous harmony of thought and movement. It is a mind prepared to fight but which prefers to nurture.

Warrior mind is a mind that has evolved beyond the need for ego and the emotional turmoils of fear and need, conflict and anger, addictions to pleasure. It is an all-encompassing awareness which reaches out and connects with the entire universe. The warrior's mind and his spirit become the same awareness.

Martial art *has to be part of your life, not just something you practice. Budo is the same as Religion.* – Pat Yoshitsugu Murosako, 7*th* Dan, Kendo

---

The warrior's ultimate task is to embrace the universe and accept its gift of infinite *Ki*. Then, in the fullness of his power, to emanate only positive energy—to reflect with compassion, to feel with empathy, and to act with as much benevolence as possible at that moment. But his constant practice prepares him for harsher choices, if they become necessary. His intent is to survive on his own terms. All his training is to clarify this intent and empower his decision.

REVIEW

The central dilemma of the warrior is how to maintain his fighting ability while evolving into a socially responsible and spiritually aware individual. In order to achieve this balance, he must continue to practice the warrior arts, but he must also learn to let go of any automatic assumption of adversarial energy on the part of people he encounters. His martial mindset and self defense training are merely tools to be used after all his other social options have failed to secure his safety. Then he will act without hesitation or regret. But in most interpersonal encounters, he must transcend this mindset and connect with people in ways that lead to more positive outcomes.

In order to transcend his martial mindset, he must examine many of his personal definitions, including the concepts of **self, intent, victory, personal strength,** and **personal energy.**

In redefining his personal energy, the warrior will become aware of his ***Ki***, or spiritual energy. He will learn to understand its nature and how to strengthen it. There are basically three ways to strengthen one's *Ki*: physically, through exercise and increasing one's vitality; mentally, by sharpening one's intent and visualizing his own success; and spiritually, through the practice of connectedness, maintaining respect and compassion for all others one encounters.

Never be like the man at the bottom of the well, who, looking up at the sky, thinks that the portion of the sky he sees is all there is of heaven. *– James Lee*

Ultimately, there is a unity to the entire universe. The warrior must learn to connect with this unity, to draw his energy from it. And once connected, to live in a way that radiates this energy outward and lights the world.

Make of yourself a light. *Sakyamuni Buddha's last words*

We are all here to help one another lead better lives. We assist our friends in their personal quests, celebrate their victories, and comfort them in their losses. We strive to achieve the most positive results, even in conflict, for the universe is continuously created from our own emanations. We hold all people in high regard, for we are connected with everyone we encounter along our way. There are no enemies; only lessons to be learned. There is no contention, for we are at peace within ourselves. There is no mistake, except compromising our integrity. There is no failure, except losing sight of our path. There is no end—there is only transformation.

You may substitute any word you wish for the words *Universe*, or *Ki*. Try out your favorite words: *Fate, Providence, Kismet, Ki, Spirit*. Try the word *God*, if you want to. That works for me. But any word will do, so long as you accept and embrace it. It's your construct, after all. And any word that you put into that spot will be absolutely right.

Now, go back to the beginning and learn to love it more.

****

Bibliography

A Book of Five Rings, by Miyamoto Musashi

Aikido, by John Stevens, Shambahala Publications, Inc, 1996.

Aikido in Daily Life, by Terry Dobson, North Atlantic Books, 1993.

Aikido and the Harmony of Nature, by Mitsugi Saotome, Sedirep Press, 1986.

Aikido and the New Warrior, by Richard Strozzi Heckler, North Atlantic Books, 1985.

The Art of Happiness, by the Dalai Lama

The Art of Peace, by Morihei Ueshiba O-Sensei, translated by John Stevens.

The Art of War, by Sun Tsu

Autumn Lightning, by Dave Lowry, Shambhala Publications, 1985.

The Deadliest Men: The World's Deadliest Combatants Throughout the Ages, by Paul Kircher, Paladin Press, 2001.

Demon Chaser, by Shannon Kawika Phelps, 10th dan, from Temple

Bell, Ltd.

"The Esoteric Principles of Judo", by Judo (Jujitsu) master Henry Seishiro Okazaki (unpublished paper).

"The Evolution of Hapkido" pub. TaeKwonDo Times Magazine, Nov. 1993.

The I Ching Handbook, by Mondo Secter, North Atlantic Books, 1993.

Karate-Do Kyushan, the Master Text, by Gichin funakoshi, Kodansha International Ltd, first edition, 1973.

Ki and the Way of the Martial Arts, by Kenji Toktsi, Shambala Publications, Inc., 2003.

Kodo: Ancient Ways, by Kensho Furuya, Ohara Publilcations, Inc., 2003.

Leading from Within, by Robert Pater.

Musashi, by Eiji Yoshikawa.

"Musashi's Void" pub. TaeKwonDo Times Magazine, July, 1996.

The Mysterious Power of Ki, by Kouzo Kaku, Global Oriental, 2000.

Precepts of the Martial Artist, by Walter Muryasz.

The Principles of Aikido, by Mitsugi Saotome, Shambhala Publications, Inc., 1989.

Profiles in Courage, by John F. Kennedy.

Quantum Healing, by Deepak Chopra.

Samurai Aikijutsu, by Toshishiro Obata, Dragon Books.

Secrets of Modern Professional Warriors: SEAL Team Combat Course, by Frank Cucci.

Sharpening the Warrior's Edge, by Bruce K. Siddle, PPCI Research Publications, 1995.

The Tao of Jeet Kune Do, by Bruce Lee.

Twelve Winds, by Karl E. Geis, Fugakukai, 1982.

The Unfettered Mind, by Takuan Soho, Kodansha International, 2002.

The Warrior's Path: *Wisdom from Contemporary Martial Arts Masters*, edited by James Sidney, Shambhala Publications, Inc., 2003.

"World Oriental Martial Arts Newsletter", (quarterly, 1990-1998).

Zen Flesh, Zen Bones, edited by Paul Reps.

Zen in the Martial Arts, by Joe Hyams.